IMAGES
*of America*

# EVANS

**On the Cover:** Gertrude Briscoe is posing with her combined third- and fourth-grade class in the fall of 1927. This is the last year the original 1874 schoolhouse was open. It was torn down and replaced with a brick building that would later become the Chappelow School, city hall, and the Jack Meakins Community Center. (Courtesy of the Evans Historical Museum.)

IMAGES
*of America*

# EVANS

Sarah Arnusch

ARCADIA
PUBLISHING

ISBN 978-1-4671-3121-6

Published by Arcadia Publishing
Charleston, South Carolina

Printed in the United States of America

Library of Congress Control Number: 2013952333

For all general information, please contact Arcadia Publishing:
Telephone 843-853-2070
Fax 843-853-0044
E-mail sales@arcadiapublishing.com
For customer service and orders:
Toll-Free 1-888-313-2665

Visit us on the Internet at www.arcadiapublishing.com

*This book is dedicated to the people of Evans, Colorado. May you continue to collect and preserve the history of this unique town.*

# Contents

# Acknowledgments

I would like to thank everyone who was so helpful in putting this Evans history together. First off, I would like to thank the City of Evans and Brian Stone, who graciously granted me permission and hours to work on this project. The Evans Historical Museum files contain so many wonderful photographs, which could not possibly all go on display at the library. I am so happy that all of these photographs can now reach the public. Unless otherwise noted, all of the images in this book are from the Evans Historical Museum.

The staff at the City of Greeley Museums has been very helpful, offering advice on collections care and help with historical research. I would like to give a special thanks to Caroline Blackburn and Melissa Gurney from the Hazel E. Johnson Research Center at the Greeley History Museum.

I would like to thank my husband, Wade Vitany, who has been very helpful and supportive throughout the process of writing this book. I would also like to thank my parents, Hans and Lucile Arnusch, who encouraged me to continue writing.

# INTRODUCTION

Evans started out like many other towns in the West during the 19th century. Railroad tracks were being laid across the prairie, followed shortly thereafter by settlers who were looking for adventure, prosperity, and new beginnings. Evans was unique to Weld County in the late 19th century for a variety of reasons. Being the oldest town in the county initially placed Evans a step above the other towns because it was the most populous and it was the county seat. A number of disagreements and a few setbacks over the years further strained the town, but Evans persevered. A thriving business district, schools, social organizations, and civic programs have provided the backbone of Evans. By the turn of the 21st century, Evans was among the fastest growing cities in the entire state.

Evans was named after the second territorial governor of Colorado, John Evans. Governor Evans was also a president of the Union Pacific Railroad and was instrumental in establishing the Denver Pacific Railroad line, which connected Denver to the Transcontinental Railroad at Cheyenne. The Denver Pacific line passed straight through Evans. So, while there is no evidence that Governor Evans actually visited the town, Evans does owe its existence in some part to Governor Evans. Without the establishment of the railroad, Evans may have never come into being.

One of the most drawn out and bitter arguments that Weld County ever saw was the contest between Greeley and Evans over the county seat position. The first county seat of Weld County was Latham, which was located east of Greeley and Evans along the Platte River, about halfway to Kersey. In the fall of 1869, Evans was platted two miles west of Latham. According to an article by Ruth Munz published in the *Weld Genealogical Quarterly* in 1978, "Everything was in favor of the new community at the very outset. Financial backing from Denver, the first railroad repair shops in Colorado, many nice buildings and residences, and a population that apparently was well coined." Evans's auspicious beginning led the county seat to be moved from Latham to Evans on January 4, 1870.

In its early years, Evans was a major hub for those traveling from the Transcontinental Railroad to Denver. The town was bustling with hotels, restaurants, saloons, and stores for weary travelers. It is said that one day's receipts for the town during its early boom time totaled over $4,500. However, this time of intense prosperity was short-lived.

About the time Evans began to enter a period of decline, a new group of settlers started to arrive at the Union Colony, which was later renamed Greeley. These colonists were more puritanical than the residents in Evans, and the two communities clashed from the beginning. The Union Colonists believed in abstaining from alcohol, while the residents of Evans enjoyed their saloons. As Greeley began to grow rapidly, residents complained of having to go to the "wet" town of Evans to conduct county business. A movement was started to have the county seat relocated to Greeley. It gained enough momentum that a countywide election was held on September 9, 1872.

Evans had a lot of support to keep the county seat. The only precinct in the county, outside of the Union Colony, that supported moving the county seat was the Green Colony, which voted

22 to 19. Erie voted unanimously against the move. The total voter turnout was 1,000, with Evans winning a little over 600 votes. Greeley was not satisfied with the results of the election and again pushed to have the county seat moved two years later. The 1874 election proved Greeley the winner by a small margin. After the election, the Weld County commissioners ordered that all books and records be moved to Greeley.

Tensions began to boil over when Evans refused to turn over the records, claiming that the election had been a fraud, and all of the locks on the vaults at the courthouse in Evans were changed. A month later, all trade and traffic between Evans and Greeley had stopped. Evans still refused to turn over the records, so under the leadership of Nathan Meeker, a group of men went to the courthouse and took all the records and furniture to Greeley before Evans even noticed. Enraged Evans citizens threatened to invade Greeley and take the records back by force, but that luckily never happened. The case between the two towns became so intense that it had to be tried in Arapaho County, where a judge ruled in favor of Greeley. Evans then appealed the decision all the way up to the Supreme Court of the Colorado Territory, which ruled that the issue should be decided at the next election. Evans won the election by 40 votes, and the county seat was moved back to Evans on October 6, 1875. Again in 1877, Greeley filed a petition requesting another election about the county seat. In the election in October 1877, Evans carried most of the county, except for Greeley, which was large enough to win on its own without the help of the rest of the county. When the votes were counted, Greeley turned out to be the winner by 64 votes. Evans contested on the grounds that the constitution of the territory prohibited an election of this type to be held more than once in a four-year period. The case was argued before a board of commissioners to no avail. In October 1877, the long battle was finally over. The county seat was moved to Greeley, where it has remained ever since.

By the 1910s, an issue that had been a matter of debate in Evans since its earliest years began to come to a head. Years before the 18th Amendment was ratified, banning alcohol in the United States, Evans was fighting its own battle over prohibition. The town government was divided into two local parties: the Citizens Party, which was in favor of keeping the saloons, and the Taxpayer's Party, which wanted to ban the sale and consumption of alcohol in the town. The town government, as well as the citizens of Evans, were divided nearly in half by the two parties.

As the April 1910 election to decide whether or not to keep alcohol in town drew closer, the disagreements between the two parties became dirty and heated. The Taxpayer's Party threatened to print the names of citizens who would sign a petition to allow the Citizens Party ticket to be placed on the ballot. This move was not taken well by the town, even among some of the temperance crowd. On January 28, 1910, the editor of the *Evans Courier*, a self-described temperance advocate, admonished the Taxpayer's Party, stating the following: "Probably one of the most Brazen attempts to rule or ruin ever attempted in Weld County was the action taken by the Taxpayer's, or Temperance Party of Evans last Friday evening when the organization held a meeting to the effect that they would publicize the names of and otherwise brand every citizen who would choose to sign the petition to permit a Citizens, or License Ticket to be placed on the official ballots at this spring election."

The issue of temperance was not isolated within the town. In the early 1900s, Evans was the only town in the northeastern part of Weld County that allowed alcohol. Windsor, Greeley, and La Salle were all temperance towns, and they worked together to pressure Evans to adopt temperance policies as well. In February 1910, the *Evans Courier* published a quotation from a minister in La Salle who advocated for an all-out boycott of all Evans businesses as long as alcohol was legal in the town. The minister affirmed, "We propose to hold up such ideals that the merchant, the doctor, the editor, or whoever he may be, who signs a petition shall do so at his own cost." He claimed that the temperance communities would not patronize businesses who worked against temperance, which he believed led to "the ruin of men and women." Those who disagreed with the temperance movement argued that the people in Evans were no different from those who lived in temperance towns. After all, it was well known that alcohol still made its way into supposedly "dry" communities. A commenter to the *Evans Courier* on March 18, 1910, pointed out, "This big howl about our sons and daughters going bad on account of saloons is only done for political purposes. Compare the sons and daughters of Evans with those of Greeley, La Salle, or Kersey, or any other of our surrounding towns and see how they class up." The commenter further argued: "I guess you will find them right up in the top class morally, intellectually, and physically."

Election day took place on March 25, 1910. The Citizens Party ran on the platform that saloons should be permitted in town, provided they not serve habitual drunks or minors, close between 11:00 p.m. and 6:00 a.m., and not allow card playing or gambling in the establishment. The Taxpayer's Party demanded that all of the saloons be shut down without exception. Martin Briggs and Albert Weinhold ran on the Taxpayer's ticket and Henry Behrens and E.W. Balfour ran on the Citizens ticket. Despite what appeared to be an easy win for the Citizens Party, the Taxpayer's Party won by 33 votes, establishing Evans as a dry town. Upon hearing the news of the election results, temperance activists from neighboring communities came to Evans to celebrate. The Salvation Army church from Greeley sang songs and gave speeches. Schoolchildren from La Salle were brought to town to march though the streets with banners touting the evils of liquor. Evans remained officially dry throughout Prohibition but reintroduced liquor after the repeal of the 18th Amendment, at which time the issue of "wet" versus "dry" was no longer nearly as heated as it had been before Prohibition.

By 1972, Evans was eligible to become a city since the population had recently reached the 2,000-person mark. The 1970 census listed the population as 2,570, but after a rapid growth spurt in the early 1970s, estimates placed the population of the town around 4,000. With a town of that size, it was necessary to reexamine the governing practices to see if they were fair and efficient to the majority of the population. After certification from the secretary of state of Colorado, Evans officially became a city and had the choice to become a statutory city or a home-rule city. In a statutory city, the local government rules and makes decisions via the legislature. In a home-rule city, voters are given much more say in how their government operates. The town government draws up a charter, which is presented to voters. They can decide whether or not to pass the charter by which the local government must abide.

In 1973, the Evans City Council presented voters with the choice on whether or not to allow a home-rule charter convention, which—if approved—would establish a 21-person panel to serve as charter commissioners. In the election held in February 1973, voters in town approved of holding a charter convention by a nearly four-to-one ratio. Two months later, the city council presented a charter for residents to vote on, which passed, establishing Evans as a home-rule city.

Individual settlers, business owners, residents, and schoolchildren who called Evans home help to bring the past alive and make the town's stories interesting. The following chapters will give closer examination of these groups of people. The information in this book has been gathered from the Evans Historical Museum files, the Hazel E. Johnson Research Center at the Greeley History Museum, and genealogical records.

# *One*

# Settlers, Steamers, and Saloons

## Evans in the Early Years

Like many towns in northeastern Colorado and the rest of the western United States, the history of Evans is directly tied to the growth of the railroad. The town is named for John Evans, who had been the second territorial governor of Colorado and was the president of the Denver Pacific Railroad (DPR) when the town was founded. In 1862, Congress passed the Pacific Railway Act, which called for the construction of a transcontinental railroad and telegraph service to facilitate westward expansion. John Evans was one of 158 commissioners appointed to help organize the Union Pacific Railroad Company. In 1867, the Denver Pacific Railroad Company was formed for the purpose of connecting Denver to the Transcontinental Railroad, which passed through Cheyenne. Construction of the DPR started in 1868, and the first train reached Evans on December 13, 1869. During this period, the town of Evans experienced an incredible boom, bringing a number of businesses and services to northern Colorado.

Evans holds the distinction of being the first in many categories in Weld County. It was the first town to be officially plotted in the county on November 22, 1867, and was also the first town to be officially incorporated two years later on November 29, 1869. Evans was off to a running start by early 1870 as business was booming and new settlers were arriving almost daily. The town boasted a dairy, a tannery, a doctor's office, civil engineers, a jewelry repair shop, a millinery, a blacksmith, a freight line, two carpenters, three general stores, several hotels, a railroad station and offices, a mail carrier, three saloons, and a brewery.

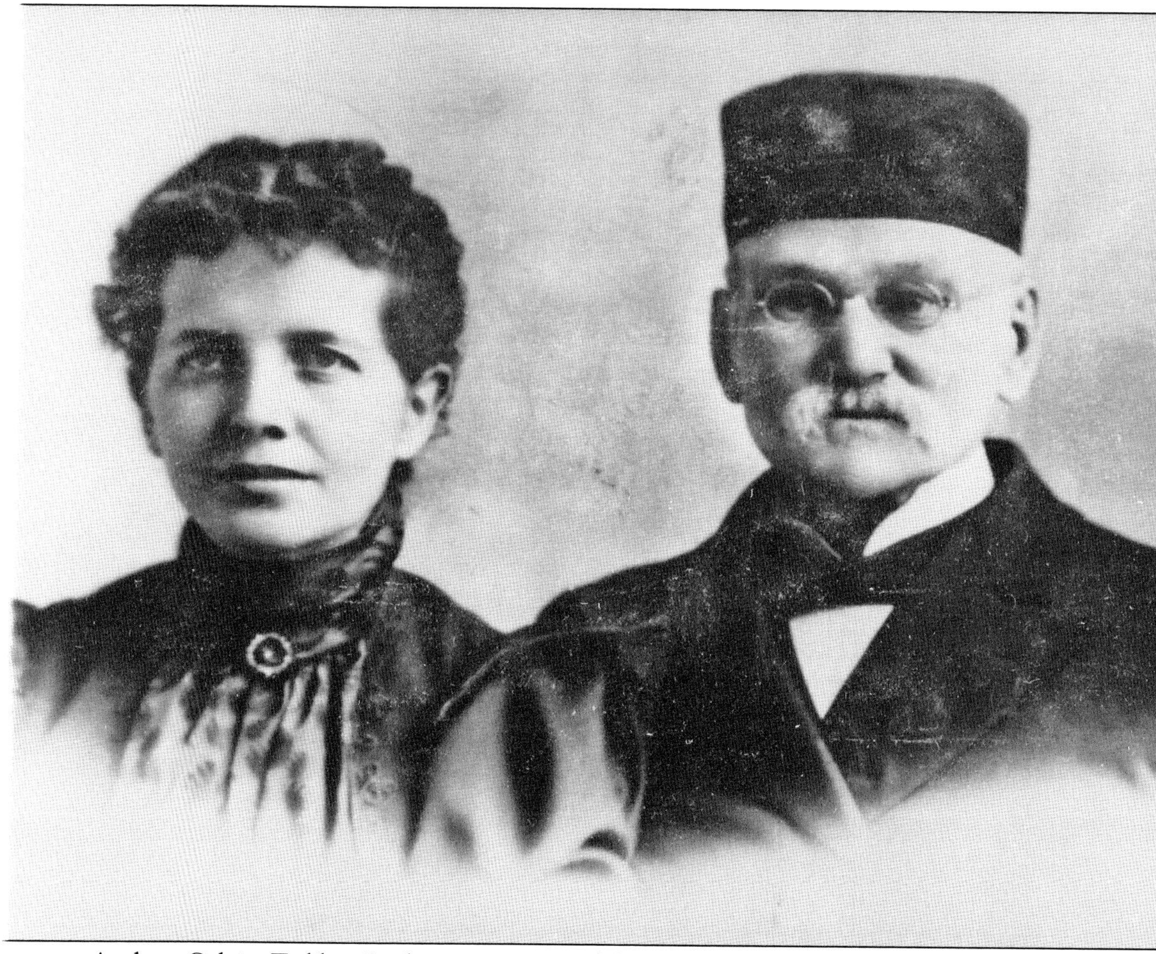

Andrew Calvin Todd, a Presbyterian reverend from Missouri, was responsible for organizing the St. Louis Western Colony, which brought large numbers of settlers to Evans in the 1870s. After a visit to Colorado in the summer of 1870, Reverend Todd and his wife, Margaret Louisa, became enamored with the natural beauty and opportunity in Colorado. He knew that families in southern Illinois and western Missouri would be interested in settling the area. His friend J.H. Pinkerton put him into contact with influential people, including Gov. John Evans and William N. Byers of the National Land Company, who could make his dream a reality. Reverend Todd returned to Missouri, and by November 29, 1870, the St. Louis Western Colony was officially formed. The first settlers of the colony arrived in Denver on February 25, 1871, and soon made their way to Evans, where Todd quickly set about establishing a Reformed Presbyterian church, a normal school, and a newspaper called the *Evans Journal*. The Todds are pictured here on March 5, 1898. (Photograph by G. Ed Anderson, courtesy of City of Greeley Museums, Permanent Collection, 1974.09.0001.)

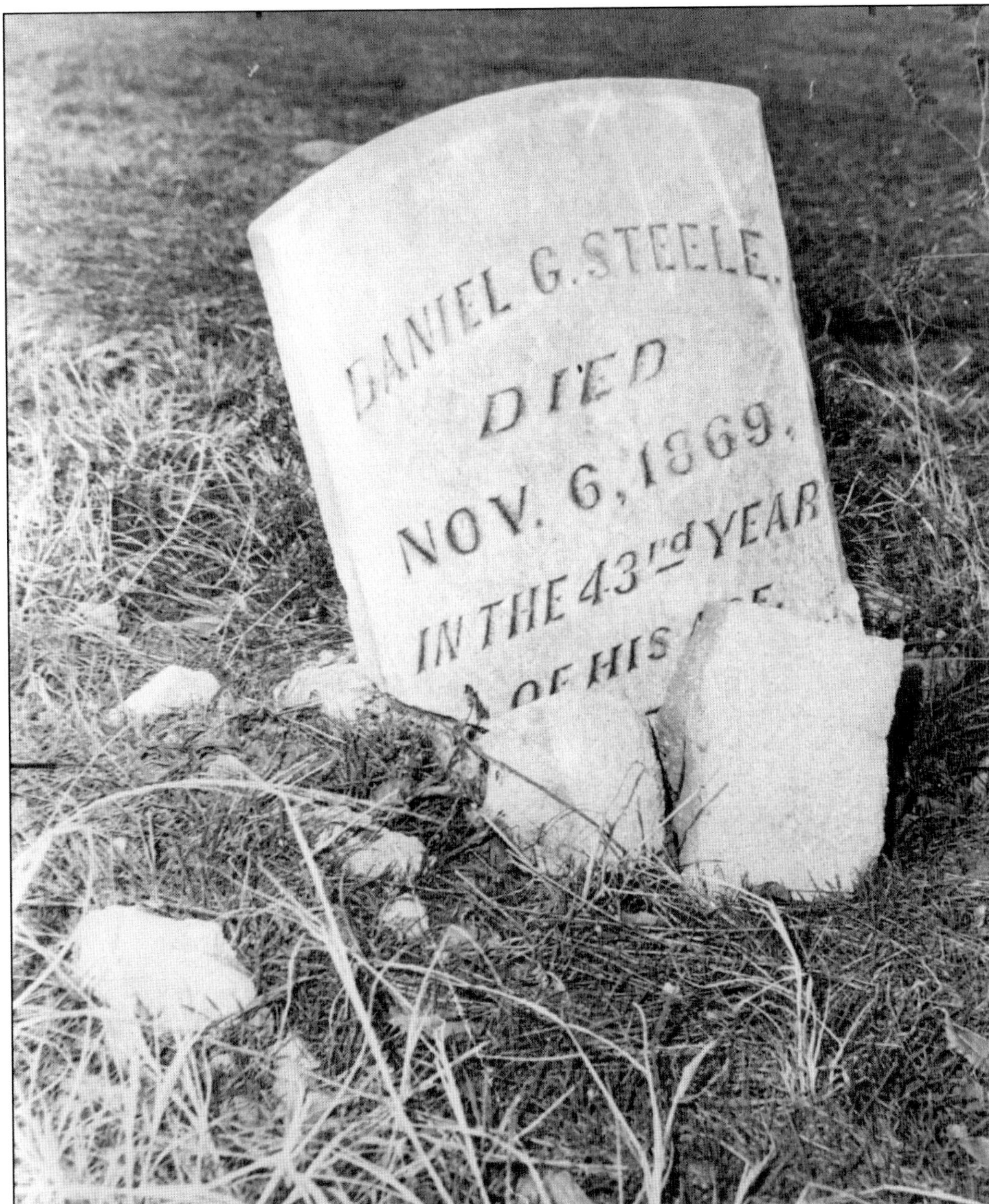


Daniel Steele, an innkeeper, was one of the first people buried at the Evans Cemetery. A drunken cowboy named Jack Carr murdered him in November 1869. Carr came to Steele's hotel a little before noon for lunch. Steele was not ready to serve yet, so Carr paid for his meal and went to a nearby tent saloon. He did not hear the dinner bell, and when he got back to the hotel there were no seats left at the table. He became enraged and Steele insisted that he leave, returning his money. Carr went back to the saloon and continued to become more inebriated. He returned to the hotel around 3:00 p.m. and shot Steele in the back of the head. A hasty "trial" was organized that very afternoon, and Carr was hung from a nearby tree. (Courtesy of City of Greeley Museums, Permanent Collection, 1983.48.004V.)

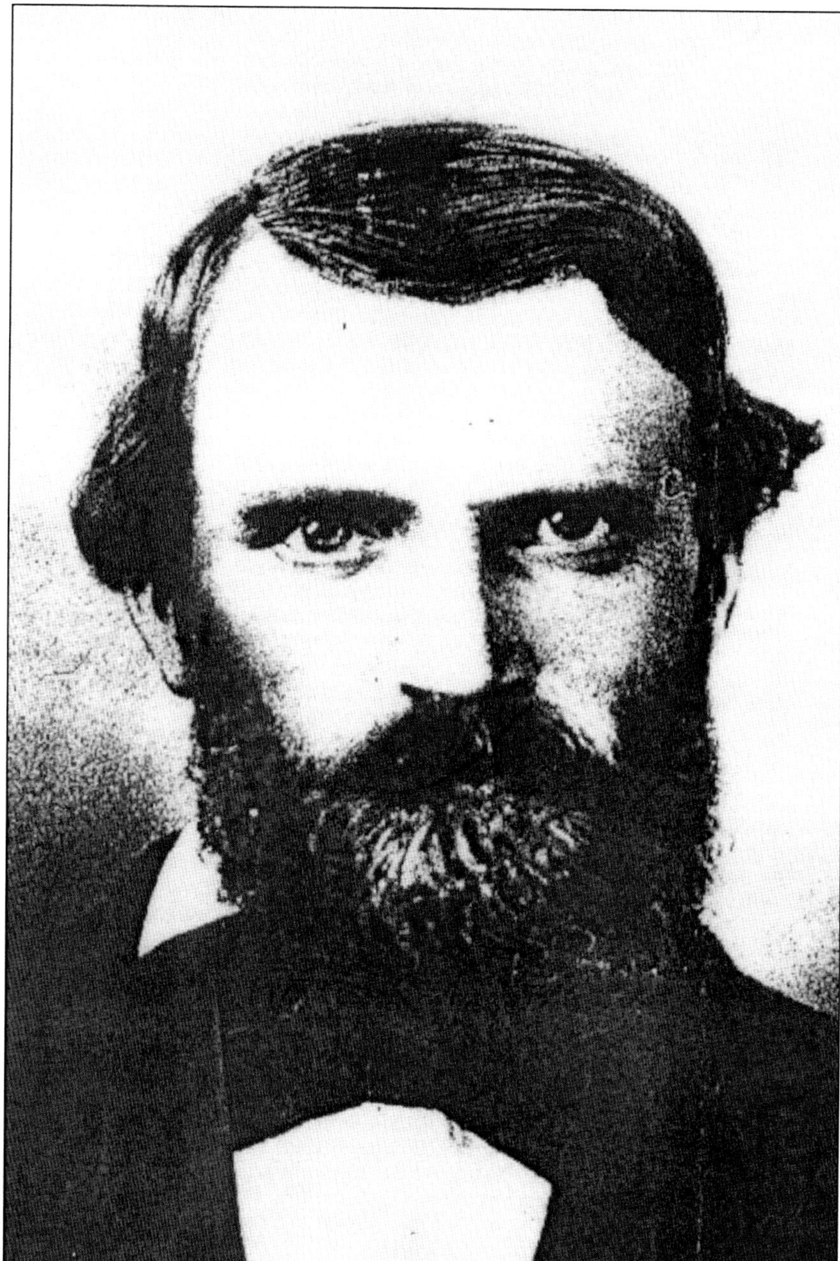

Elbridge Gerry was the first Anglo settler of Weld County. Born in Massachusetts in 1818, Gerry ran away from home at a young age and eventually found his way west with a group of fur trappers and traders. He arrived in Colorado in the 1830s and settled down along the South Platte River northeast of Evans, where he established a successful trading post and ranch. Gerry had several wives, all of whom were American Indians, including several daughters of Chief Swift Bird of the Ogallala tribe. He is sometimes referred to as the "Paul Revere of the West" because he once rode to Denver in the middle of the night to warn about a planned Indian raid on the town that he learned about from his wife. It is rumored that he is a descendant of the Elbridge Gerry that signed the Declaration of Independence, but the relation has never been confirmed and is unlikely.

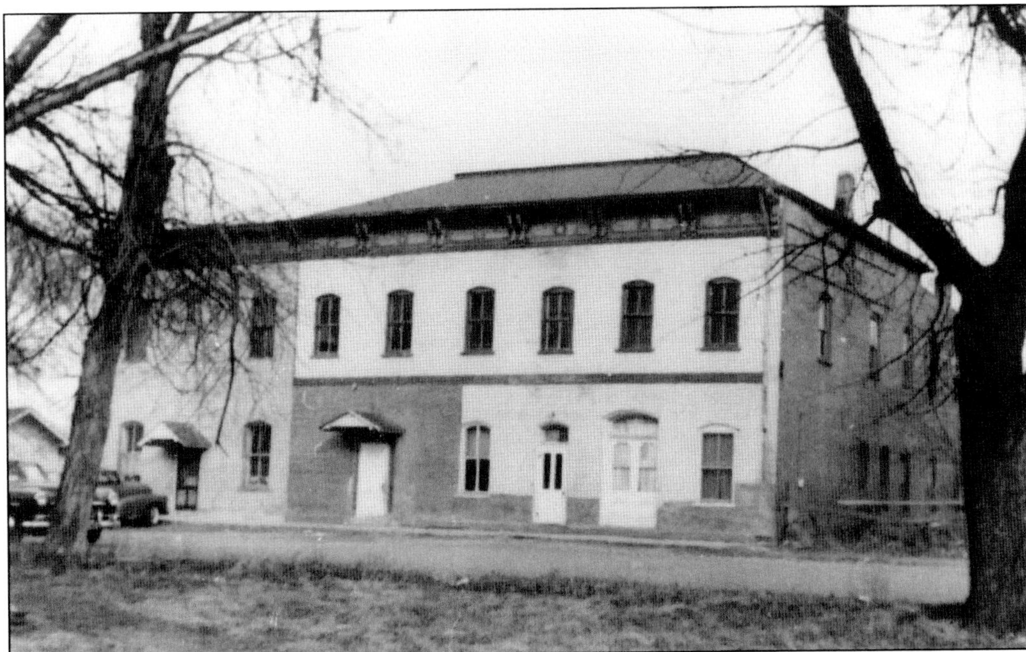

Elbridge Gerry and Fritz Niemeyer built the Gerry House Hotel in 1872 at a cost of approximately $17,000. Gerry received the money from the federal government as compensation for property that was destroyed in an Indian raid. It was located on Denver Street just a few buildings south of Seventh Street (now Thirty-ninth Street).

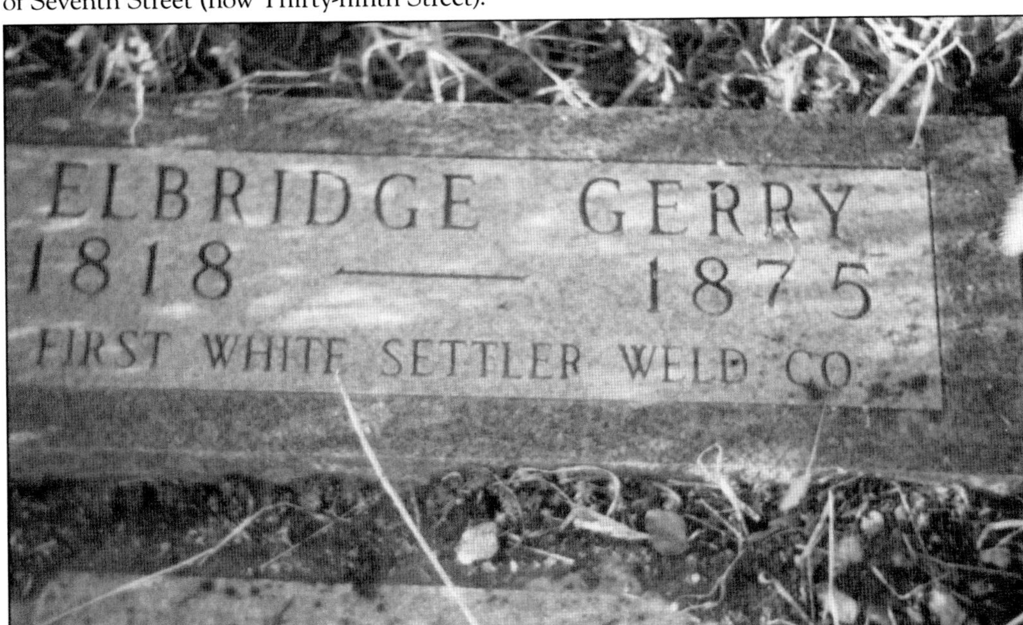


Elbridge Gerry passed away after a brief illness at the age of 57 in 1875. He is buried on his old ranch, located along Crow Creek and the South Platte River just a little north of Kersey. There was an adobe house and a trading post at this ranch, neither of which are still standing. One of Gerry's wives (it is unknown which one), his daughter Lizzie, and her husband Seth Ward are also buried at the site.

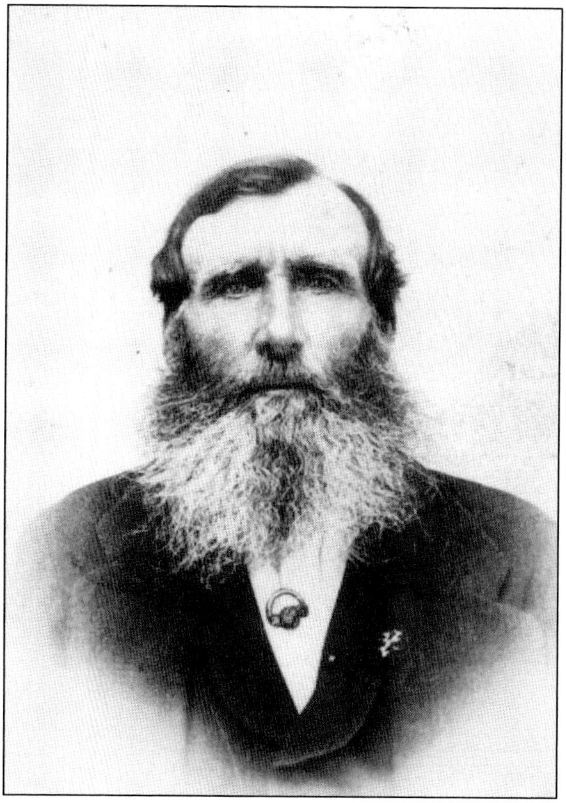

Holon and Matilda Godfrey farmed along the South Platte River between Evans and La Salle in an area that came to be known as Godfrey Bottoms. Holon was instrumental in the development of agriculture and irrigation in Weld County. In 1869, he was the primary organizer of the Section No. 3 Ditch Company, known as the Godfrey Ditch. He served as president of the company for 10 years. While active in local politics and economic development, the Godfreys were known as a colorful bunch. Holon's friend Jimmy Chambers noted that he was known all over for his use of "vigorous and picturesque" profanity. Eugene Williams described the family, saying, "Godfrey was rather tall, and somewhat slight, wore whiskers. Wife, a white woman. Typical pioneer, easy to meet, somewhat gruff, not especially jolly. Large family. Not too polite. When drunk was rather mean."

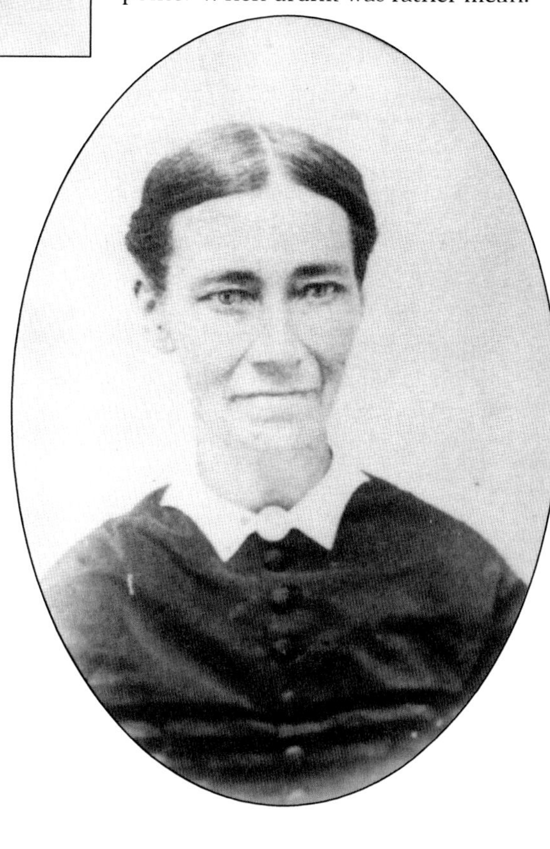

W.D. French was a wealthy cattleman who owned a home in Evans and a ranch near BeeBee Draw. In 1887, an Evans shoemaker named Harry Woodbury (right) entered into a business partnership with French, which only lasted a year. Woodbury agreed to purchase 850 pounds of flour from French, but only 250 pounds were delivered to his home. A fight erupted between the two men over the remaining flour, causing Woodbury to file a civil suit against French, which he won. On December 14, 1888, French, furious about the judge's ruling, stormed into the Woodbury home and shot Harry in the abdomen. He died the next day. Rumors that French may be released because of insufficient evidence to convict him of the murder angered many residents of Greeley and Evans. After midnight on December 29, 1888, a group of vigilantes broke into the jail and hanged French from the nearest tree.

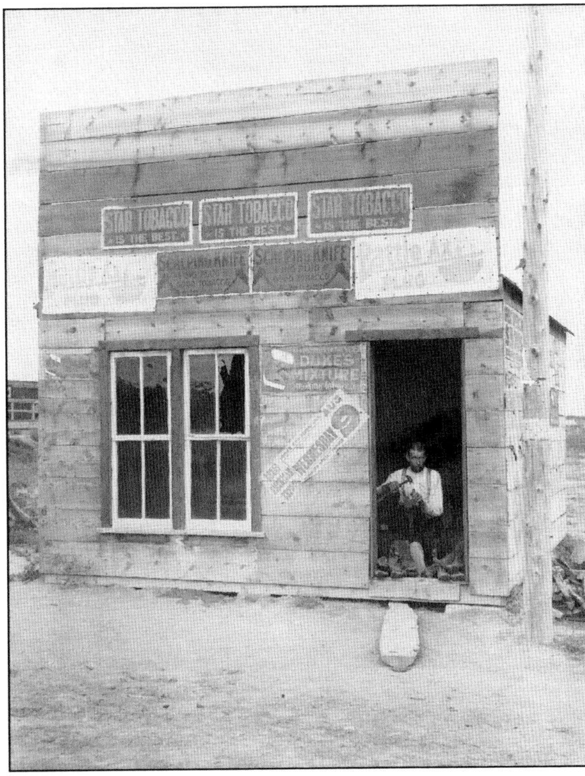


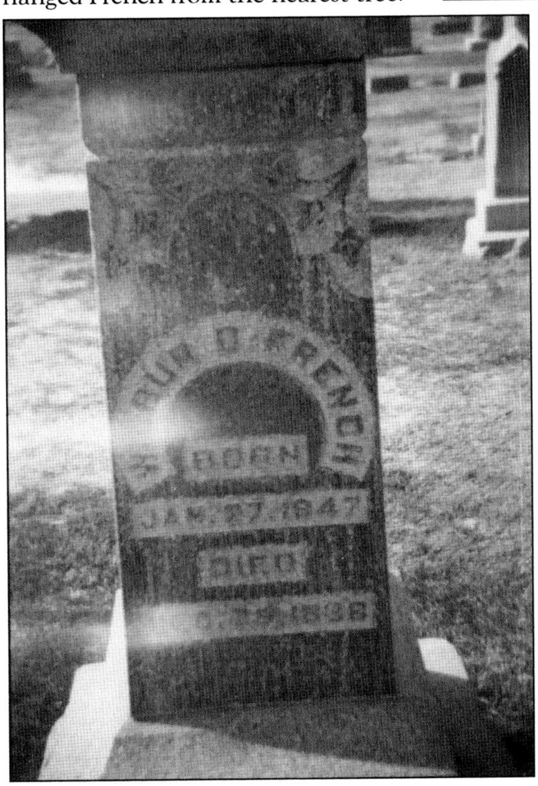

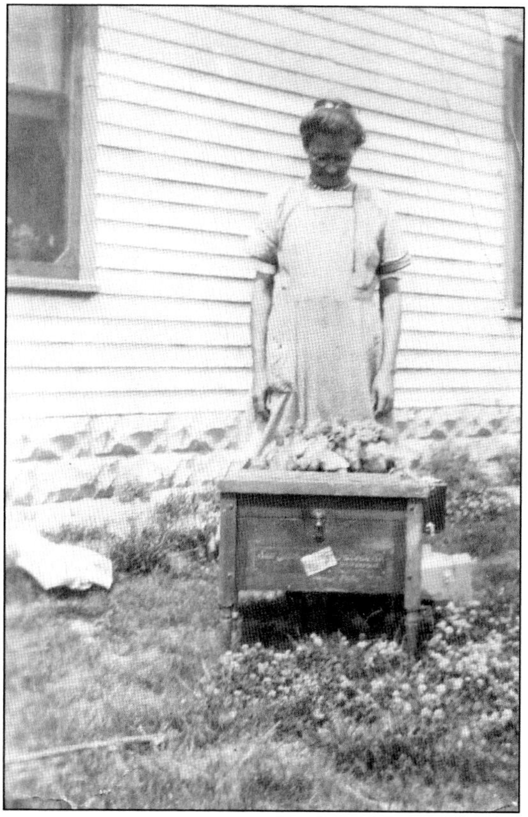

May and Melintus "Lint" Earl Kealiher farmed a few miles east of Evans in a rural area known as Auburn. May and Lint had three children: Rachel, Richard, and Fay. Here May is tending to some goslings that she hatched in an incubator around 1928.

Potatoes and sugar beets were two of the most commonly grown irrigated crops in Weld County for many years. After about 1940, a bout of potato blight as well as increased livestock production made feed corn the dominant crop. Lint's father, David Stewart Kealiher, is seen here digging potatoes on the Kealiher farm around 1928.

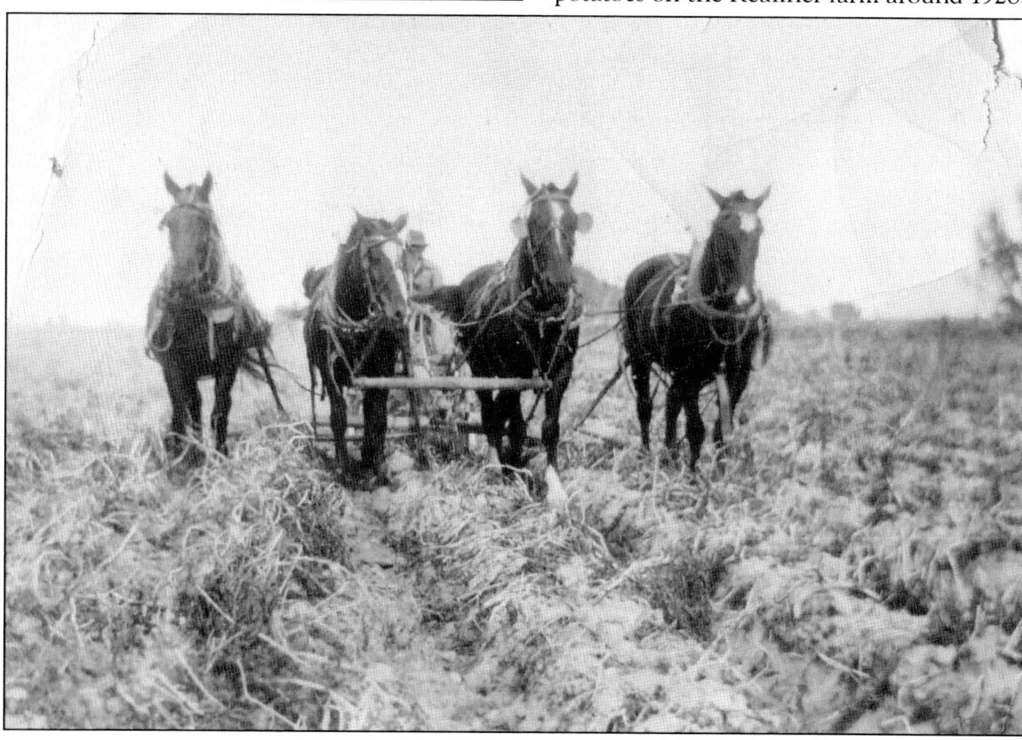

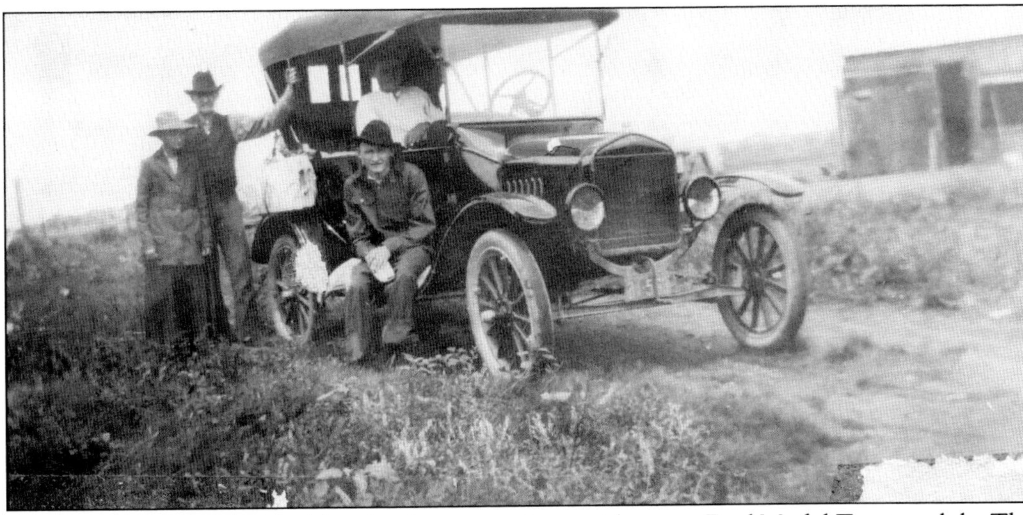

Several members of the Kealiher family are seen here with a new Ford Model T automobile. The Model T was extremely popular because it was the first affordable car geared toward the average American consumer. This photograph was taken on the Kealiher farm near Auburn in 1921.

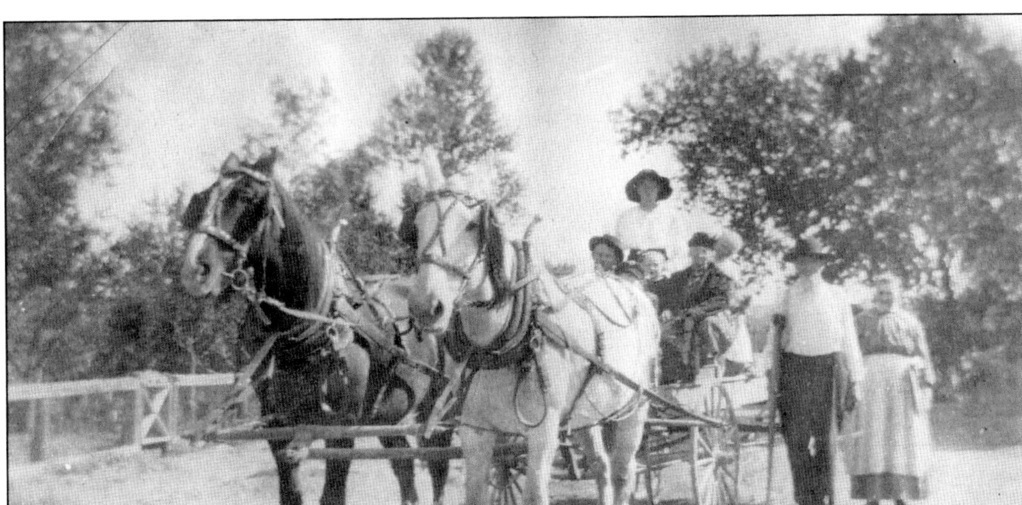

This 1921 photograph, taken east of Evans, shows several members of the Keahiler family with a horse-drawn carriage. The two people standing on the ground next to the carriage are identified as Grandma and Grandpa Kealiher. The little girl riding in the carriage (center) is Fay Kealiher Garner.

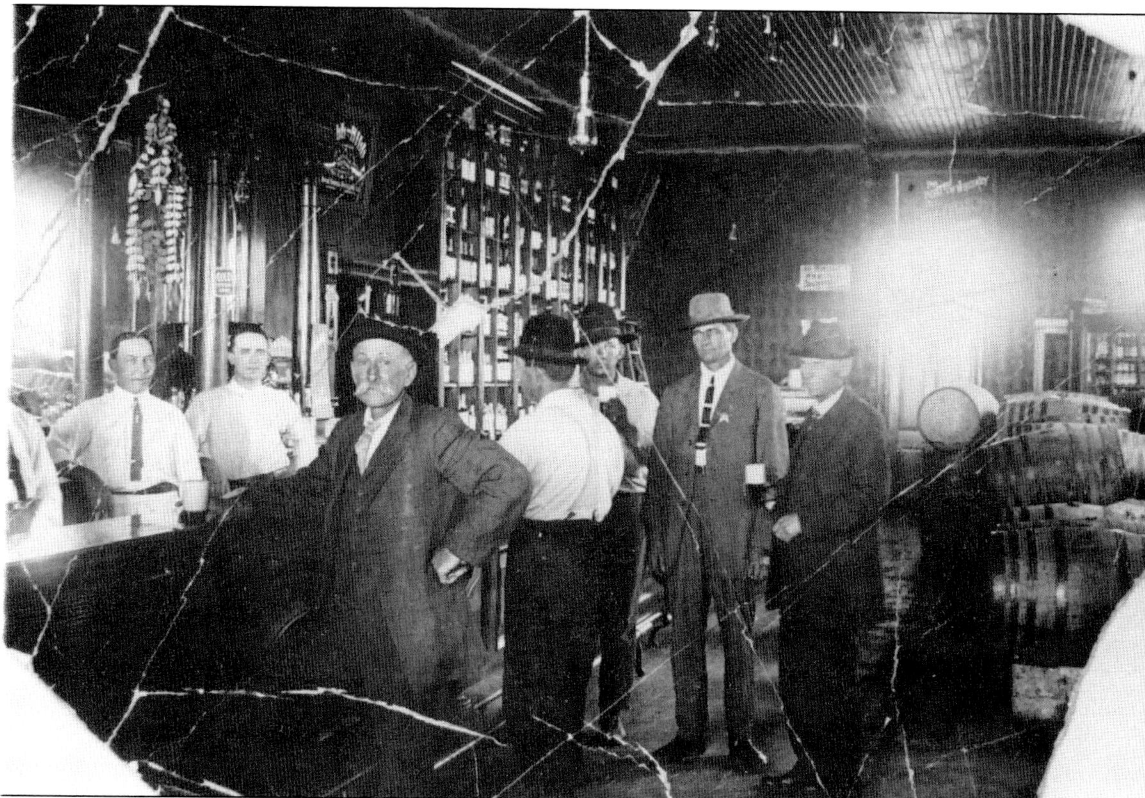

For many years, Evans was the only town in northeastern Weld County to have licensed saloons. Efforts from temperance people to close down the saloons in 1889 led to a landslide vote in favor of keeping the town "wet." The *Greeley Tribune* stated that "Liquor is going well in Evans, not as much action as could be expected, however. The saloons get all the spare dollars and dimes leaving little for the merchants; temperance people prefer to trade in Greeley." Despite the *Tribune*'s claim, bans on the sale and consumption of liquor in neighboring towns brought a good deal of business to Evans. The above photograph shows a man enjoying a drink in Jack O'Grady's Saloon around 1910. (Courtesy of City of Greeley Museums, Permanent Collection, 1978.06.006.)

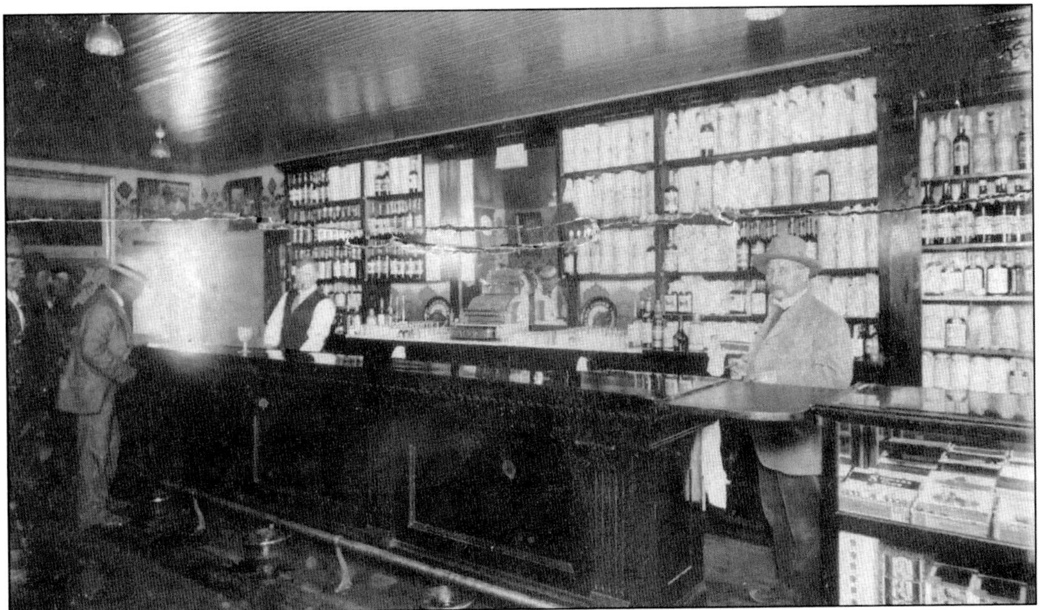

Morris Camnitzer came to the United States from Germany in 1876. He lived in Denver and was the proprietor of a saloon. Later, with the help of his son Peter and a business partner named Lucas, the business expanded. Camnitzer and Lucas ran saloons and sold package liquor at several locations around Colorado, including Milliken, Evans, and Denver. The above photograph is of the inside of the Camnitzer saloon in Evans, which was located across the street from Jack O'Grady's. The photograph below is of the main saloon owned by Camnitzer and Lucas, which was located near Seventeenth and Larimer Streets in Denver.

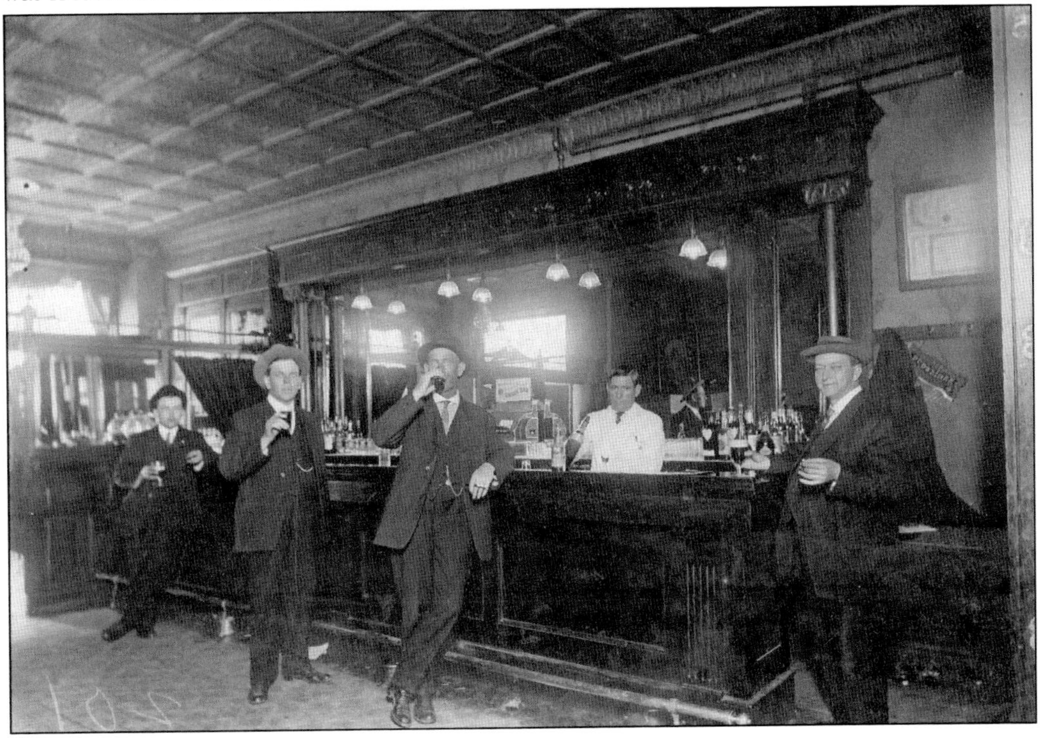

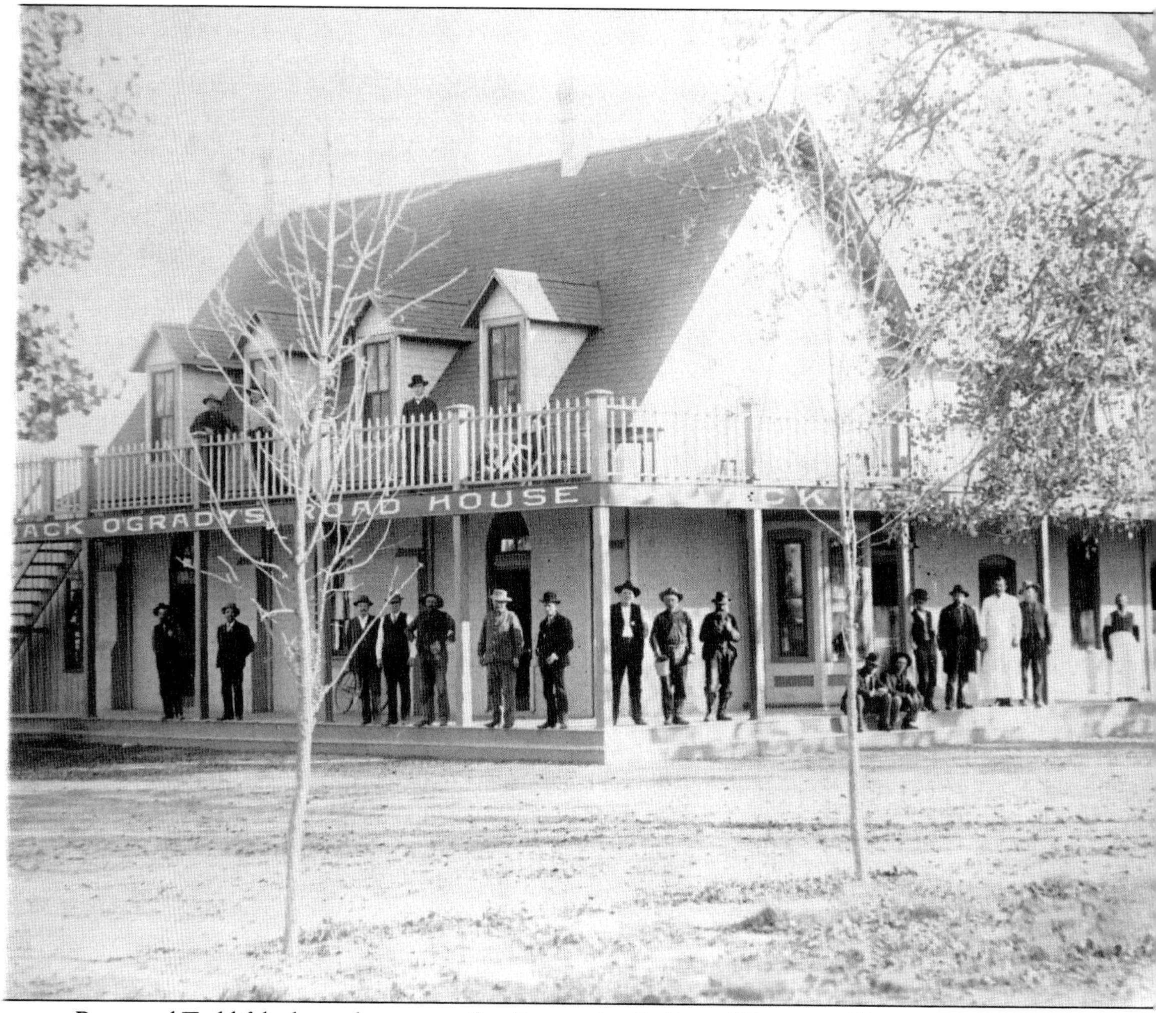


Reverend Todd felt that saloons were leading to the decline of Evans, and he is quoted as saying: "The Devil had a mortgage on the town, and it looks as if he would foreclose." After Todd left for Utah in 1891, his Reformed Presbyterian church was turned into a saloon. The men standing on the porch of the saloon are, from left to right, Jim O'Grady, Bill Merser, Fred Mins, Steve O'Grady, Mr. Camnitzer, three unidentified people, Shortie Shoemaker, Jack O'Grady, Ed Macintyre, John Olsen, Mr. Brenner, John Mahoney, Earl Baker, Fred Blumenthaw, and unidentified.

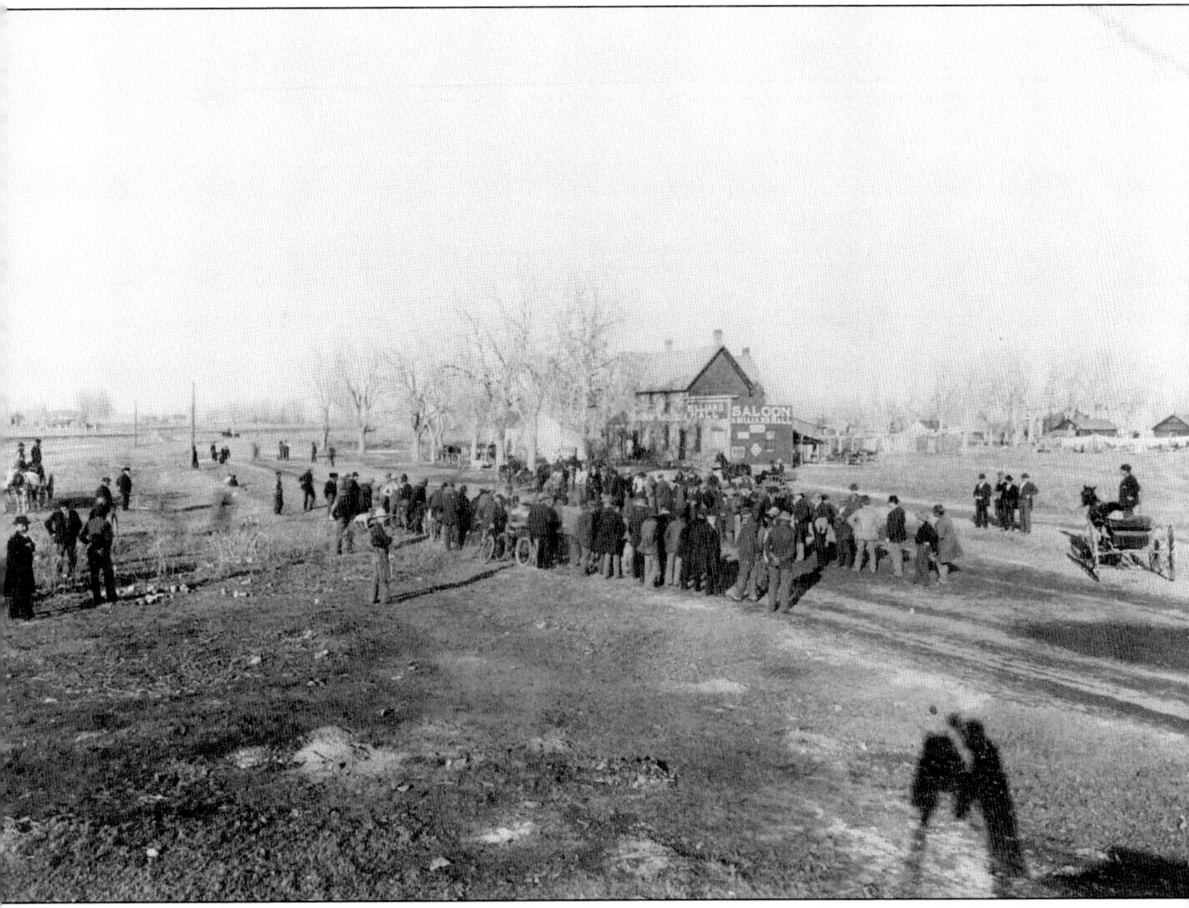


In the early 1900s, it was common for saloons to have music, dances, dinners, and other forms of entertainment, but they were only open to men. It was not considered appropriate or ladylike for women to drink in public, let alone patronize saloons. Katie Moore, a longtime resident of Evans, recalled that when she was a child all the saloons in town had signs in the windows that said, "No Women Allowed." Women were expected to socialize at church, women's gatherings, or places geared toward family entertainment. A large group of men is gathered outside of Jack O'Grady's to watch a footrace in 1903.

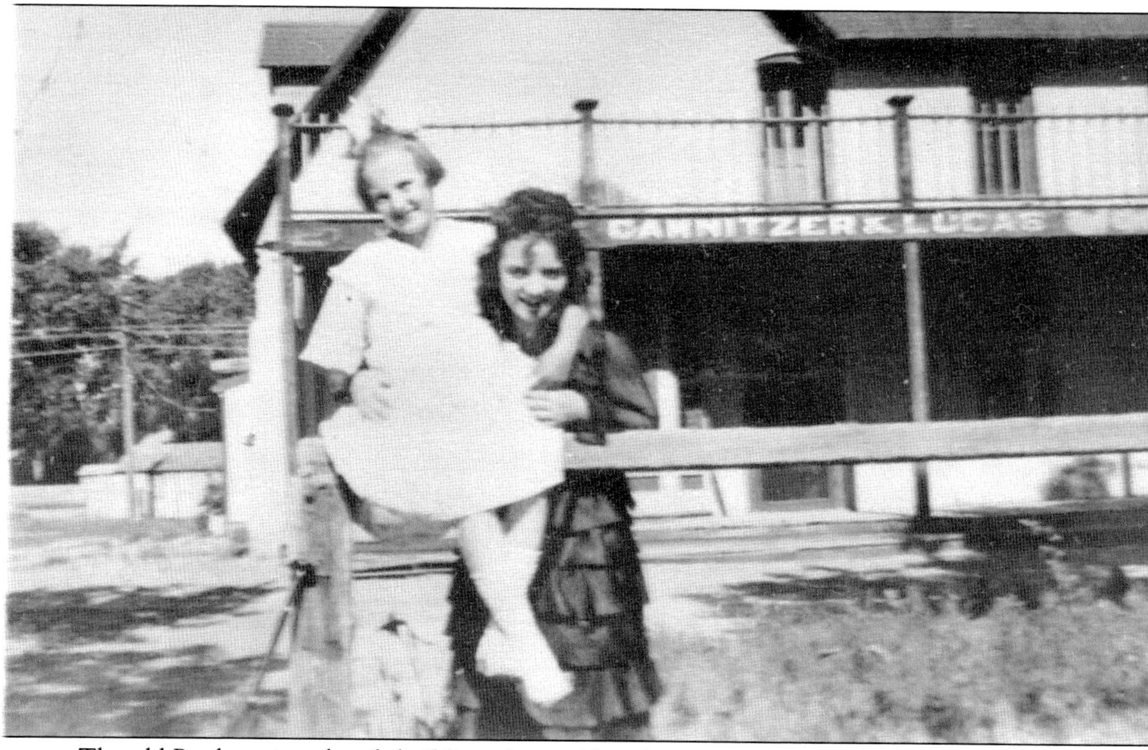


The old Presbyterian church building changed hands many times over the years and served a variety of purposes in town. The building was used as a cement factory when Fred Minns owned it. The structure was also, of course, Jack O'Grady's for many years. In 1930, it appears that the building was used for storage or was possibly an industrial building of some kind. The owners, Jack and Lillie Barton, are standing out front. The old Camnitzer Saloon building was located across the street from O'Grady's, and it is visible on the right side of the photograph.

While Jack O'Grady's was the largest and most popular saloon in Evans, there were several concentrated on Central between Thirty-eighth and Thirty-ninth Streets. The Camnitzer Saloon, Jordinelli's, Paul Hentchell's, and Fritz Niemeyer's were hangouts for thirsty residents and travelers. This photograph of the outside of the Camnitzer Saloon was taken around 1907. A woman purchased the building and turned it into a restaurant sometime around World War I.

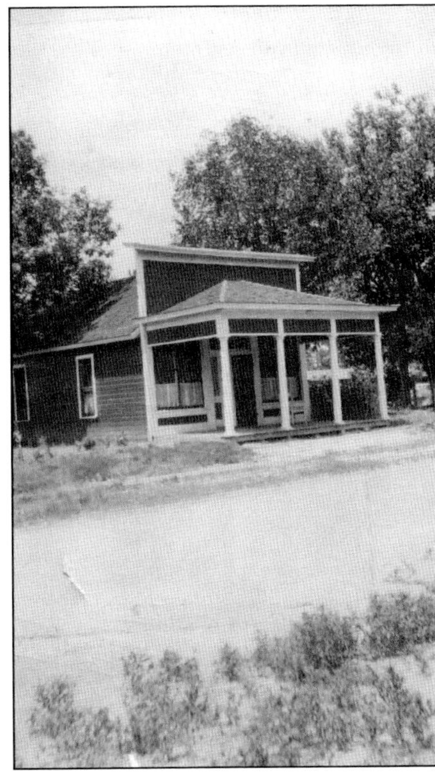

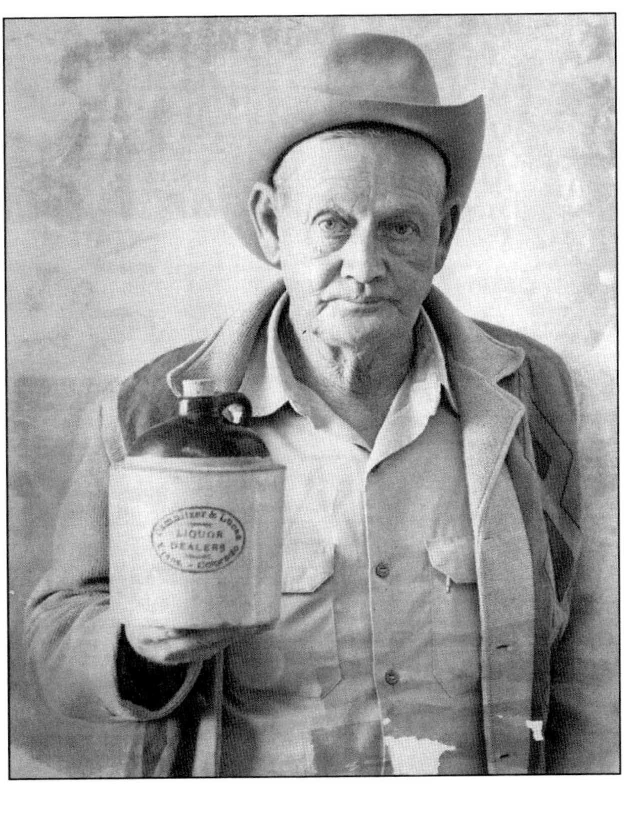


For a period of time, Evans had its own distillery. Camnitzer and Lucas, of the Camnitzer Saloon, made whiskey. A whiskey jug from Camnitzer and Lucas like this one was dug up in Greeley during the construction of the water sanitation plant in 1965. The photographer and the date the image was taken are unknown. (Courtesy of City of Greeley Museums, Permanent Collection, 1983.48.0004T.)

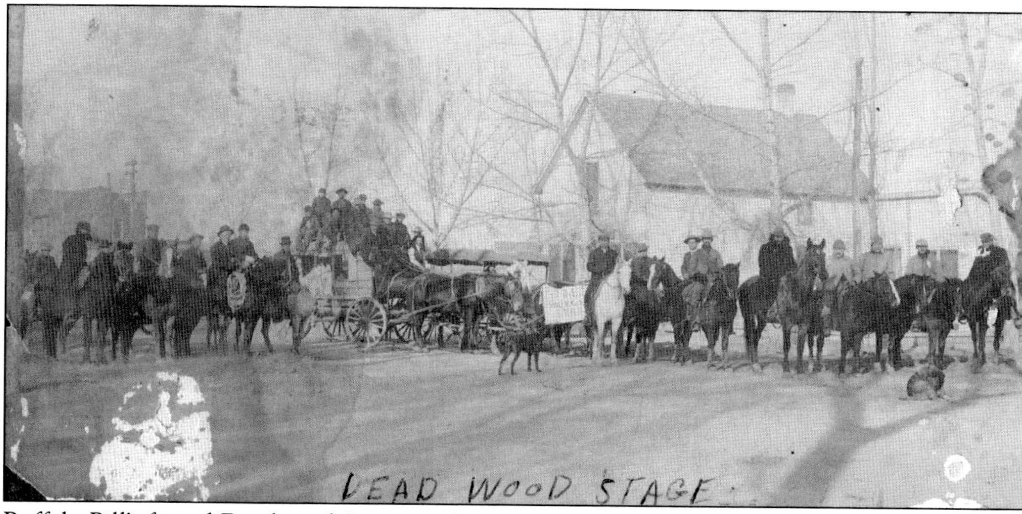


Buffalo Bill's famed Deadwood Stage made a trip to Evans on at least one occasion. It arrived in town to a warm welcome from the residents, who gathered around to catch a glimpse of the stagecoach. The banner in the front is advertising a dance to be held in the evening at Young's Hall, the principal event venue in town.

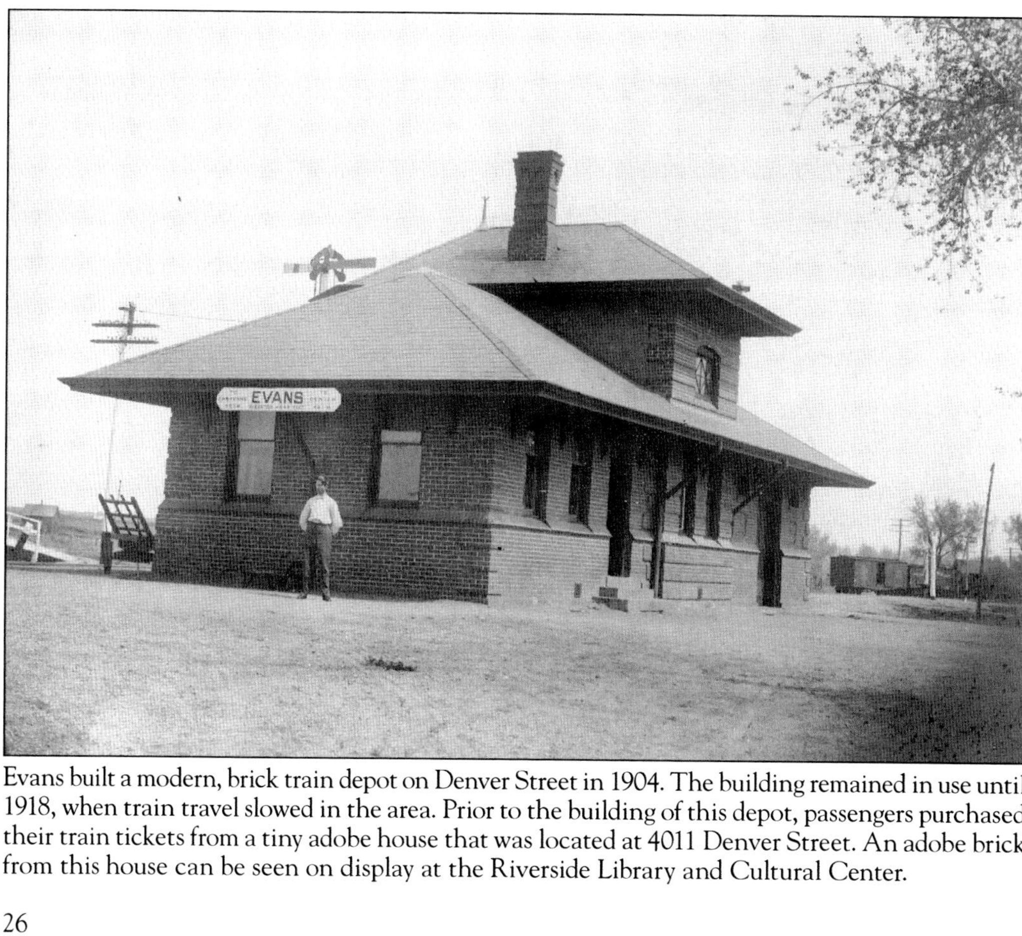


Evans built a modern, brick train depot on Denver Street in 1904. The building remained in use until 1918, when train travel slowed in the area. Prior to the building of this depot, passengers purchased their train tickets from a tiny adobe house that was located at 4011 Denver Street. An adobe brick from this house can be seen on display at the Riverside Library and Cultural Center.

# *Two*

# Everything You Need
## Living and Working in Evans

Evans had a bit of a wild start in the early years with saloons, cowboys, and a few instances of vigilante justice, but the true heart of Evans lies with the people who worked hard and made a life for themselves and their families here. By the turn of the century, Evans had a population of 400 residents, modern businesses, and many beautiful homes. Like most small towns, those who ran the town and helped it grow wore many hats. It was not at all uncommon for a businessman in town to run one or more businesses, be a member of a fraternal organization, and also serve on the school board, or hold a public office.

In a business brochure from the turn of the century, Evans is described as "a healthy locality" and is listed as having "five public soft water wells and six private, two churches, good grade schools with three competent teachers located only 3 miles from the State Normal, fine public park, taxes low and town out of debt, two telephone systems, nine secret organizations, two good public halls, one weekly newspaper, three general merchandise stores, one clothing store, one drug store, two blacksmith shops, one feed and coal store, two hotels, one lumber yard, one harness shop, two meat markets, two confectionary stores, one shoe shop, one dentist, two doctors, one jeweler, two real estate offices, one livery stable, one barber shop, one billiard hall, four saloons at a revenue of $4,000 per year, one mill (not in operation), located only 4 miles from the sugar beet factory, town is owner of a ditch of 30 cubic feet capacity which furnishes an abundance of water for all purposes."

There are several prominent families that made significant contributions to the town of Evans. They ran businesses that served the needs of the community, but they also gave back to the community and invested in the future of the town. The Behrens, Young, Reed, and Wiggins families, and many others that might not be mentioned here, helped to shape Evans into what it is today.

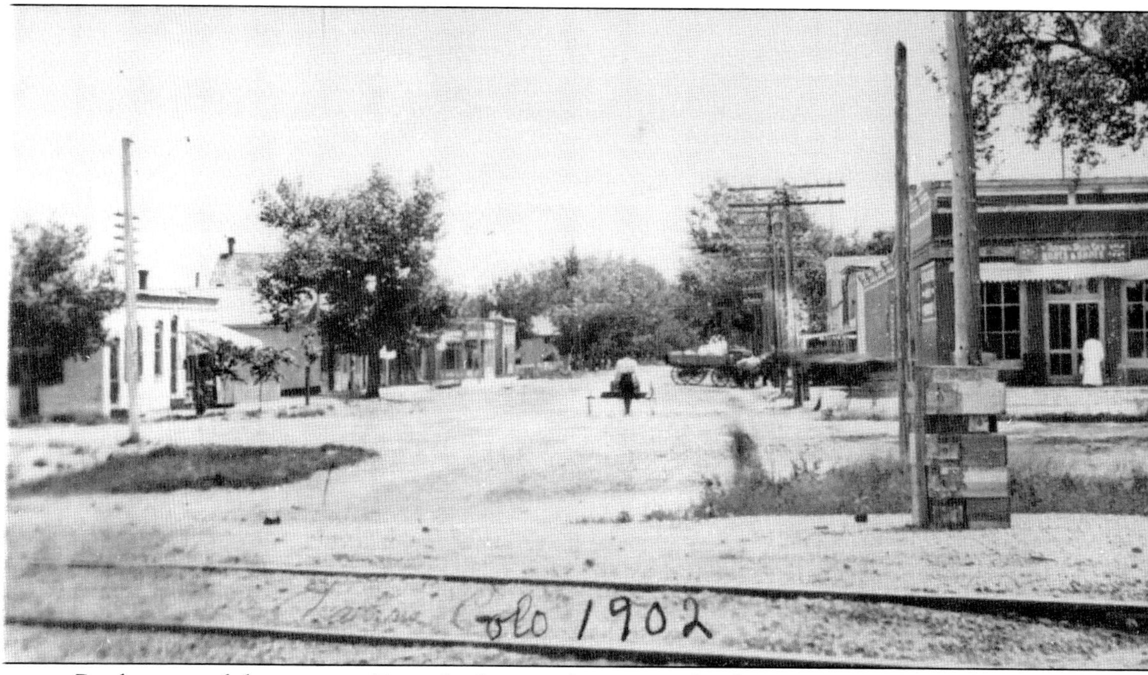


By the turn of the century, Evans had grown from just a few houses scattered near the railroad tracks to a full-service town. Evans had everything from drugstores to general merchandise stores, restaurants to hotels, garages to feed stores, banks to doctors, and a variety of other businesses. Nearly every necessity could be met in Evans. This is how the Evans business district appeared in 1902, looking east down Thirty-eighth Street from the railroad tracks at Denver Street. Though there are just a few houses and businesses there now, this was once the center of activity in town.

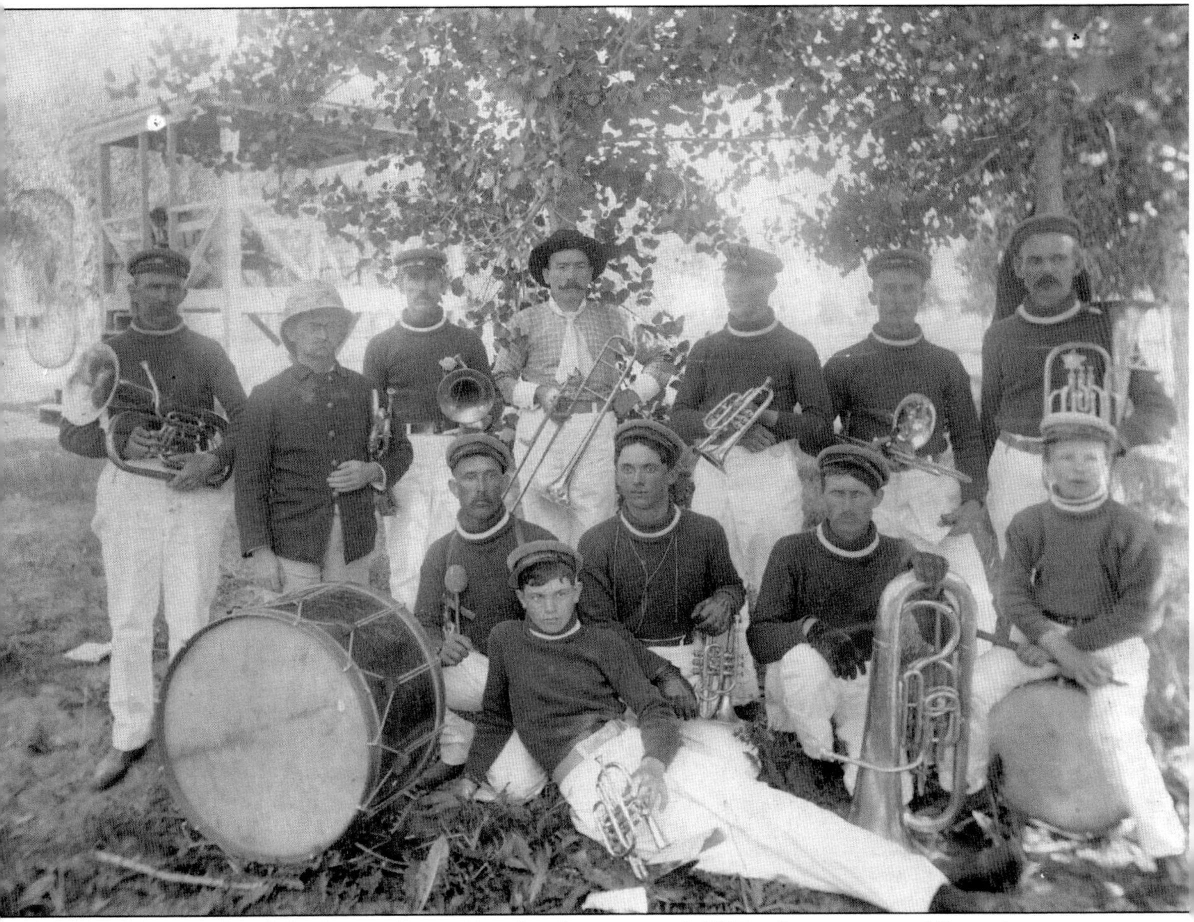

This photograph of the Evans Brass Band, taken around 1900, shows some of Evans's most prominent residents and business owners. The band members are, from left to right, (first row) Ralph Richard; (second row) Robert Redman, unidentified, Henry F. Behrens, and William Scott; (third row) William E. Morrison, "Professor," Charles C. Huffsmith, James O'Grady (saloon proprietor), Charles O. Behrens (lumber yard), David S. Kimzey, and Harry Hunter.

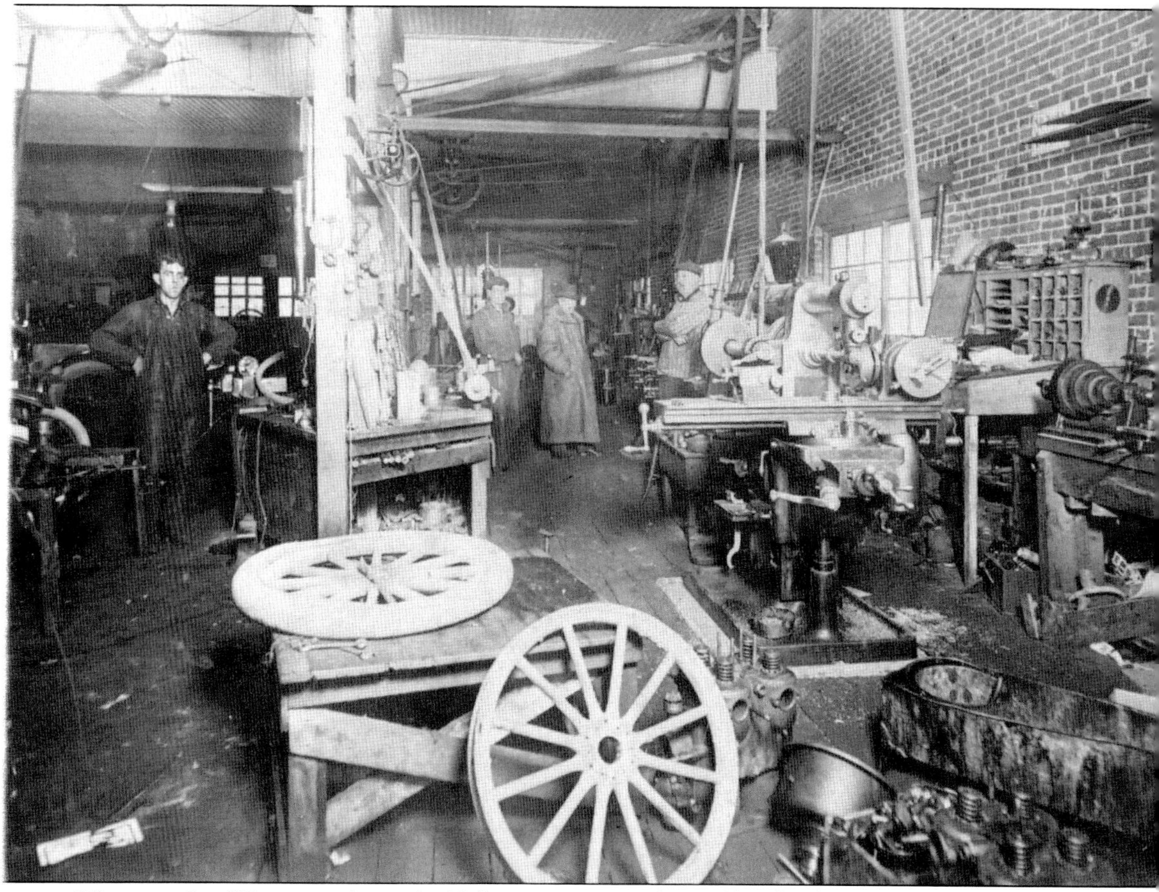

The growth of Evans in the early 20th century is evidenced by the fact that there were two of many of the same types of businesses in town. Pictured above is the W.A. Jack Blacksmith and Auto Repair shop, located on what is now Thirty-ninth Street. Note the front of the automobile that is visible on the far left side of the photograph, just to the left of the man in bib overalls. There was also the W.F. Smith Blacksmith and Implement Dealer on Boulder Street. Since Evans is located in a largely agricultural area, many of the businesses in town catered to farming and ranching needs.

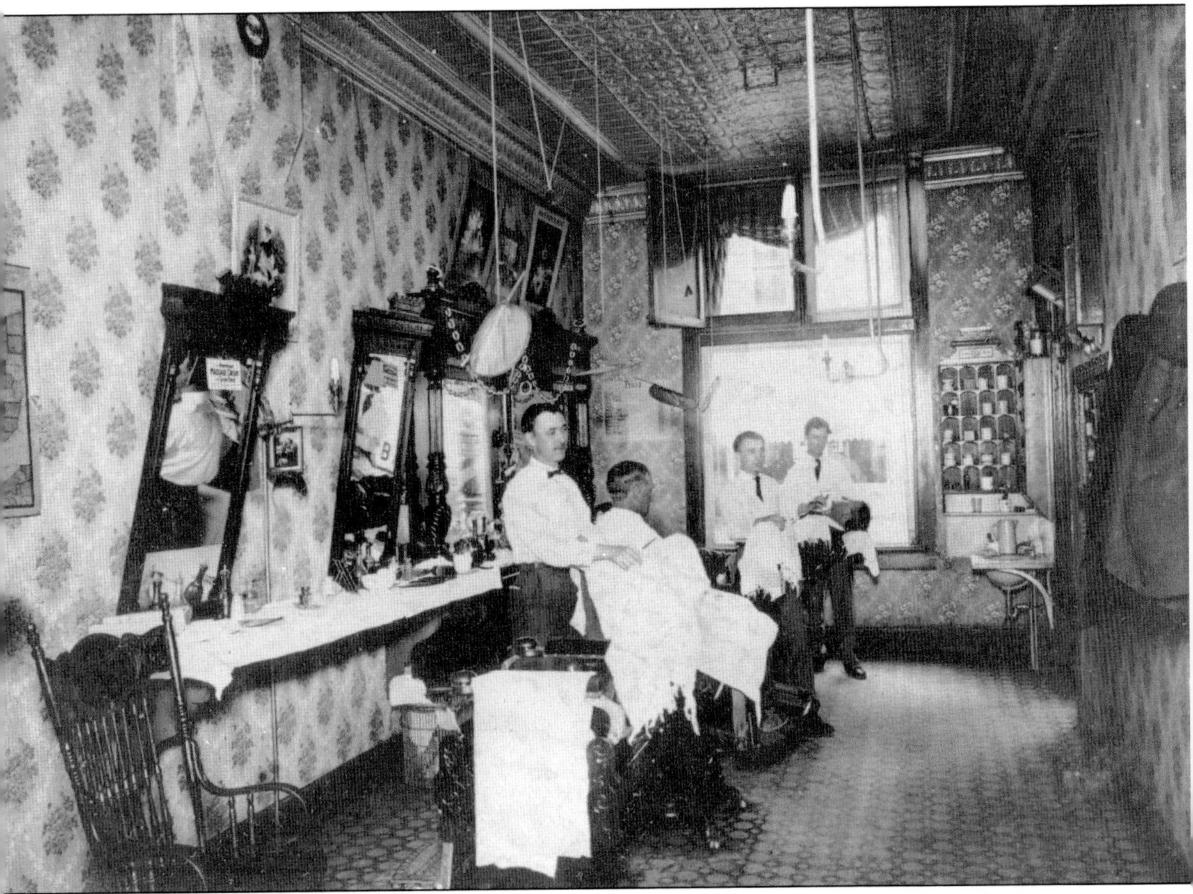

Evans had several different barbers over the years. This unidentified photograph from the Evans Historical Museum collection is quite possibly of the Parks Barber Shop. According to the 1910 census, George and his son Melvin were both working as barbers in Evans in 1910, and the 1911 business directory states that Melvin was the proprietor of the business.

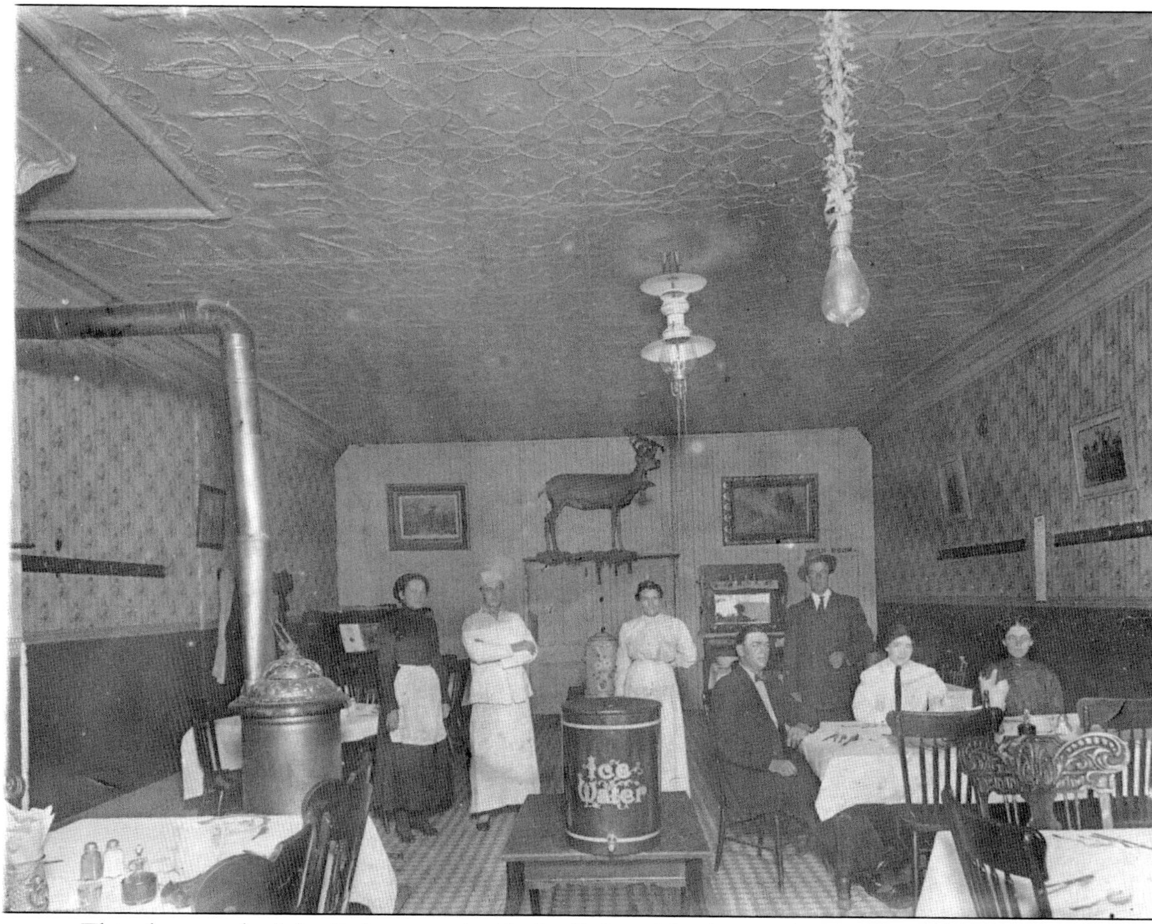


This photograph of the dining room inside the Perkins Hotel, owned and operated by Mary Cahill in Evans in the late 1800s, shows the gradual transition from gas to electric lighting—note the two different light fixtures hanging from the ceiling. Pictured from left to right are Hazel Sherman, Charlie Koalinz, Mary Cahill, John Brickman, unidentified, Nell Cahill, and Minnie Randall.

John Behrens was born in Germany on November 25, 1839. He came to the United States in 1857 with his parents, first settling in New York City. He married Caroline Hibschile in 1865 and operated a mercantile business in New York. In 1871, John and Caroline moved to Evans, where he was a business owner and leader in the community. The Behrens family attended the Lutheran church and was active in many local improvements in the town over the years.

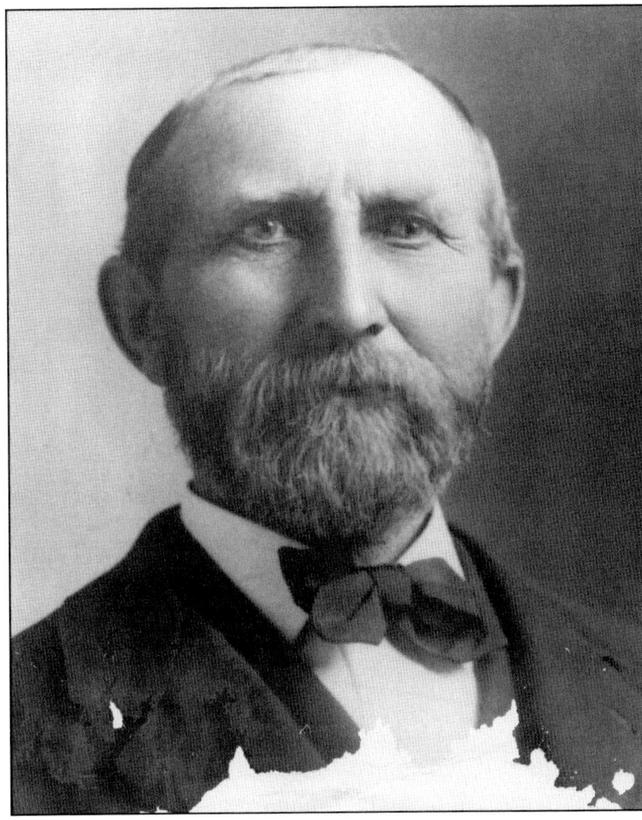

The Behrens Lumber Company was owned and operated by John H. Behrens and was one of the first businesses in Evans. The business was taken over by John A. and Charles Behrens, sons of John H. John A. Behrens moved the lumberyard to La Salle, where he lived until his death in 1959.

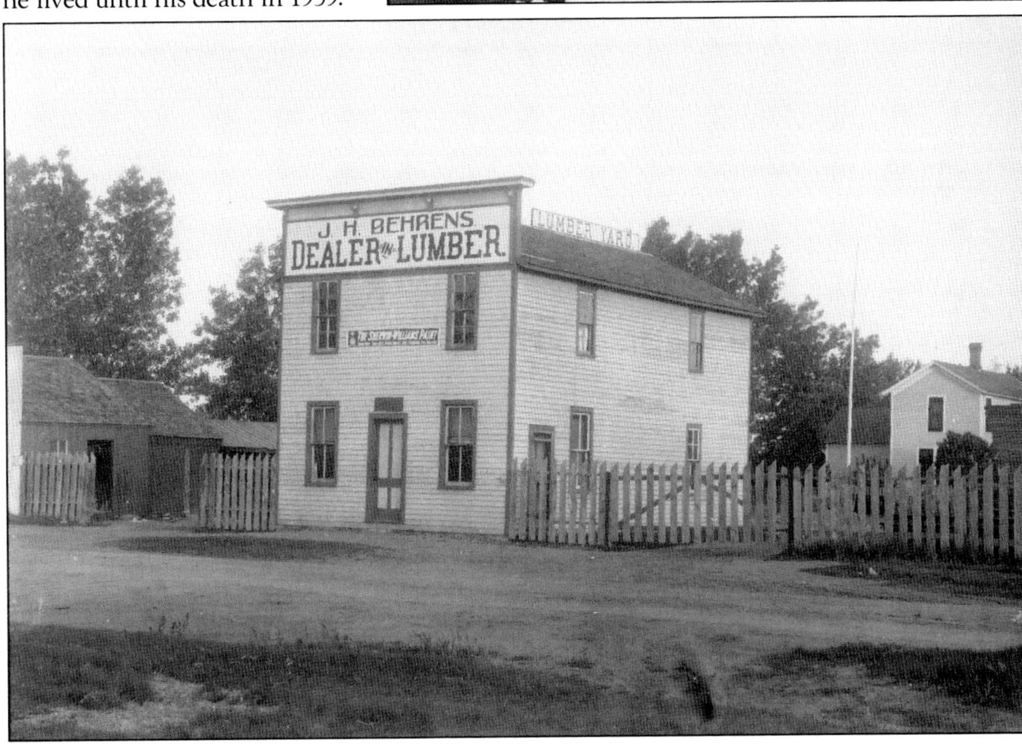

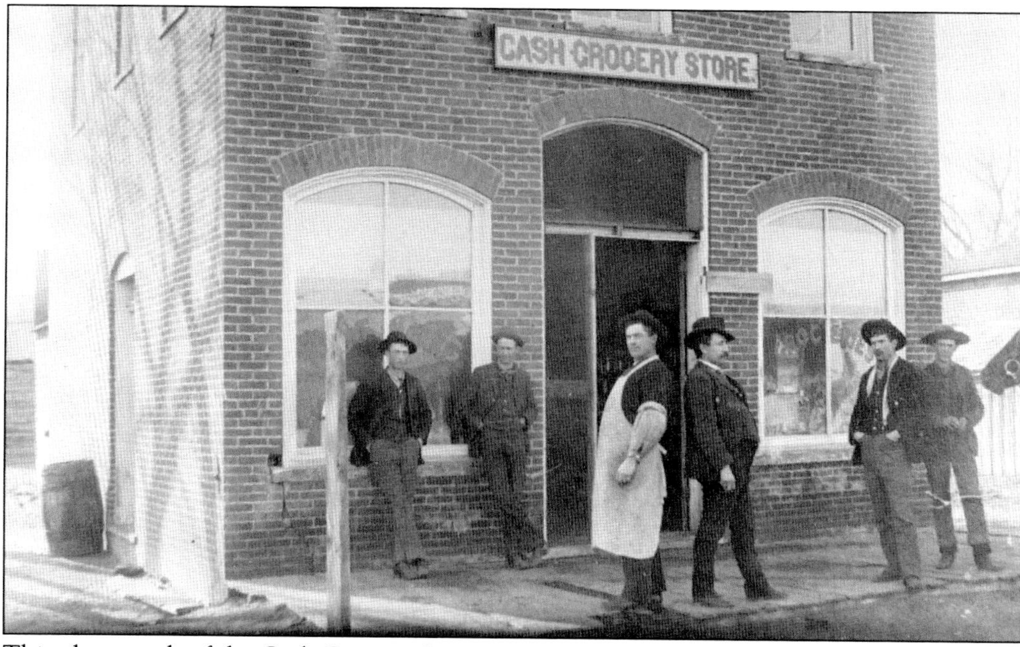


This photograph of the Cash Grocery Store in Evans was likely taken sometime between 1880 and 1900. The man standing in the center front wearing a butcher's apron is identified as Alex Lucas, though it is unknown if he is the same Lucas as in the Camnitzer and Lucas liquor dealers. The photographer and date of the image are unknown. (Courtesy of City of Greeley Museums, Permanent Collection, 1982.62.0001.)

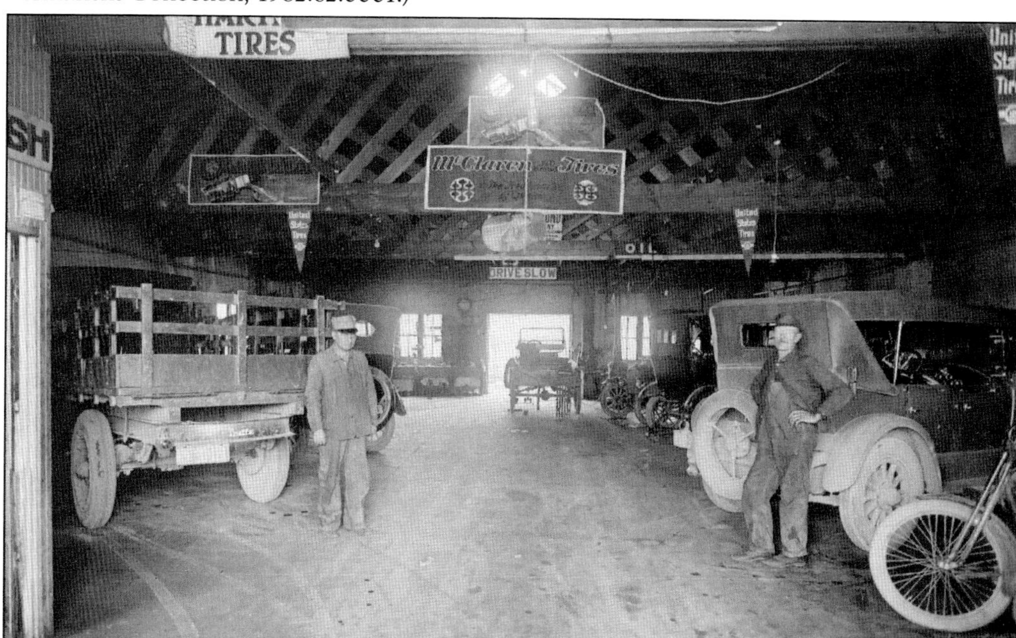


The F.F. Hart Garage was located in the heart of the business district on Thirty-ninth Street in the building that was formerly the W.A. Jack Blacksmith shop. In 1922, a fire spread through downtown that required the efforts of the Evans, Greeley, and La Salle fire departments. Many of the oldest buildings in town, including Hart's Garage, were destroyed.

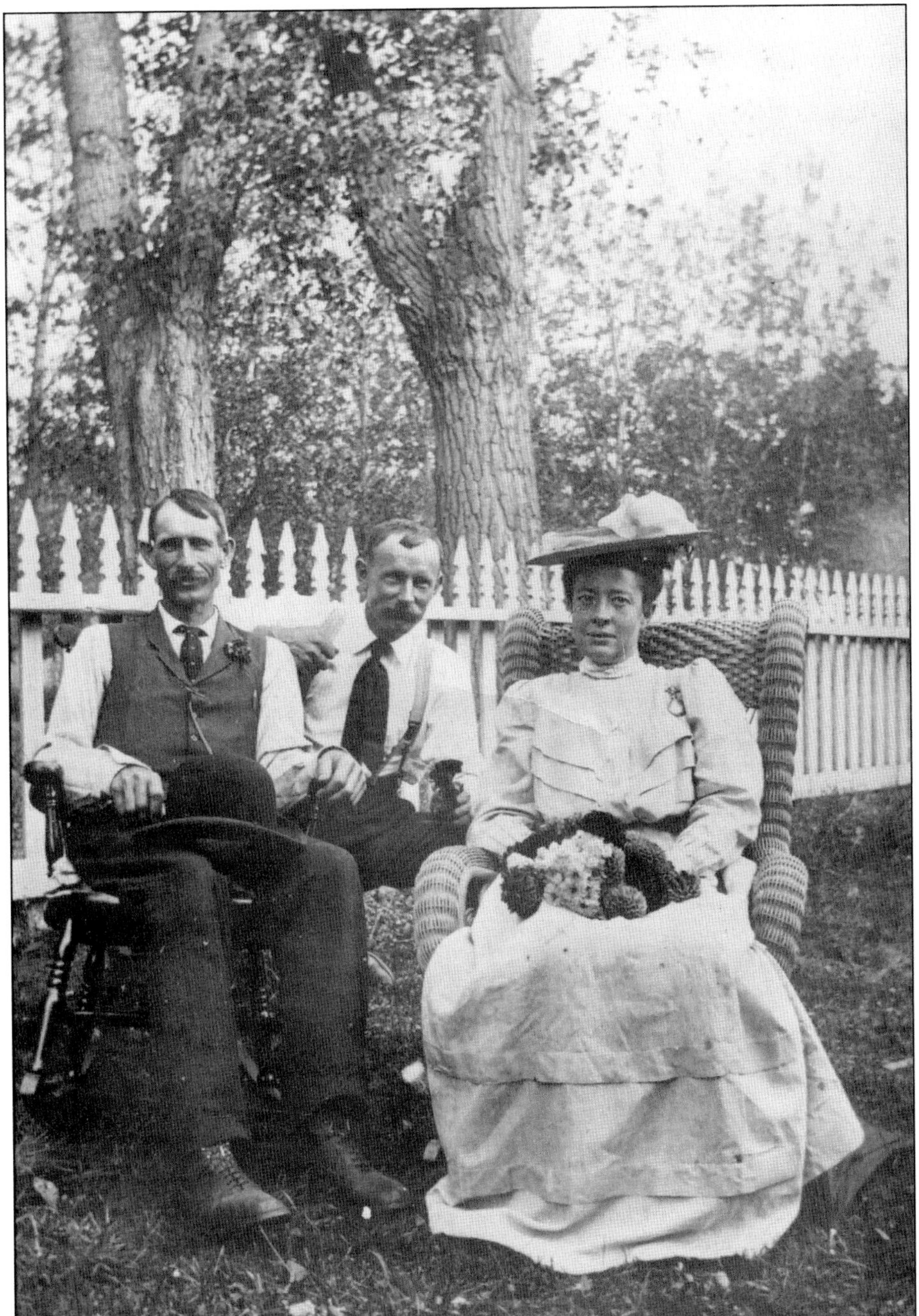

Martin Van Buren Briggs came to Evans in 1889 and began work as a clerk at his brother's general store. After six years, he purchased the French and Parks flour and seed business, and soon after that, he purchased his brother's coal business. In 1903, the *Evans Courier* described his business practices: "Mr. Briggs attributes his success in large measure to the fact that he buys for cash and sells for cash and points very proudly to the fact that, by following this rule, he is able to look the whole world in the face as he owes no man." He is pictured here in the center, along with his friends Henry and Elizabeth Behrens.

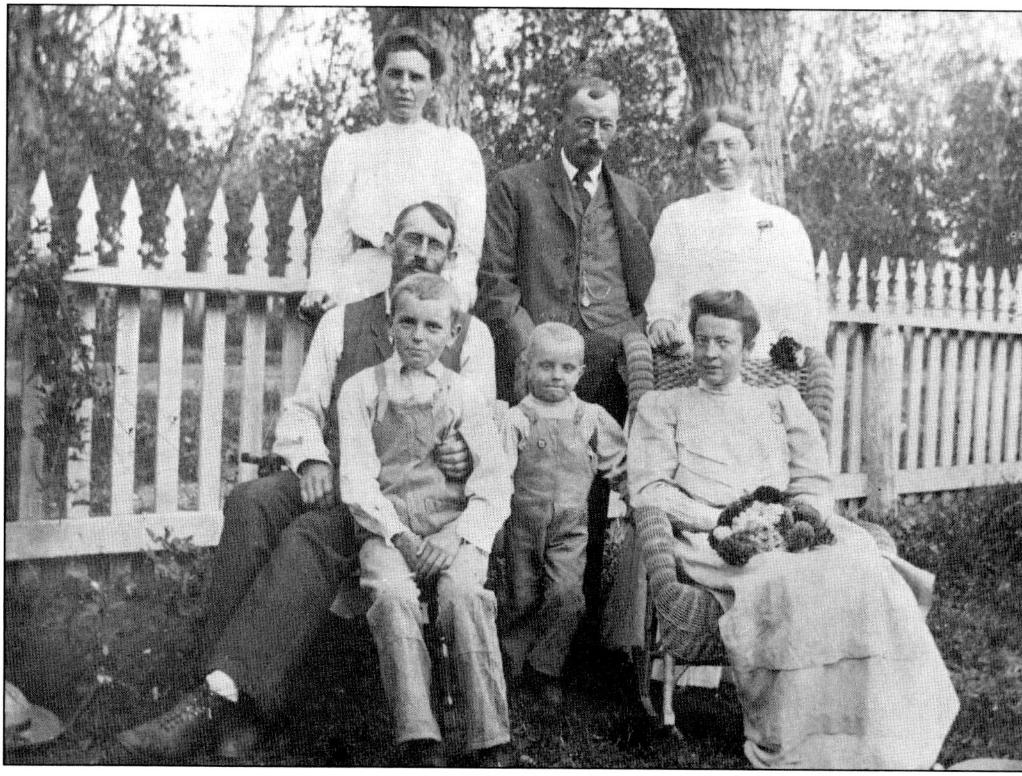

The Briggs and Behrens families are enjoying and afternoon together in Evans on an unknown date. Pictured from left to right are (first row) Henry Behrens, Ralph Reid Briggs (seated on Henry's lap), Roy Martin Briggs, and Elizabeth Behrens; (second row) Nellie May Reid Briggs, Martin Van Buren Briggs, and Elizabeth Morrow.

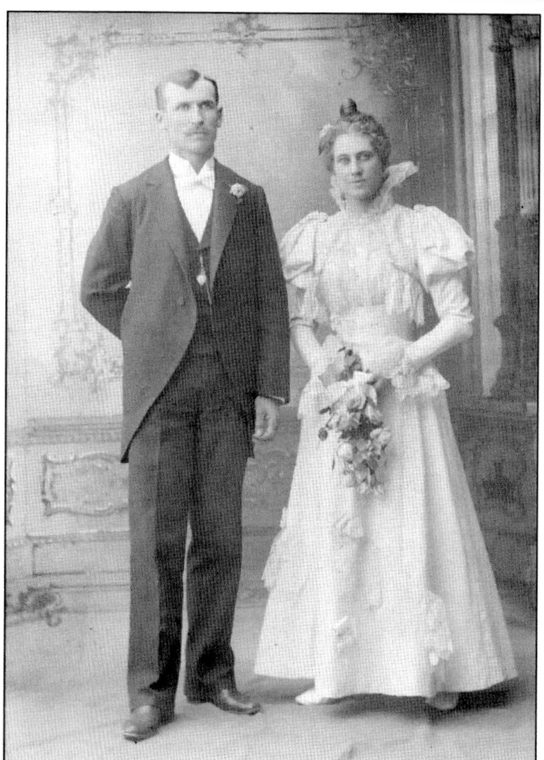

Elizabeth Behrens passed away in 1924 at the age of 35 after an illness. Henry F. Behrens was remarried two years later to Amelia "Allie" Smith, a dressmaker who had been a boarder at his parents' home. This photograph was taken on their wedding day, November 17, 1926.

Grace Jay and her friend Lovenna Vanderlip are playing outside in 1903. Grace married John A. Behrens, son of John H. Behrens. John took over the Behrens lumber and tanning business for a number of years with his younger brother Charles. John and Charles later moved the lumberyard to La Salle. Lovenna's father, L.C. Vanderlip, ran a general merchandise store and a blacksmith shop and manufactured gasoline and acetylene lighting devices.

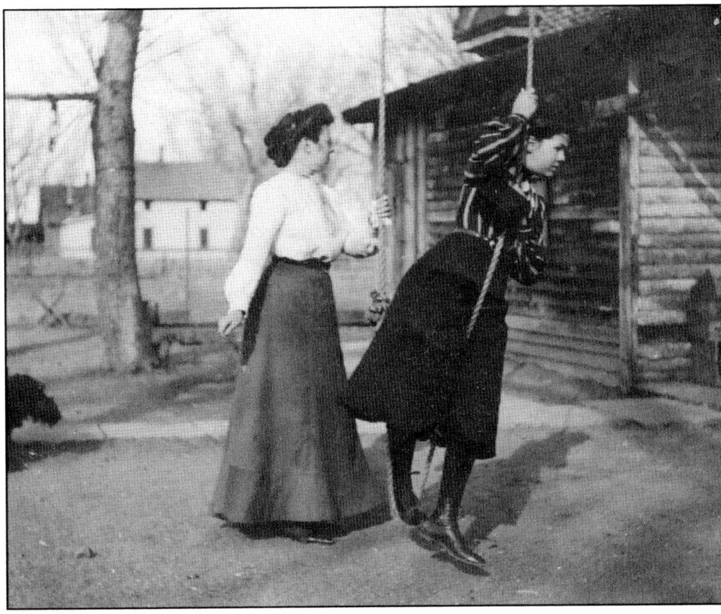

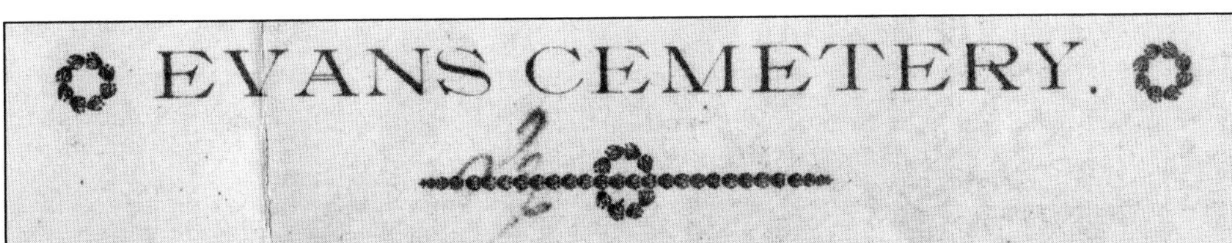

EVANS CEMETERY.

KNOW ALL MEN BY THESE PRESENTS, *That for and in consideration of the sum of* Five *Dollars, the receipt of which is hereby acknowledged, the Trustees of the Town of Evans, Weld County, Colorado, granted, bargained and sold, and do by these presents convey to* Christian Miller, *his heirs and assigns, to have and hold forever, Lot No.* 38 *in Block No.* (2) Two *(as laid off and platted according to the approved map, filed in the Town Clerk's office,) in the EVANS CEMETERY of the said Town of Evans, with all the privileges and appurtenances thereto belonging, for the sole use and purpose of a burial ground.*

WITNESS WHEREOF, *We have hereunto set our hands and the seal of said Town of Evans this* 29 *day of* May *A. D.* 1914.

A. V. Balfour, *Mayor.*
Chas. O. Behrens, *Clerk.*

The Behrens family was very active in city government and civic affairs in Evans. This cemetery certificate, dated May 29, 1914, is signed by town clerk Charles Behrens, son of John H. Behrens. This certificate shows that Christian Miller purchased plot 38 in block 2 of the Evans Cemetery for $5. Charles's older brother Henry F. Behrens later donated land to the cemetery.

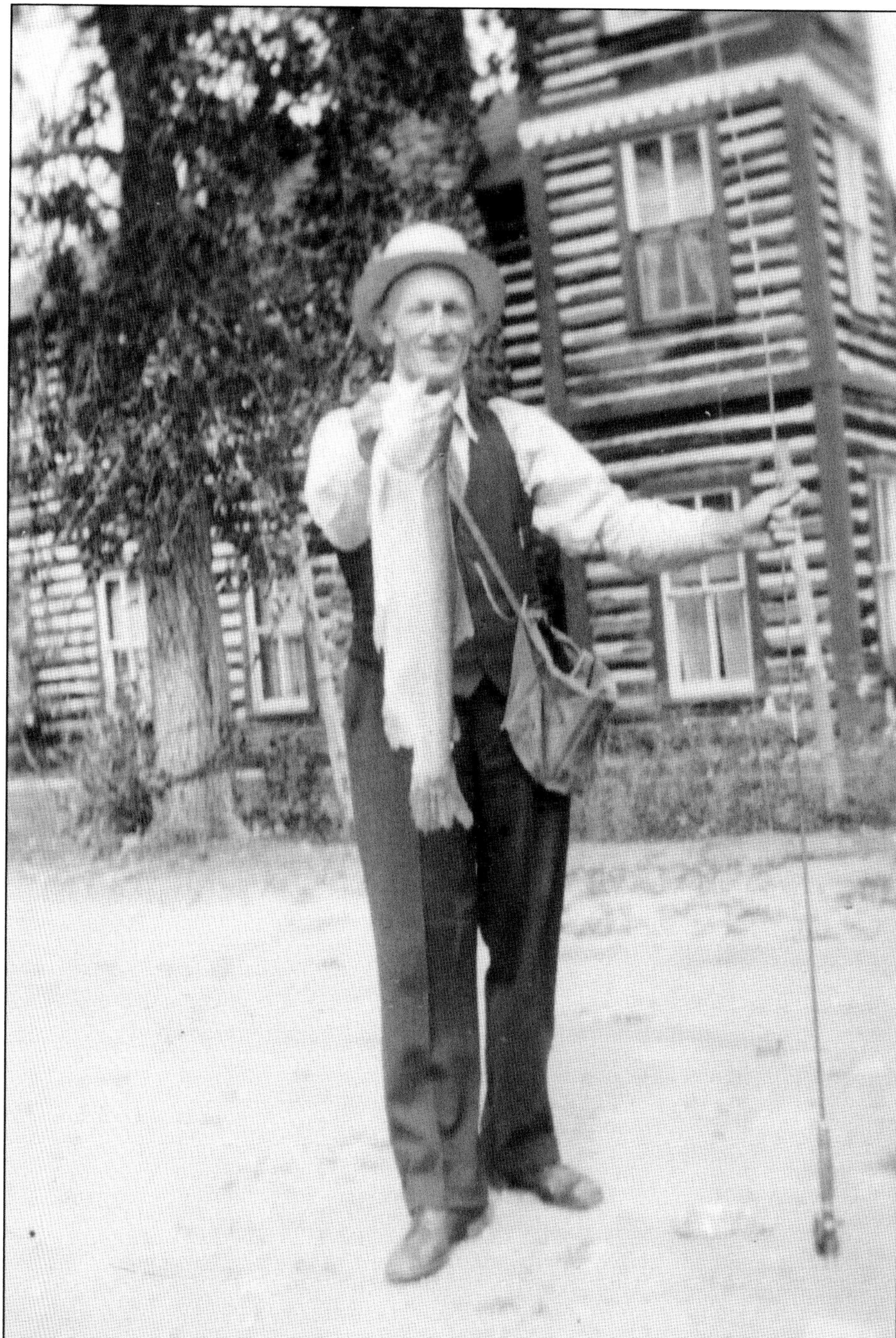

Charles O. Behrens was the son of John H. and Catharine Behrens and brother to Henry and John A. Behrens. Charles lived in Evans and helped run the family lumberyard with his brothers after the passing of their father. Charles was united in marriage to Flossie M. Dove on August 19, 1902, in Denver. Charles enjoyed being outdoors, fishing, and camping. This 1935 photograph was taken at a cabin in Cherokee Park, northwest of Fort Collins and just south of the Wyoming border. The fish he caught measured 20 inches long and weighed four and a half pounds.

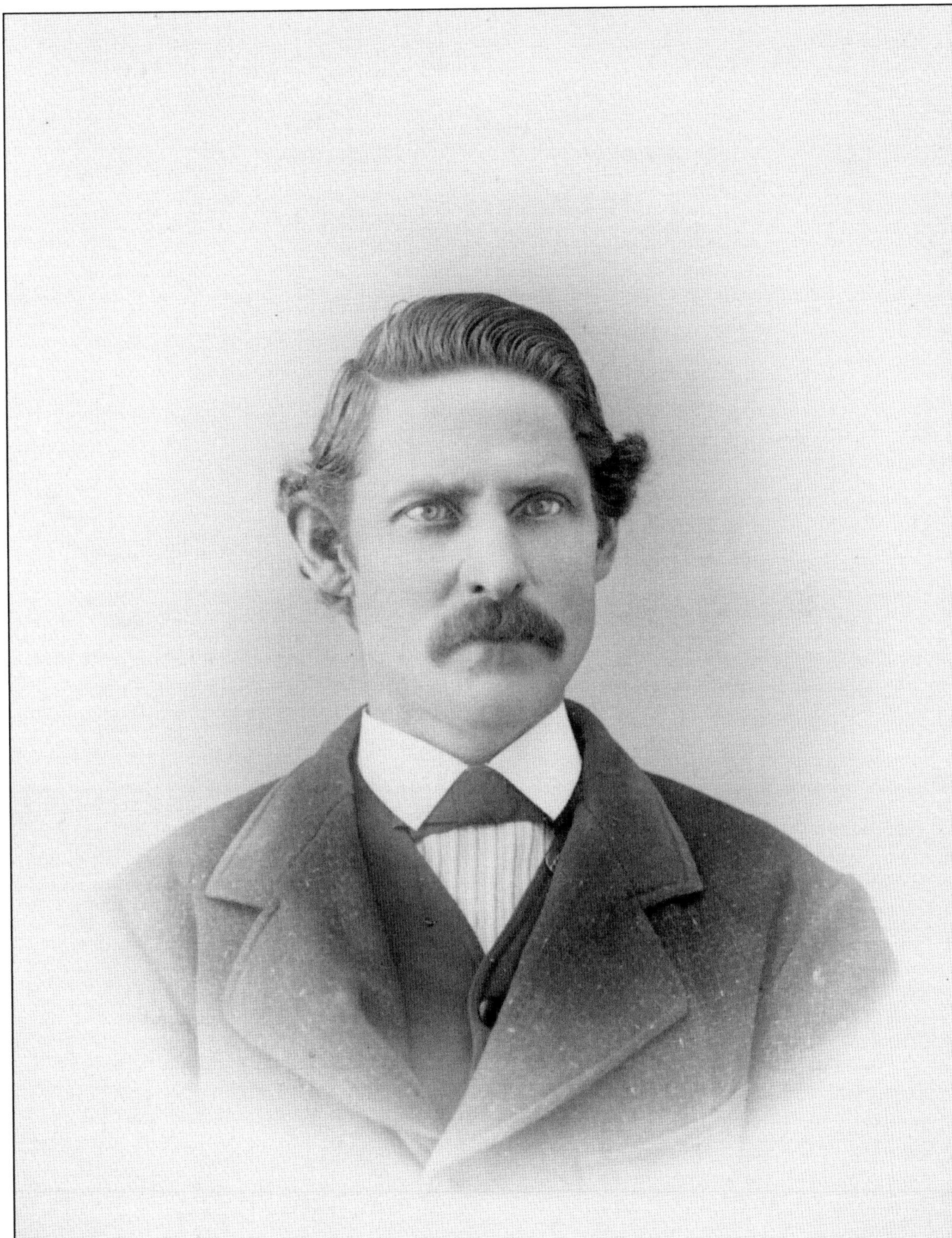

George H. Young is perhaps the most active, civic-minded, and business-oriented person in the history of Evans. He also has a fascinating personal story. Born in Columbus, Ohio, in 1844, he enlisted in the Company A of the 95th Ohio Infantry of the Union army in 1862.

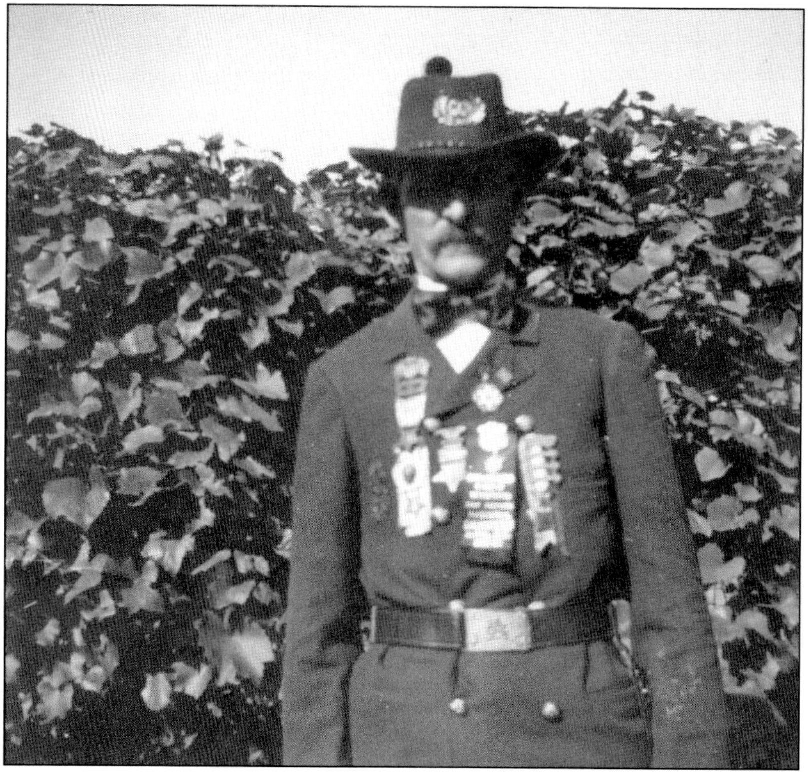

Young served in the Western Division of the Union army until the end of the Civil War in 1865. He wounded his left arm in Kentucky at the Battle of Richmond in August 1862. Young then served under Gen. Ulysses S. Grant in the Vicksburg campaign, though he was mostly on hospital duty due to his injury.

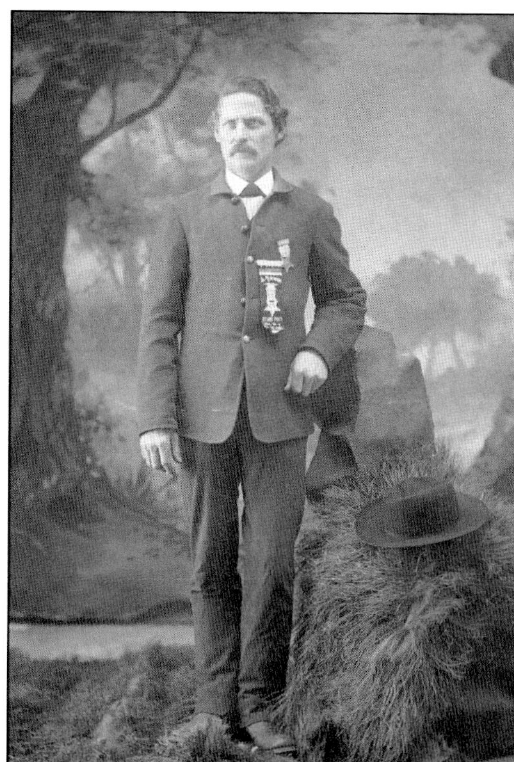

Young was captured by Confederate soldiers in Mississippi and held prisoner at several Confederate POW camps for nine months, including Andersonville, Millen, Blackshire, and Thomasville. After the end of the war in April 1865, Young was onboard the *Sultana*, a large paddleboat, traveling up the Mississippi River. The vessel exploded, killing 1,500 of the 2,200 passengers. Though badly scalded, Young survived and returned to Ohio for a short period of time before heading west for Colorado.

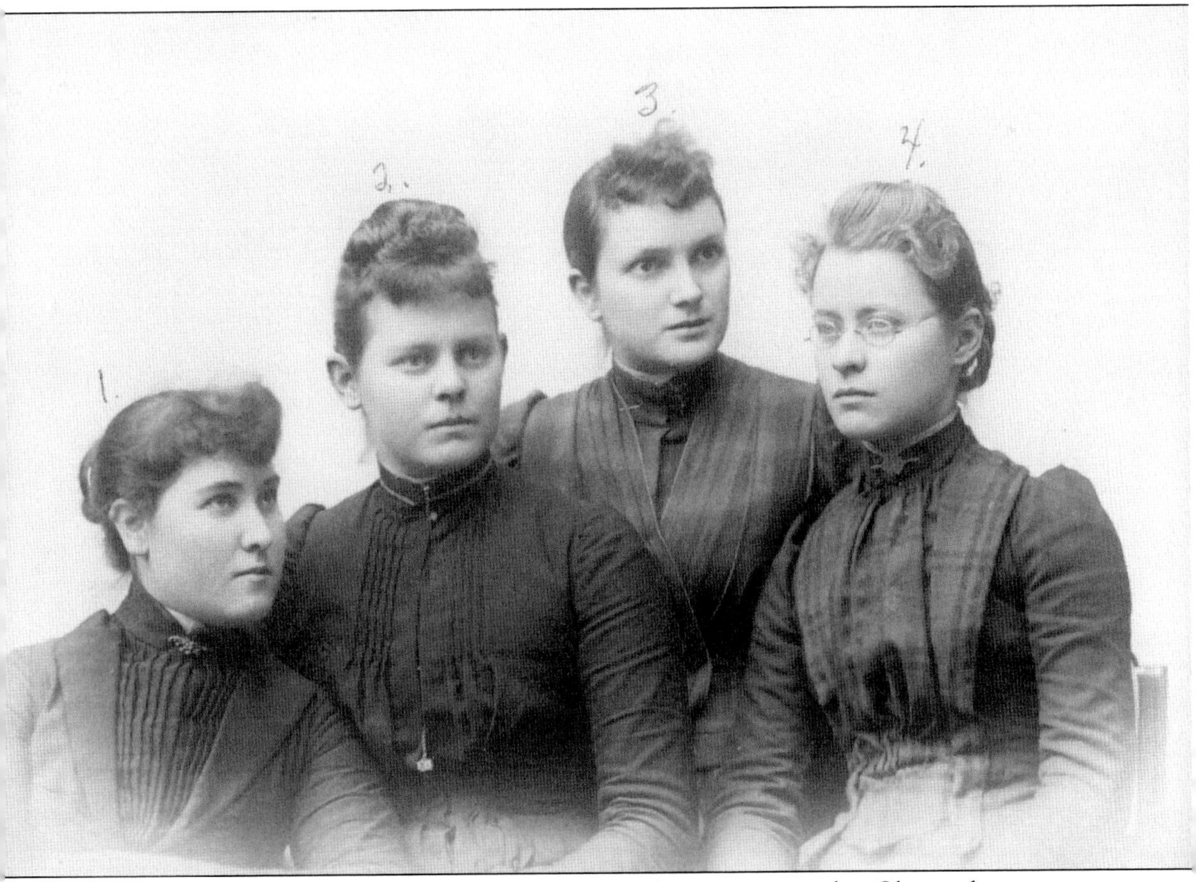

George H. Young's first wife was Martha Mills Young. They were married in Ohio and came out west to Colorado together. The Youngs had four daughters, Grace, Edna, Sadie, and Cora, as well as a son, William. They also had another daughter named Martha, who was born in Evans in 1883, but she died in infancy. This photograph, taken in Columbus, Ohio, shows three of the Young daughters with their cousin Jenne Orr. From left to right, the women are Grace Young, Jenne Orr, Cora Young, and Sadie Young. Edna is not in the photograph.

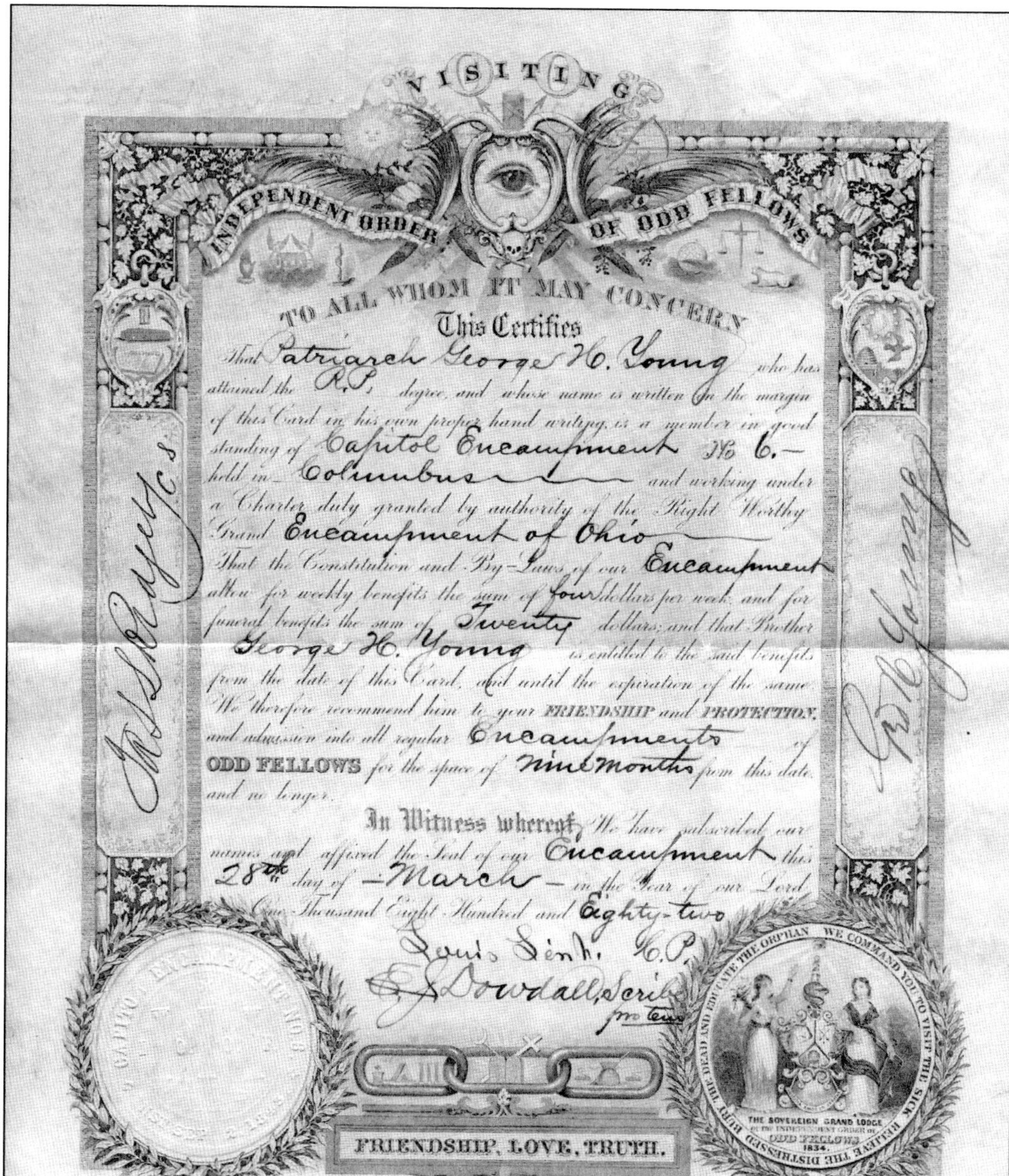

VISITING

INDEPENDENT ORDER OF ODD FELLOWS

TO ALL WHOM IT MAY CONCERN

This Certifies

That Patriarch George H. Young who has attained the R.P. degree, and whose name is written in the margin of this Card in his own proper hand writing, is a member in good standing of Capitol Encampment No 6.— held in Columbus and working under a Charter duly granted by authority of the Right Worthy Grand Encampment of Ohio

That the Constitution and By-Laws of our Encampment allow for weekly benefits the sum of four dollars per week, and for funeral benefits the sum of Twenty dollars; and that Brother George H. Young is entitled to the said benefits from the date of this Card, and until the expiration of the same. We therefore recommend him to your FRIENDSHIP and PROTECTION, and admission into all regular Encampments of ODD FELLOWS for the space of nine months from this date and no longer.

In Witness whereof We have subscribed our names and affixed the Seal of our Encampment this 28th day of March in the Year of our Lord One Thousand Eight Hundred and Eighty-two

FRIENDSHIP, LOVE, TRUTH.

BURY THE DEAD AND EDUCATE THE ORPHAN WE COMMAND YOU TO VISIT THE SICK RELIEVE THE DISTRESSED

THE SOVEREIGN GRAND LODGE OF THE INDEPENDENT ORDER OF ODD FELLOWS

George H. Young was an active member of the Evans chapter of the Independent Order of the Odd Fellows. The Odd Fellows is a service organization comprised of men who claim belief in a Supreme Being and who also wish to help their communities through outreach and service. This March 28, 1882, document certifies that George H. Young received the Royal Purple Degree—a distinguished honor for members of the organization. According to the Odd Fellows, one who receives the Royal Purple Degree "aims to teach alertness and determination as a basis for a possible success in the journey called life."

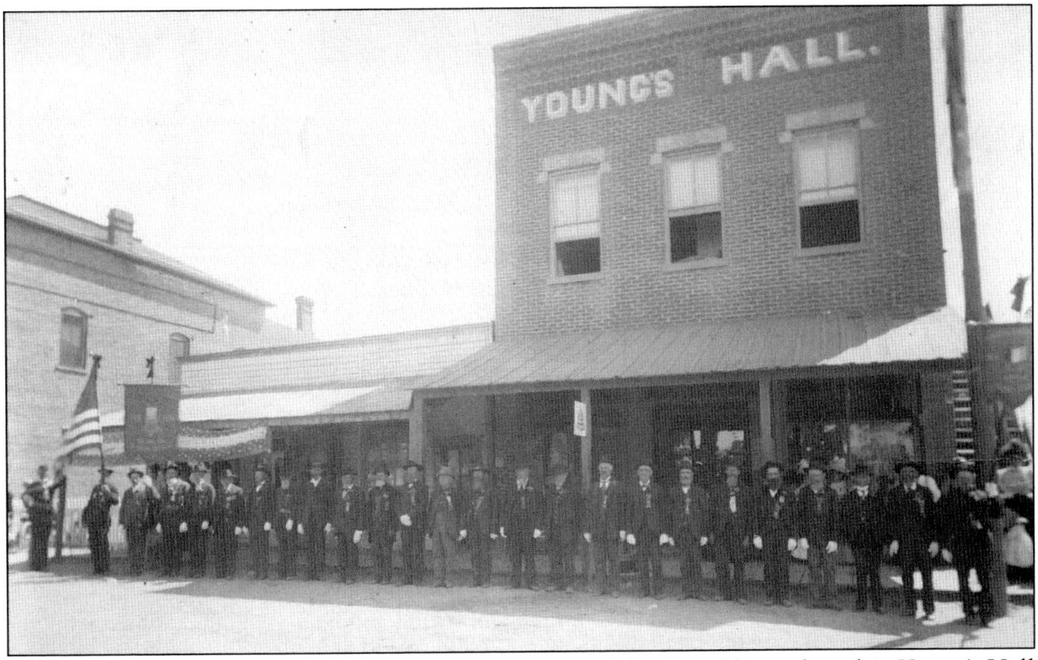


In 1902, the W.T. Sherman post of the Grand Army of the Republic gathered at Young's Hall to celebrate Decoration Day. Decoration Day is the original name for Memorial Day, a holiday started in 1868 by Gen. John Logan, head of the GAR, to honor the veterans of the Civil War. The holiday later evolved to honor veterans from all American wars.

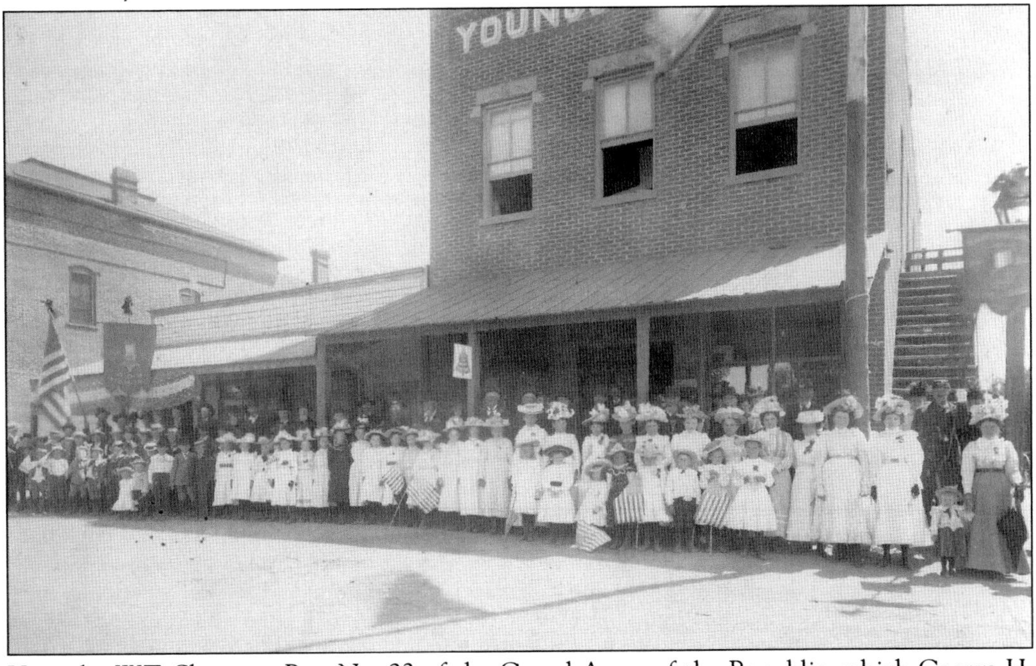

Here the W.T. Sherman Post No. 23 of the Grand Army of the Republic, which George H. Young helped to establish, is gathered together for an encampment in front of Young's Hall. Encampments were gatherings that typically lasted for several days. Veterans would bring their families for dinners, camp outs, and memorial events.

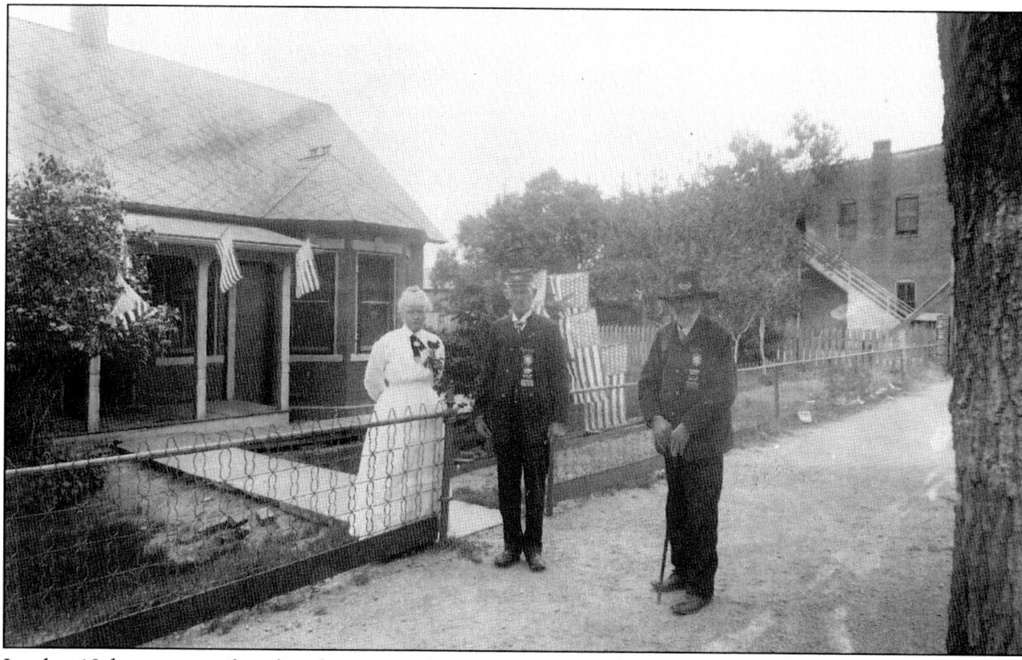

In the 19th century, few families owned a camera. Traveling artists sometimes made money by taking photographs of people and selling them the prints. This photograph of George H. Young, Lydia Young, and their friend Thomas Markle (right) was taken in front of the Young home in Evans on May 30, 1912.

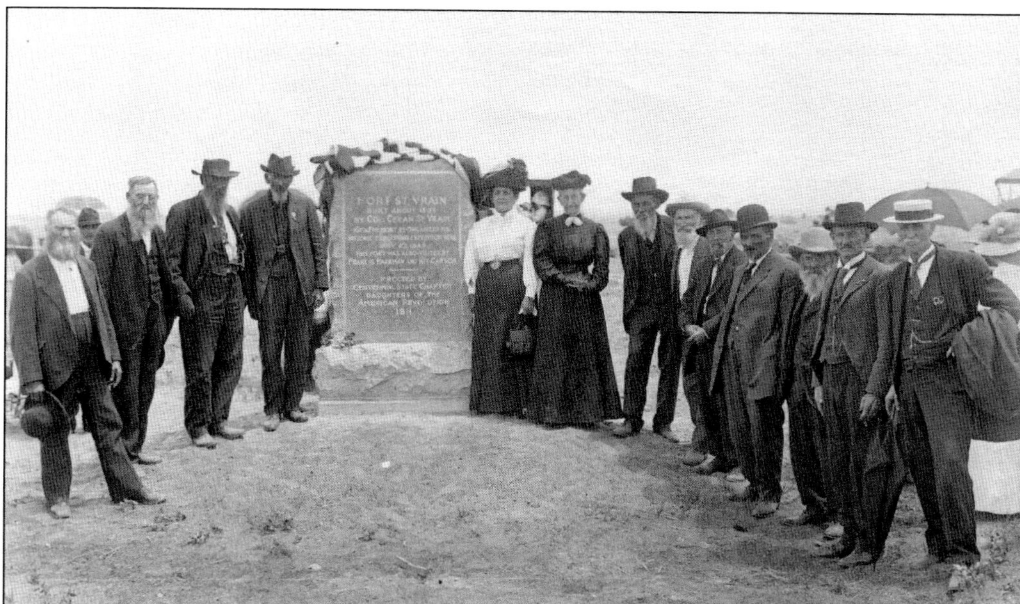


Always active in veteran and civic affairs, George H. Young attended the unveiling of the Fort St. Vrain Monument near present-day Platteville. Fort St. Vrain is important in Weld County history, as it was the location of the first courthouse in the county. The Daughters of the American Revolution erected this monument in 1911. George H. Young is second standing second from the right.

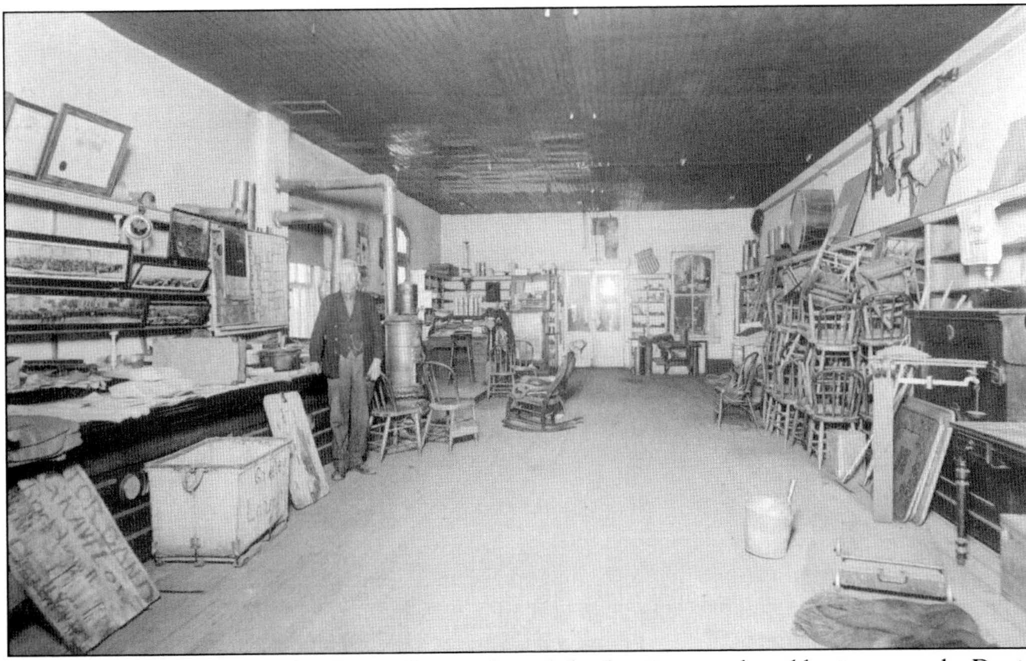

Shortly after Young arrived in Evans, he purchased the furniture and coal business run by David McMechan. This undated photograph shows George working inside of that shop. Having had some experience in the mercantile business back in Ohio, Young also opened a general store called The Pioneer in 1885. He continued to run both stores until 1895, when he quit the furniture and coal store.

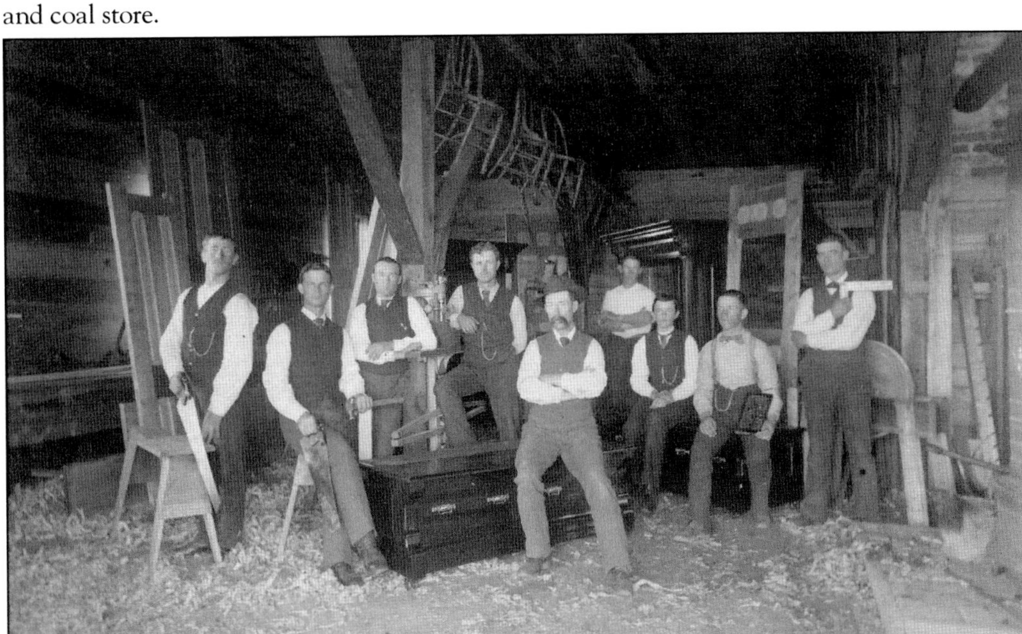

Before there were factories that mass produced goods, most everything was made locally when possible. This photograph of a woodworking class in Evans was taken in the workshop at George H. Young's furniture store. The chairs in the shelves above the students match the chairs by the wall in Young's furniture store. This class appears to have made wooden caskets.

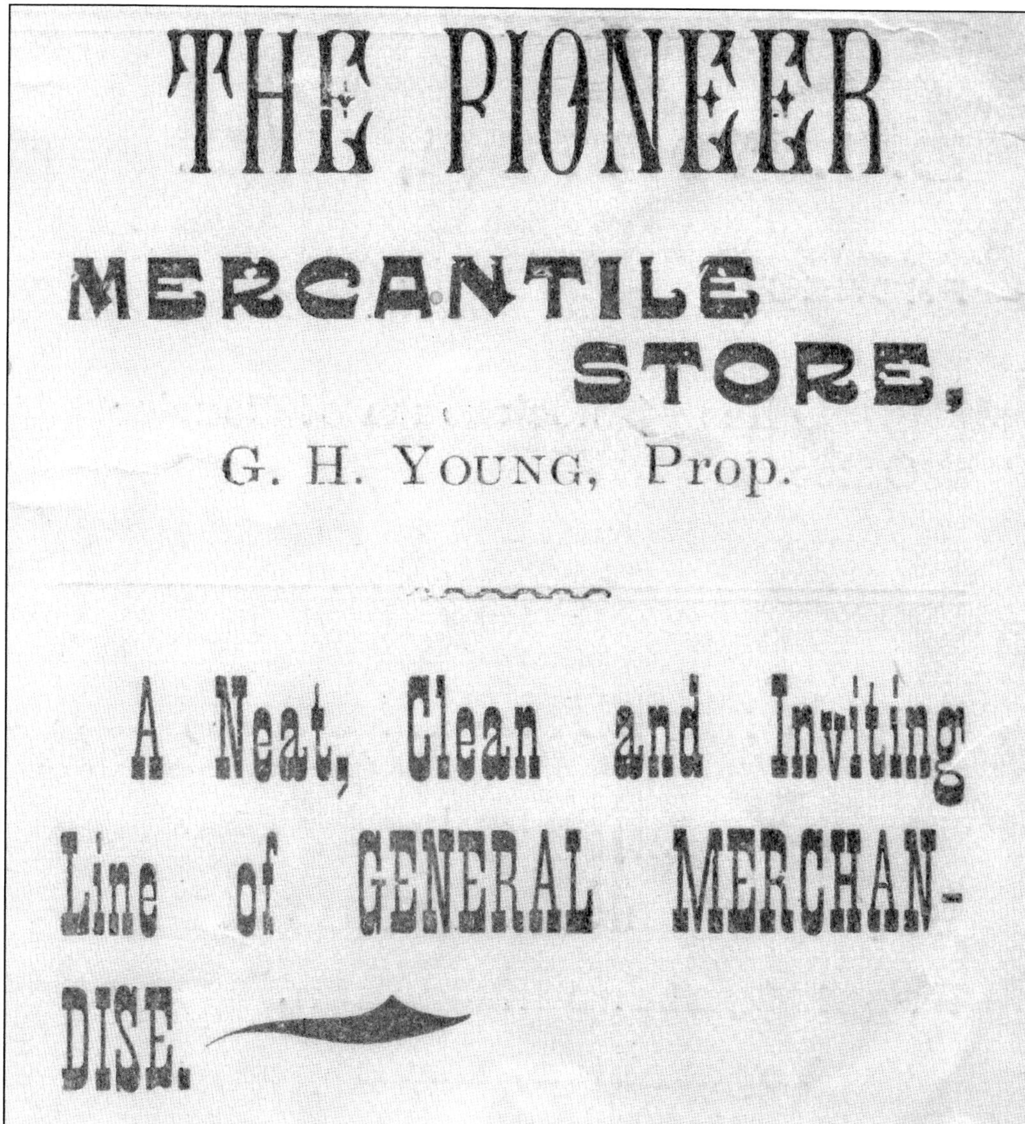


This advertisement is from George H. Young's general store, called The Pioneer. The store carried a variety of goods, including shoes, clothing, and household items. The Pioneer was located on Denver Street, two doors south of the Gerry House Hotel. The large meeting room above the store was called Young's Hall. It was the main gathering place for Evans. Dances and ceremonies took place there, and various clubs and organizations used the space as a meeting facility. School classes were held at Young's Hall between when the old school was torn down and the new one was built.

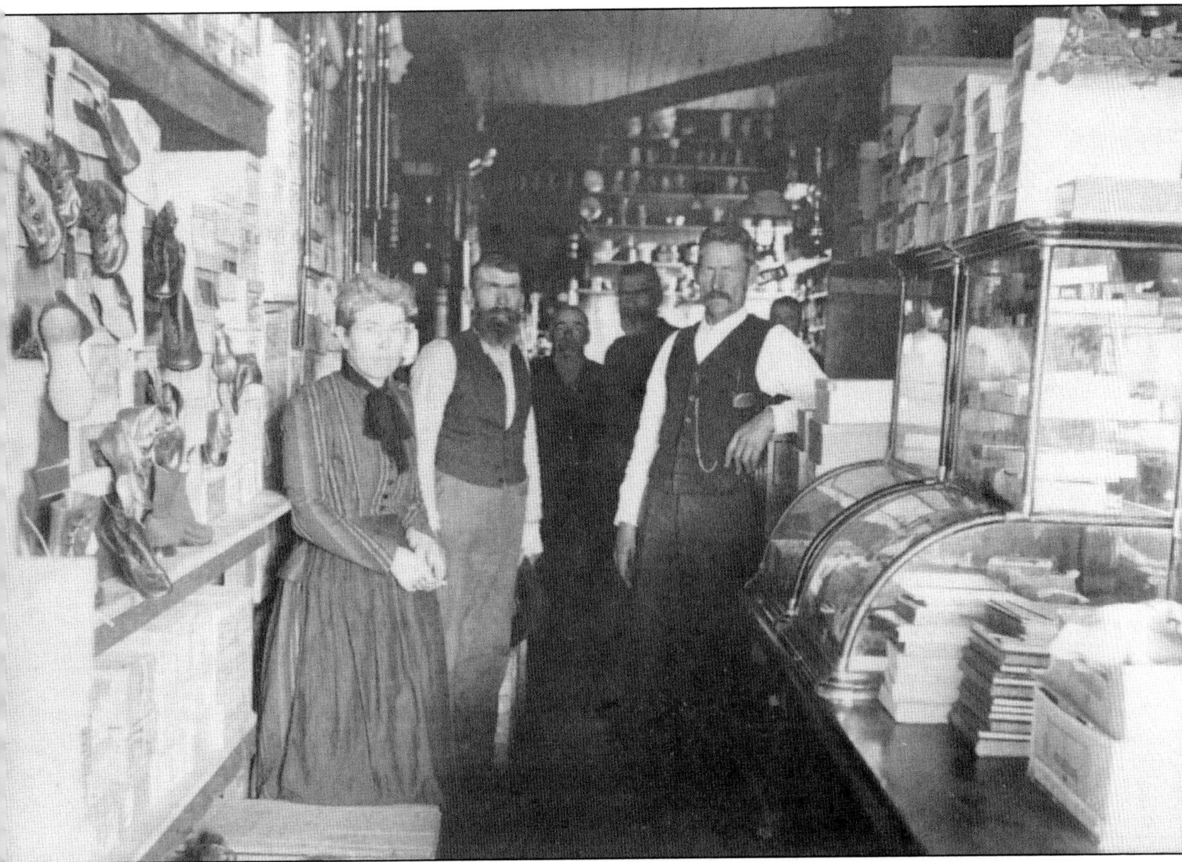

Evans was home to several general stores. In the days before the advent of the big-box stores, general stores like The Pioneer would stock a smaller number of goods, so several small stores could survive in a town together. Some stores also tended to specialize in certain items, such as clothing, kitchen items, or linens. As seen in this photograph, the Youngs carried shoes and other accessories. Lydia and George H. Young pose with employees of the store, who are only identified by their last names. From left to right, they are Lydia Young, Pris, Beeson, Drake, and George H. Young.

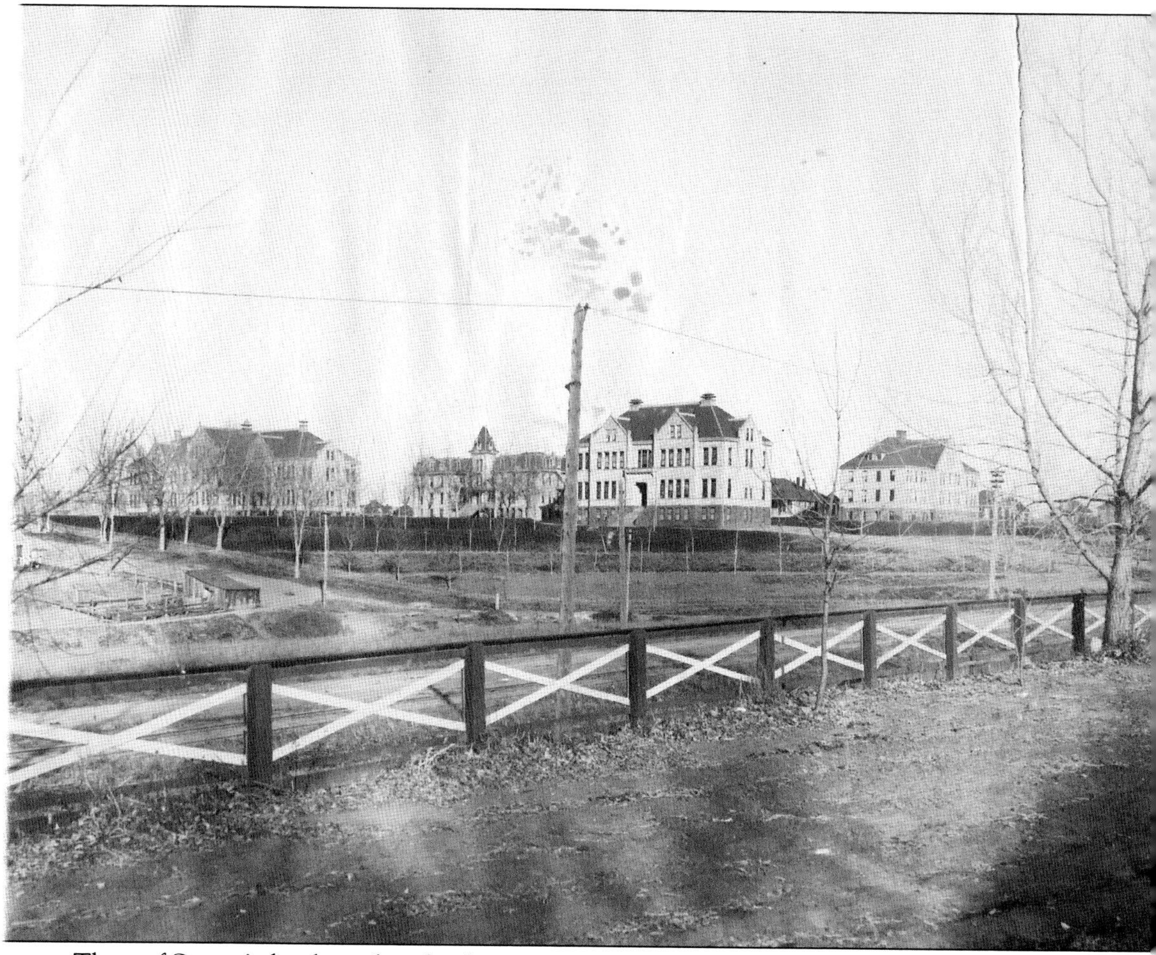

Three of George's daughters from his first marriage, Grace, Sadie, and Cora, were deaf. The Evans School was unable to provide educational services that they would need. All three of the girls attended the Colorado School for the Deaf and Blind in Colorado Springs, which was one of the premier schools for deaf and blind children at the time. Jonathan Kennedy founded the school in 1874. The school started out small, occupying a rented home in Colorado Springs. Three of the first students at the school were Kennedy's children. The school quickly grew to an entire campus, complete with dormitories, classroom buildings, and vocational education buildings.

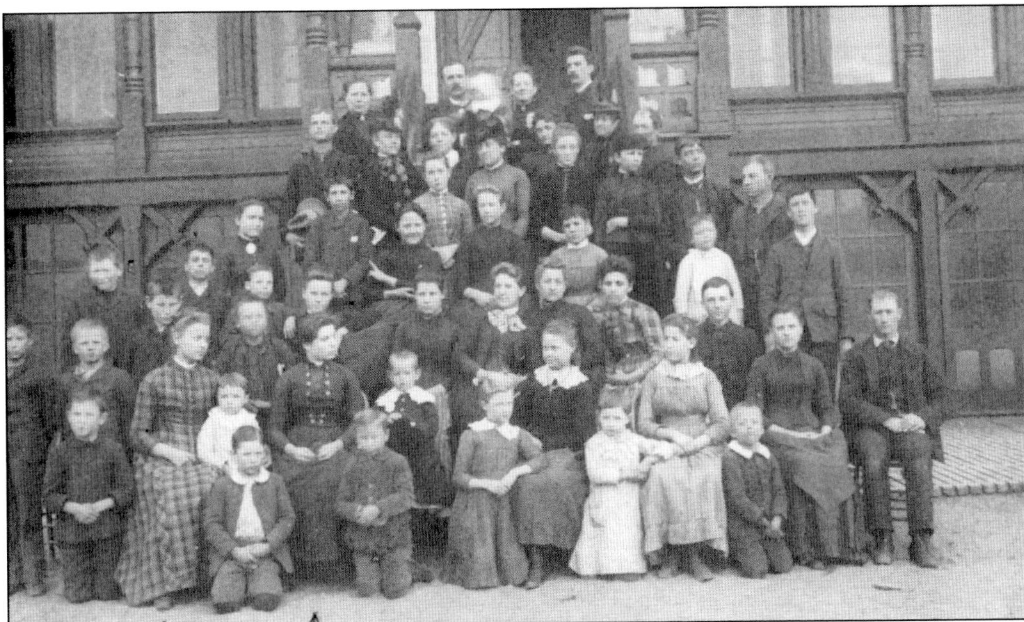

The Colorado School for the Deaf and Blind's motto was "Learn to Do By Doing," meaning that there was a great deal of emphasis on vocational education and practical skills. Classes at the time that the Young daughters attended the school included dressmaking and housekeeping for the girls and carpentry and mattress making for the boys, among other trades. Grace and Sadie are shown here with some of their classmates in 1888.

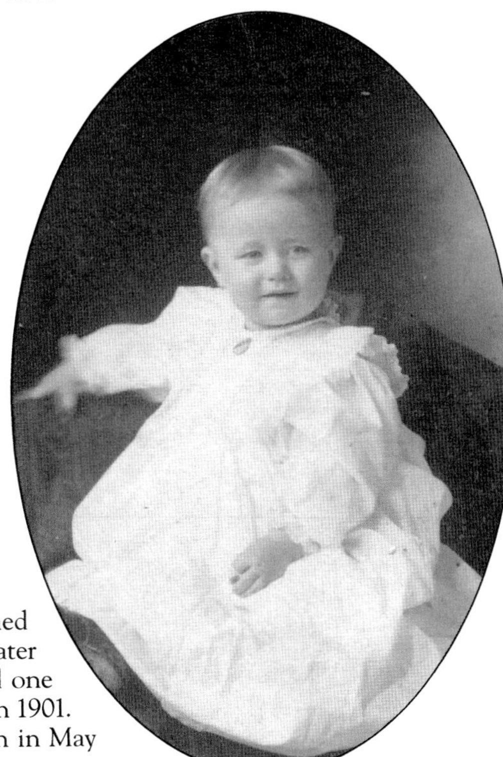

Grace Young moved back to Evans and married David Wolpert on November 23, 1898. They later farmed near Henderson, Colorado. They had one child, a daughter named Lucile, who was born in 1901. This photograph of Lucile as a baby was taken in May 1902, when she was 17 months old.

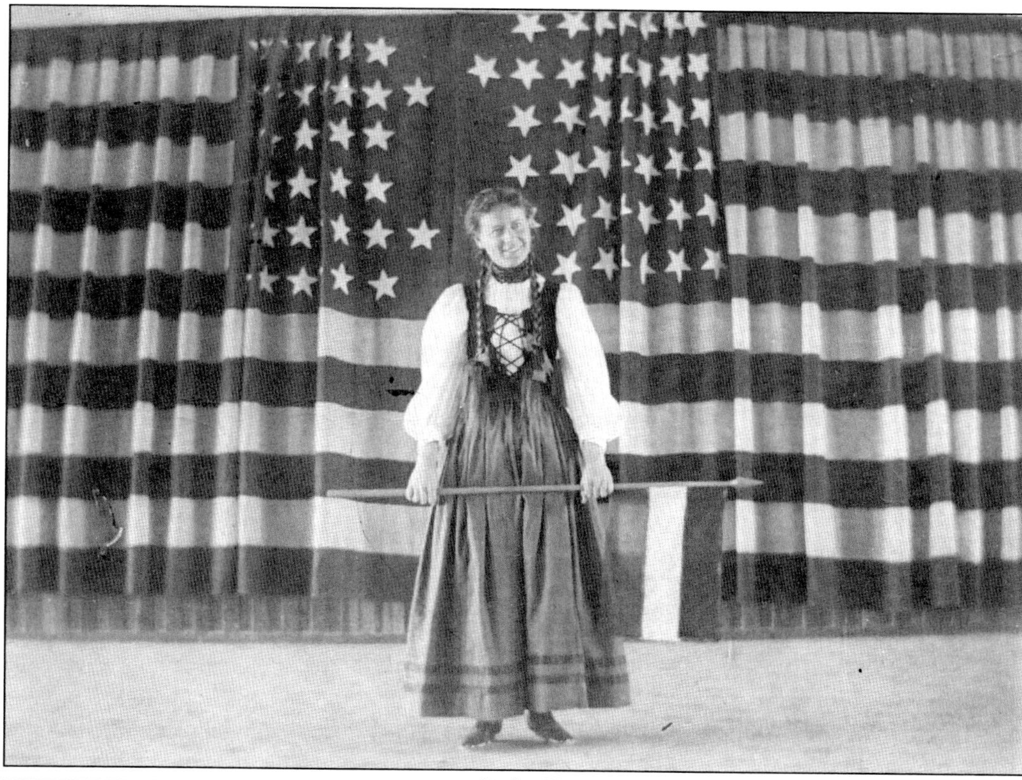

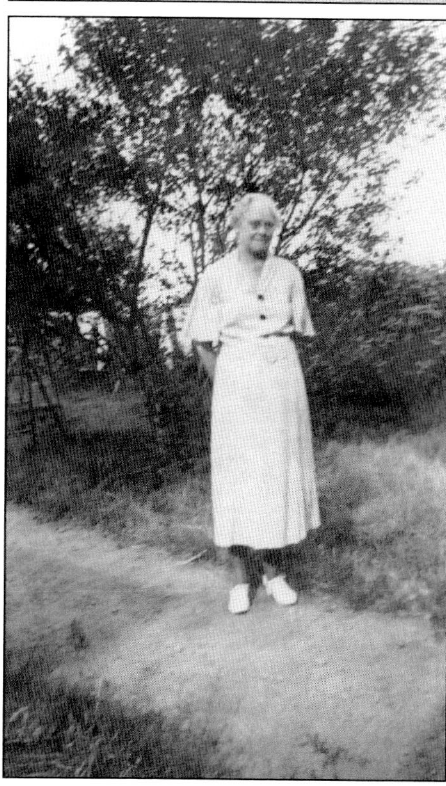

Sadie Young never returned to live in Evans. She stayed in Colorado Springs throughout school and began teaching at the same school she attended right after graduation. This 1889 photograph shows Sadie in her early years of teaching.

Sadie Young was passionate about educating deaf children, and she spent her entire career as a teacher at the school she had attended as a child. This 1937 photograph was taken in Colorado Springs. Sadie Young passed away in Denver on April 15, 1961, at the age of 87.

George H. Young married his second wife, Lydia Herriott, in Evans, Colorado, in 1889. Together they had four children: George P. Young, Charles (who passed away when he was 11 days old), Edwin Harriott Young, and Benjamin Young. Lydia was active in the Woman's Relief Corps, which was the auxiliary to the Grand Army of the Republic.

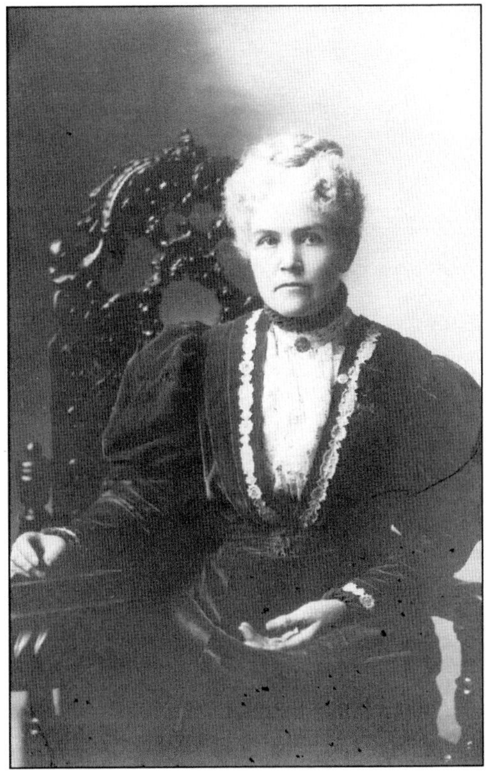

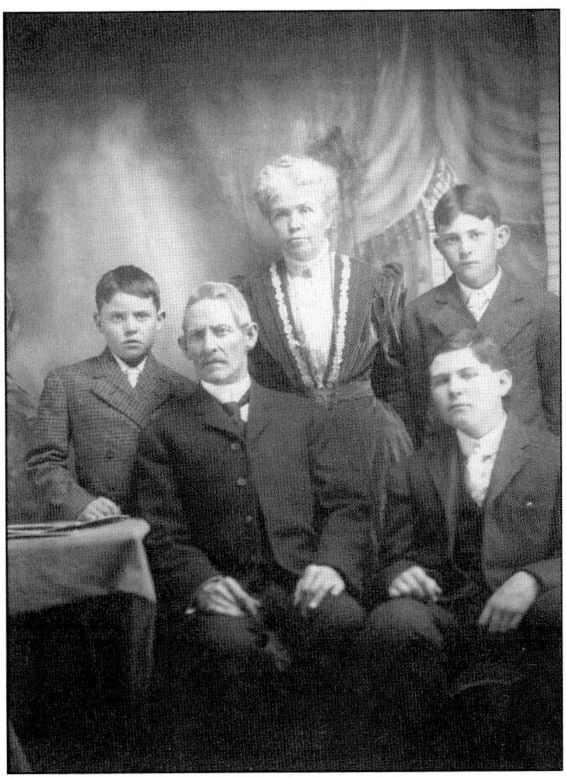

This undated portrait of the young family, probably taken sometime between 1910 and 1915, shows the three youngest children and the only sons of George H. Young. From left to right are Benjamin U. Young, George H. Young, Lydia C. Young, Edwin Harriott Young (standing), and George P. Young.

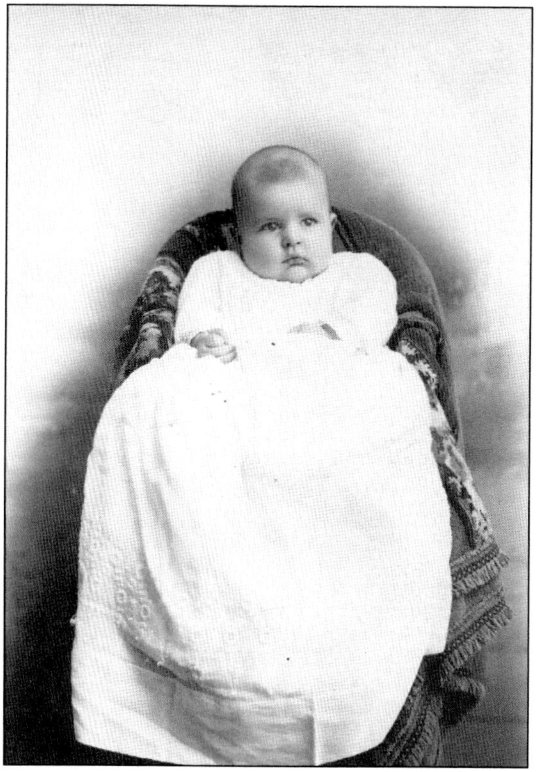

The child in this photograph is Edwin Herriott Young, the middle child of George and Lydia Young. He was born in Evans on April 8, 1894. He was admitted to the Greeley Hospital on April 7, 1910, for appendicitis surgery. He contracted peritonitis and passed away five days later, on April 12. School classes were cancelled in Evans so that his classmates could attend his funeral.

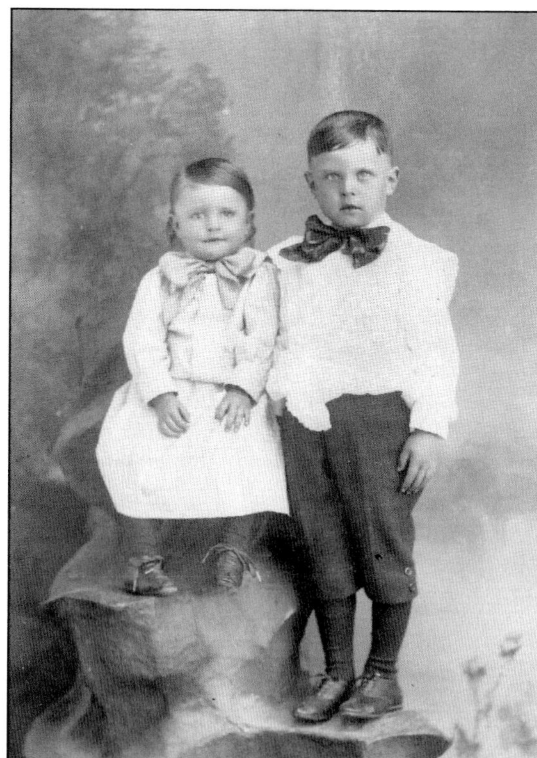

Benjamin and George Young are shown here around 1900. Benjamin is wearing a dress, which was quite common for young boys into the first decades of the 20th century. Fasteners that exist today, like Velcro and snaps, did not exist at that time, and the hook-and-eye fasteners commonly used then were difficult for children to use. It was a rite of passage for young boys to get their first pair of breeches.

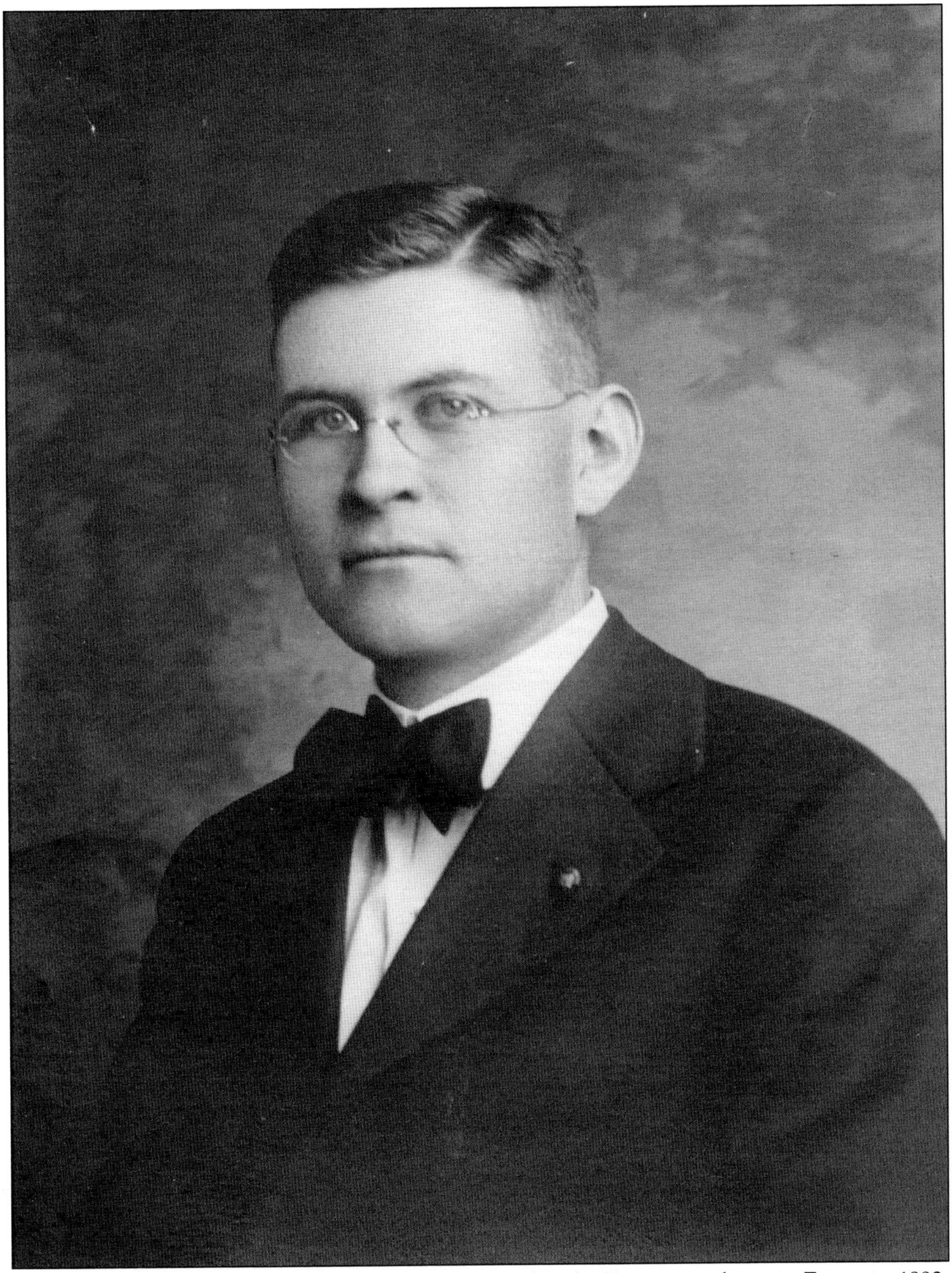

George Prestley Young, the oldest son of George and Lydia Young, was born in Evans in 1892. He served in the military during World War I and later attended college and pursued a career in education. This photograph was taken while he was working as superintendent of schools in Dix, Nebraska, in the early 1920s. He returned to Colorado just a few years later, relocating to the southwestern part of the state, where he worked as superintendent of schools in Cortez. George Young married a schoolteacher from Durango named Mary Meller on August 31, 1926.

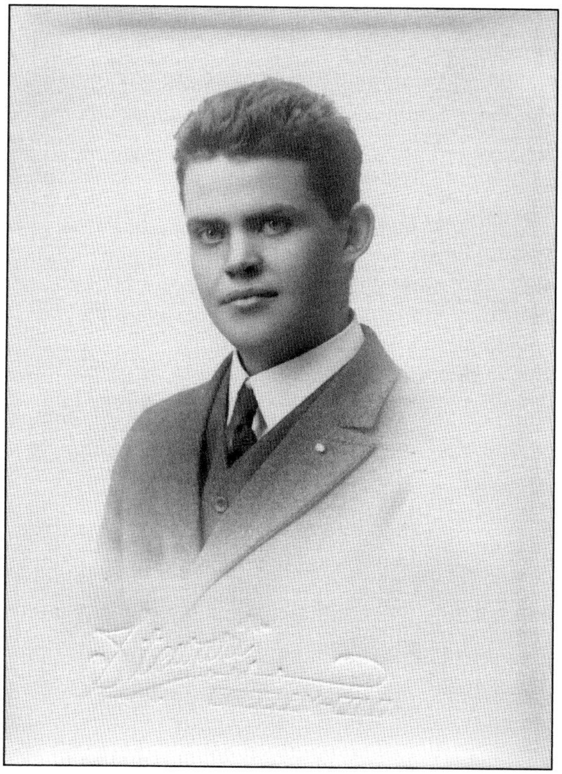

Benjamin Uel Young was the youngest son of George H. and Lydia Young, born in Evans in 1897. He received a draft notice to serve in World War I, but he was excused from service because of paralysis in his right leg.

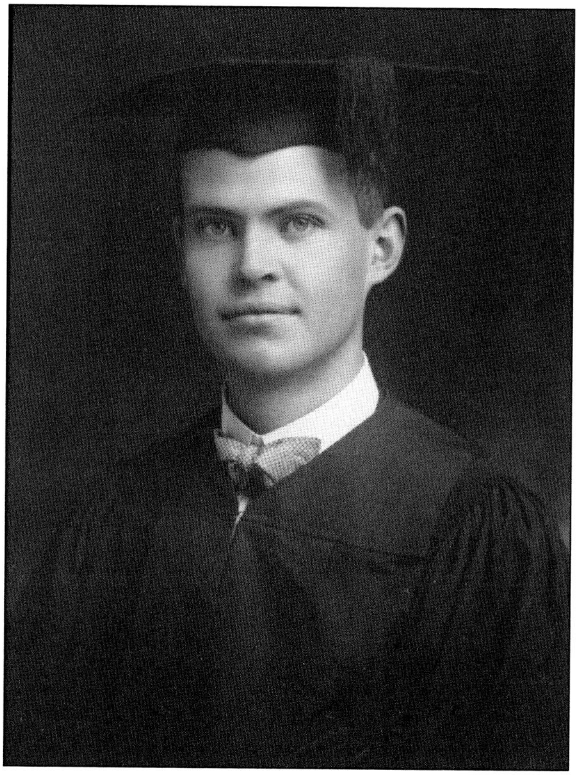

Benjamin Young attended college in Boulder, Colorado, and worked as an electrical engineer for the duration of his career. He married Isabel Smallhurst on September 3, 1921, and together they had two children, named Benjamin Jr. and Douglas. He died in 1987 in Maricopa County, Arizona.

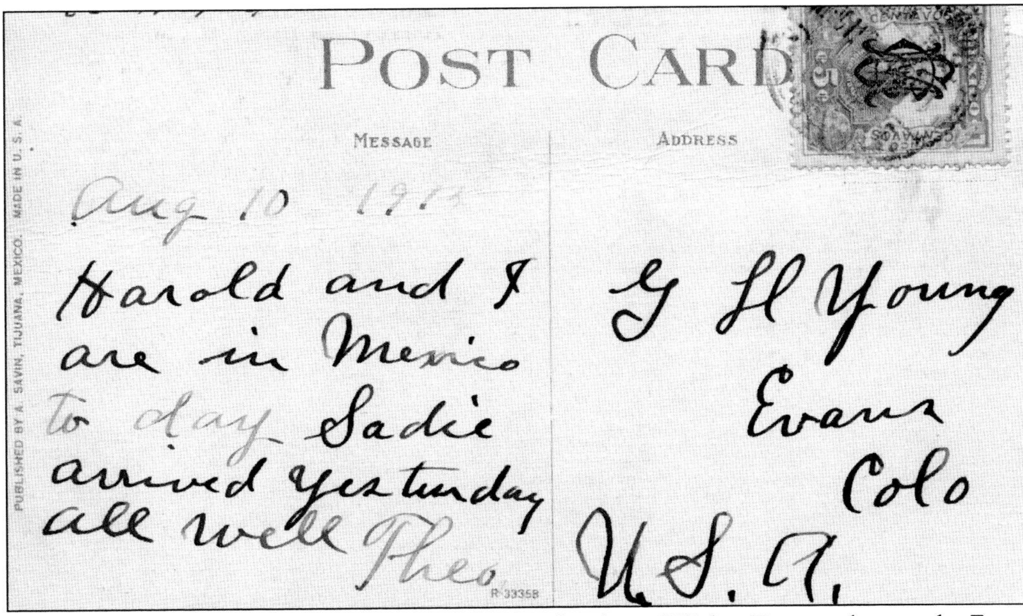


Theodore Ennes, son of Oscar Ennes and younger brother of Walter Ennes, who ran the Ennes Dairy, married Edna Young, daughter of George H. Young and Martha Mills Young. He sent this postcard to George from Mexico on August 10, 1913. He wrote, "Harold and I are in Mexico today. Sadie arrived yesterday. All Well, Theo."

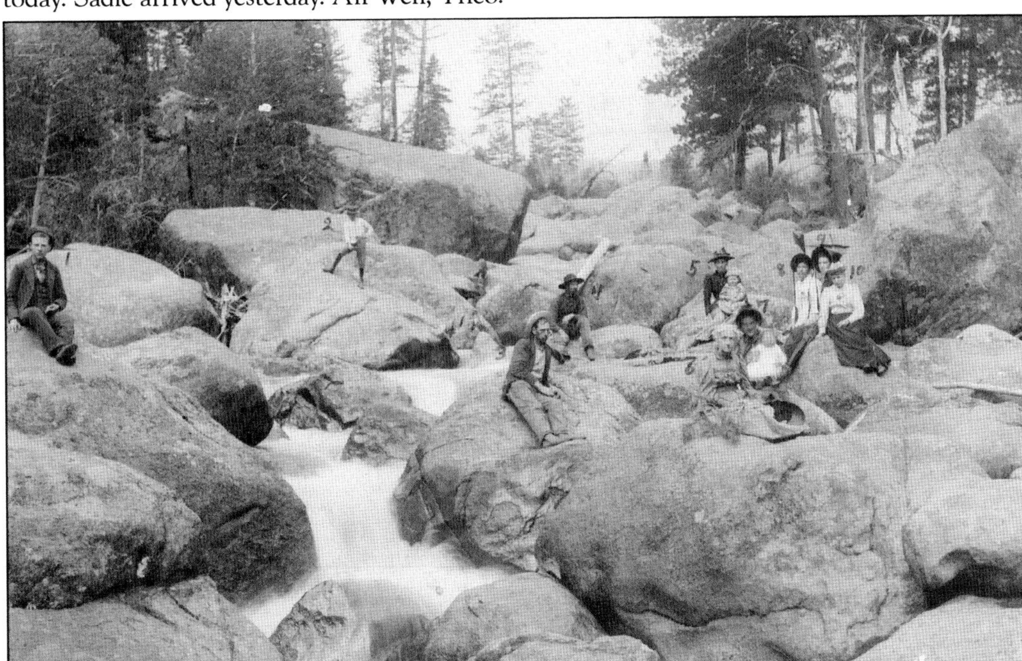

This photograph shows the Ennes and Doney families on an outing to Buffalo Creek. Evans's close proximity to the mountains provides many opportunities for hiking, camping, and picnicking. Pictured from left to right are two unidentified people, Jesse Doney, unidentified, Fannie Baker Ennes, Lovinia Ennes, Celia Ennes Doney, and three unidentified people.

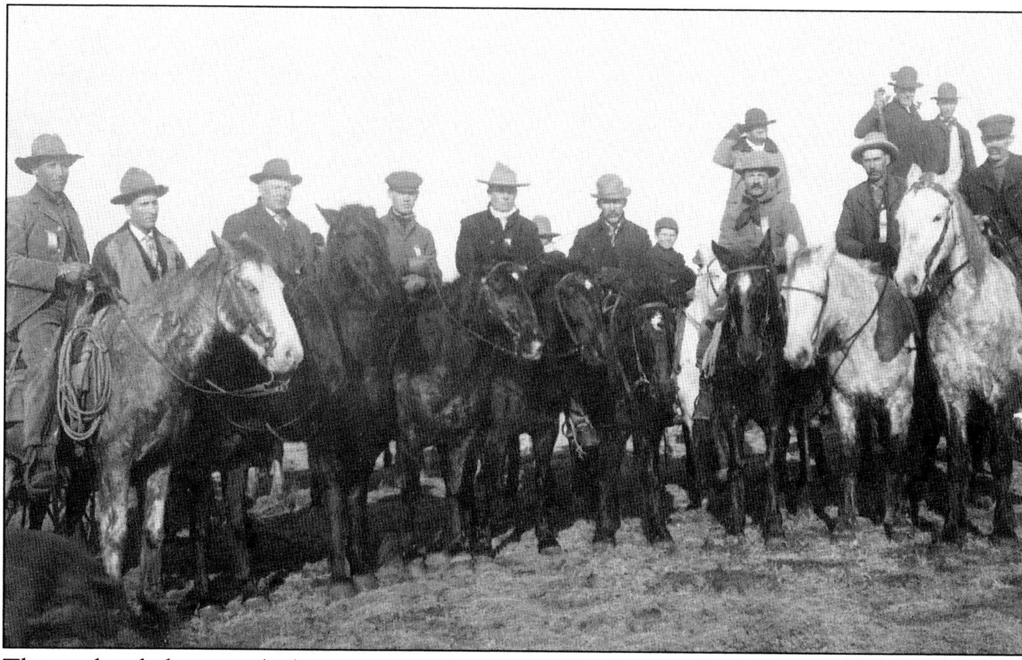

This undated photograph shows a coyote hunt near Greeley in which Jesse Doney participated. Coyote hunts are commonplace in rural areas even today because, when their population increases too much, packs of coyotes move in closer to farms and ranches in search of food, often killing a great number of livestock.

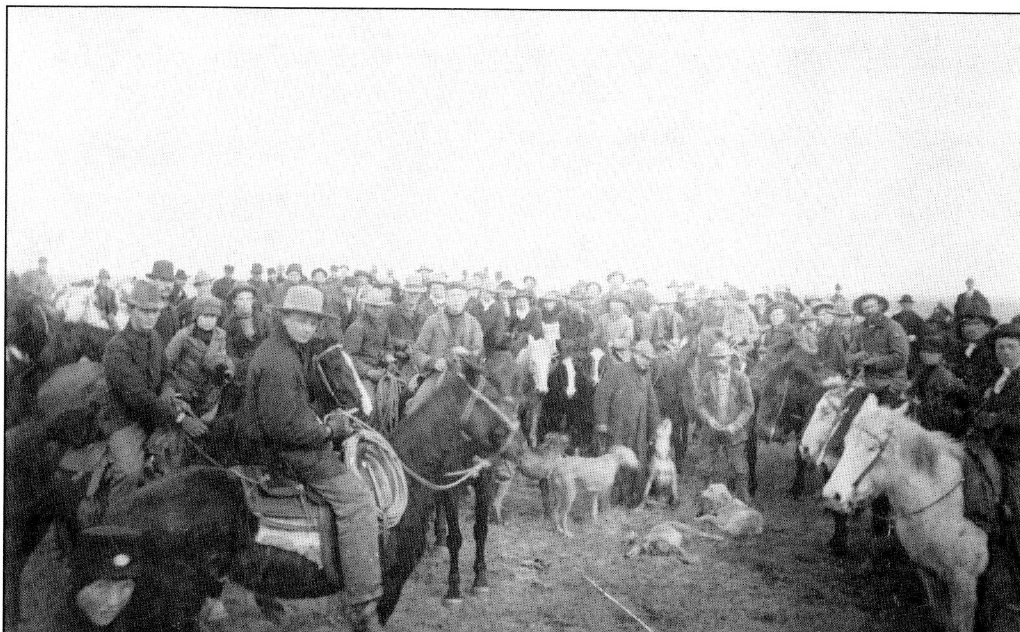

Jesse Doney also participated in a rabbit roundup near Greeley. Rabbits, like coyotes, were considered farm pests, as they would eat plants and dig holes in fields and pastures. Just like with the coyotes, farmers would plan hunts or roundups of the animals when they became pests to the farms and ranches in the area.

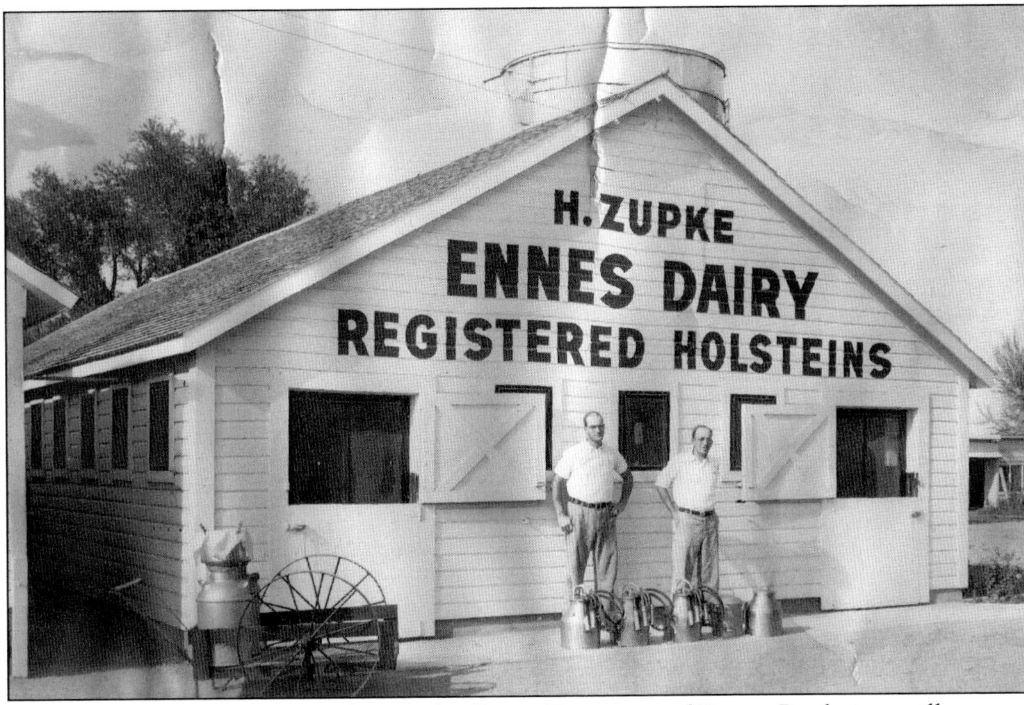


Oscar Ennes and Herman Zupke ran the Ennes Dairy east of Evans. Producing milk, cream, ice cream, cottage cheese, and orange juice, the Ennes Dairy was one of the largest and most successful businesses in Weld County for many years. The Ennes and Doney families are related through Celia Ennes, who married Jesse Doney.

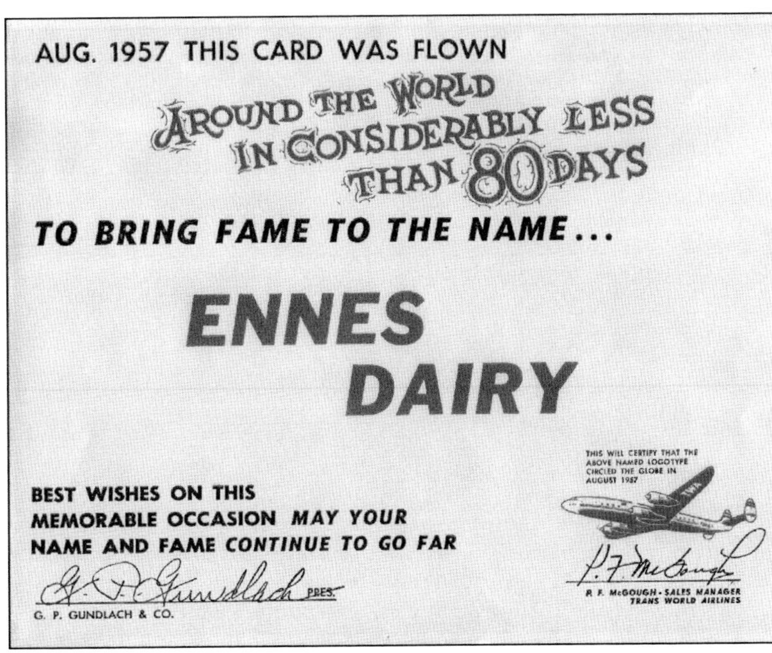


In August 1957, the G.P. Gundlach Company, makers of dairy products, flew this card around the world on a TWA flight. The promotion, called "Around the World in Considerably Less Than 80 Days," is a play on the 1956 movie *Around the World in 80 Days*, an adaptation of the Jules Verne novel by the same name in which a man attempts to fly around the world in a hot air balloon.

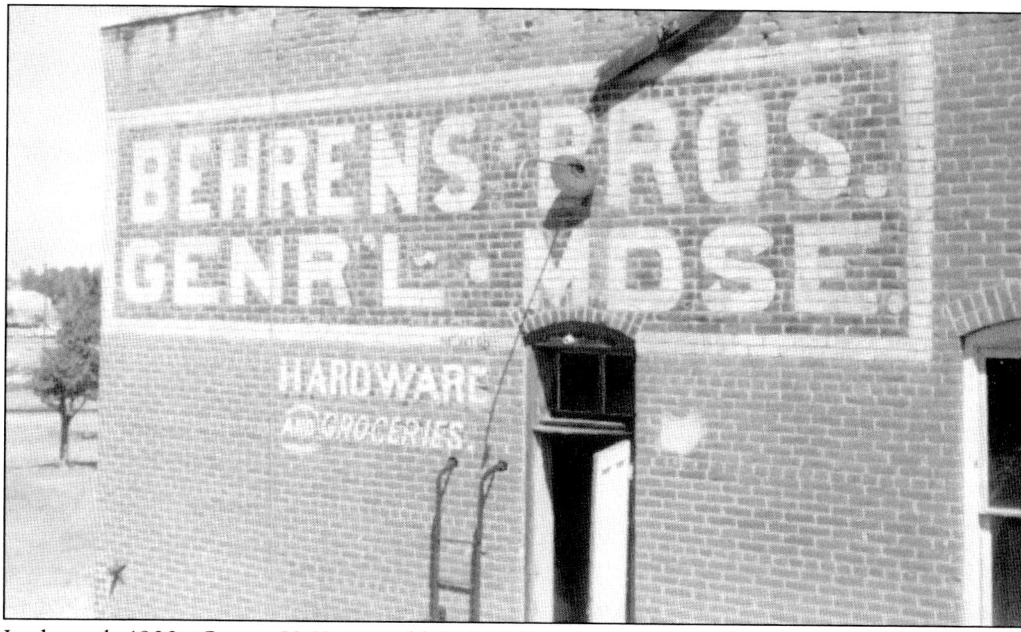


In the early 1900s, George H. Young sold the building that contained his store and Young's Hall to Charles and Henry Behrens. Together they operated the Behrens Brothers General Merchandise store while Henry continued to farm and Charles also worked at the lumberyard with his other brother, John. By the 1940s, this building had become the Evans Fire Station.

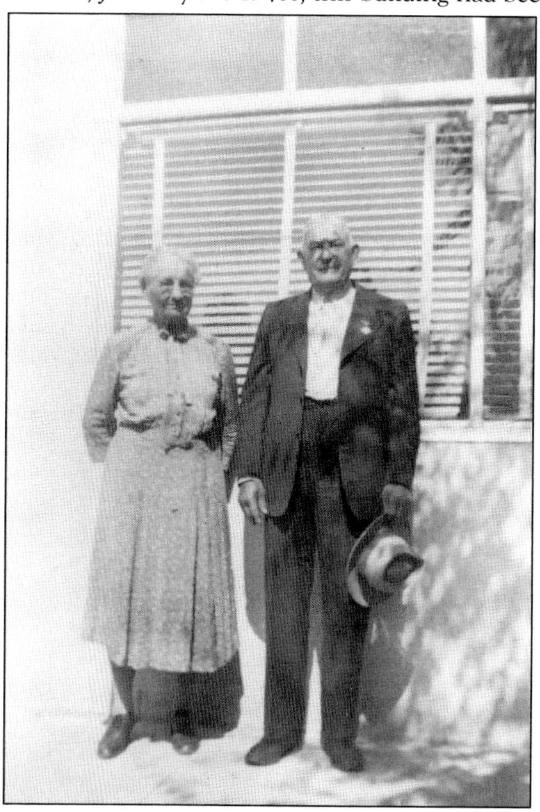

Minnie and Joseph Morriss Kinsinger were respected members of the early Evans business community. They moved to Greeley with their three children in 1894. Morris worked at the J.J. Inman Meat Market for several years before opening a meat market in Evans with William Southwell. Kinsinger later bought out Southwell and operated a successful business here for many years.

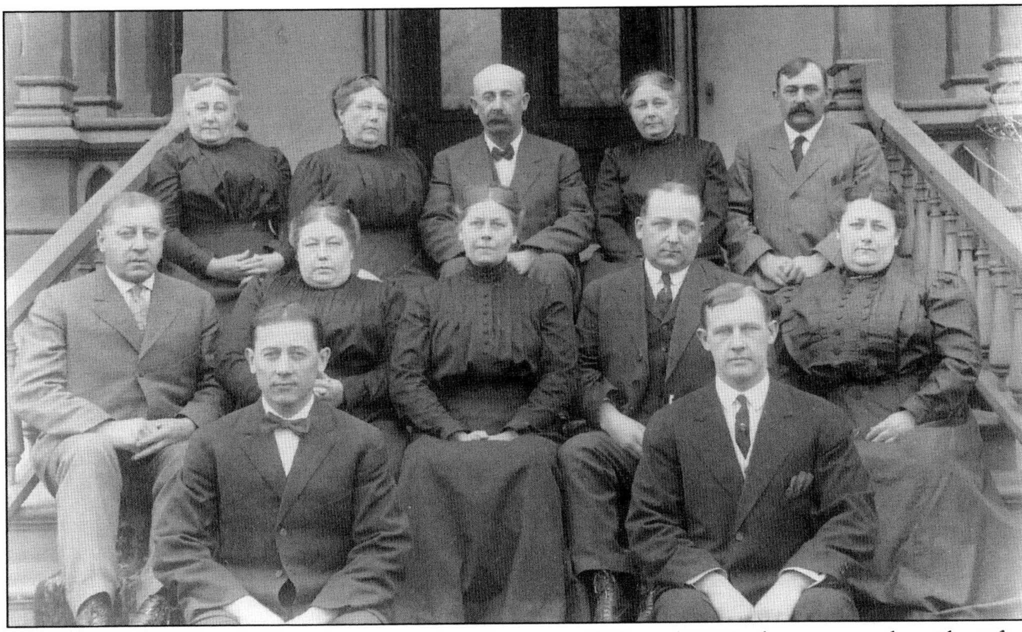

This photograph, probably taken sometime between 1910 and 1920, shows several unidentified members of the Kinsinger family in Peoria, Illinois. After the death of Peter Kinsinger, several members of the family, including Catharine, Susan, Lydia, and Amelia, moved to Peoria, where they earned money by housekeeping and taking in boarders. It is likely that Joseph Kinsinger is the man in the front row on the left side of the photograph.

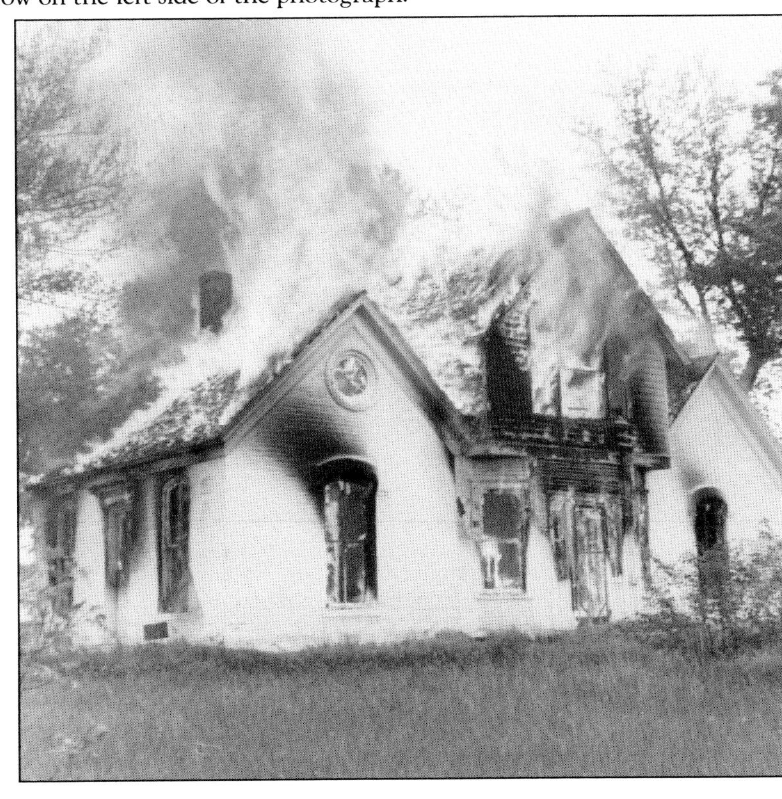

The home that Minnie and Joseph Kinsinger lived in in Evans for many years was located on Boulder Street. At one time, it had been one of the finer homes in town. The Evans Volunteer Fire Department burned down the home as a training exercise in the late 1960s.

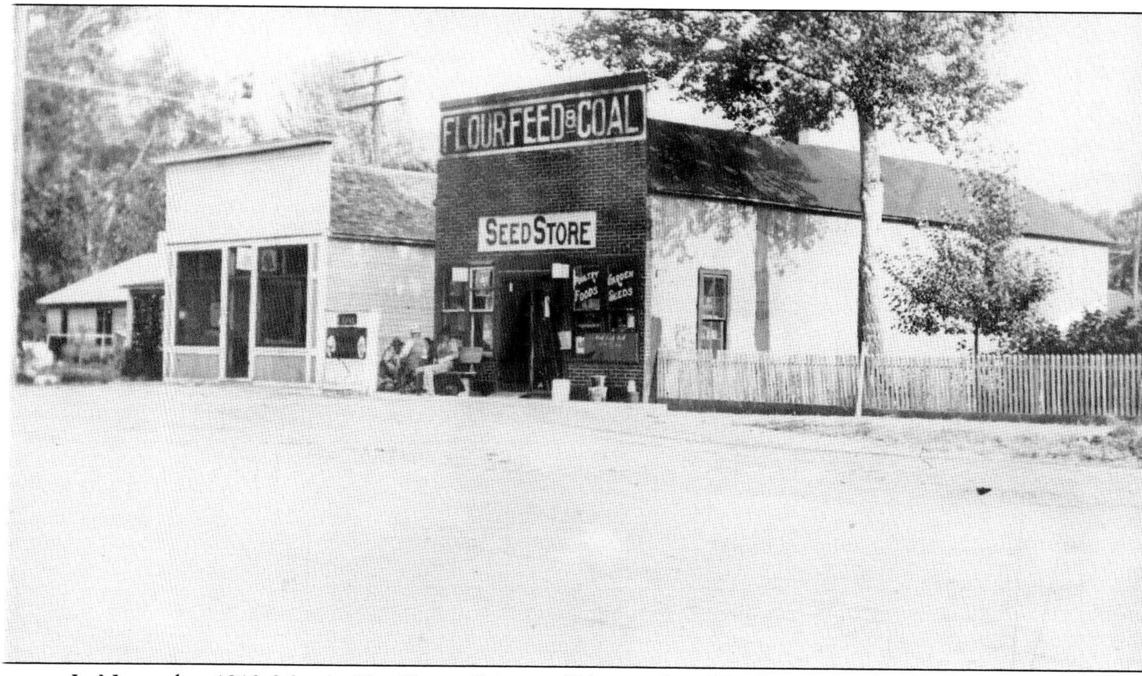


In November 1912, Martin Van Buren Briggs sold his coal and feed store to Albert R. Weinhold Sr. Weinhold kept the business basically the same as Martin Briggs had. He continued to supply Evans with animal feed and coal until his death in February 1920. He was active in community affairs and was the superintendent of Evans School District 15 for a number of years. The back of the C.H. Reed General Merchandise store is visible on the far left side of the photograph, and the telephone office and exchange is directly to the left of the feed store.

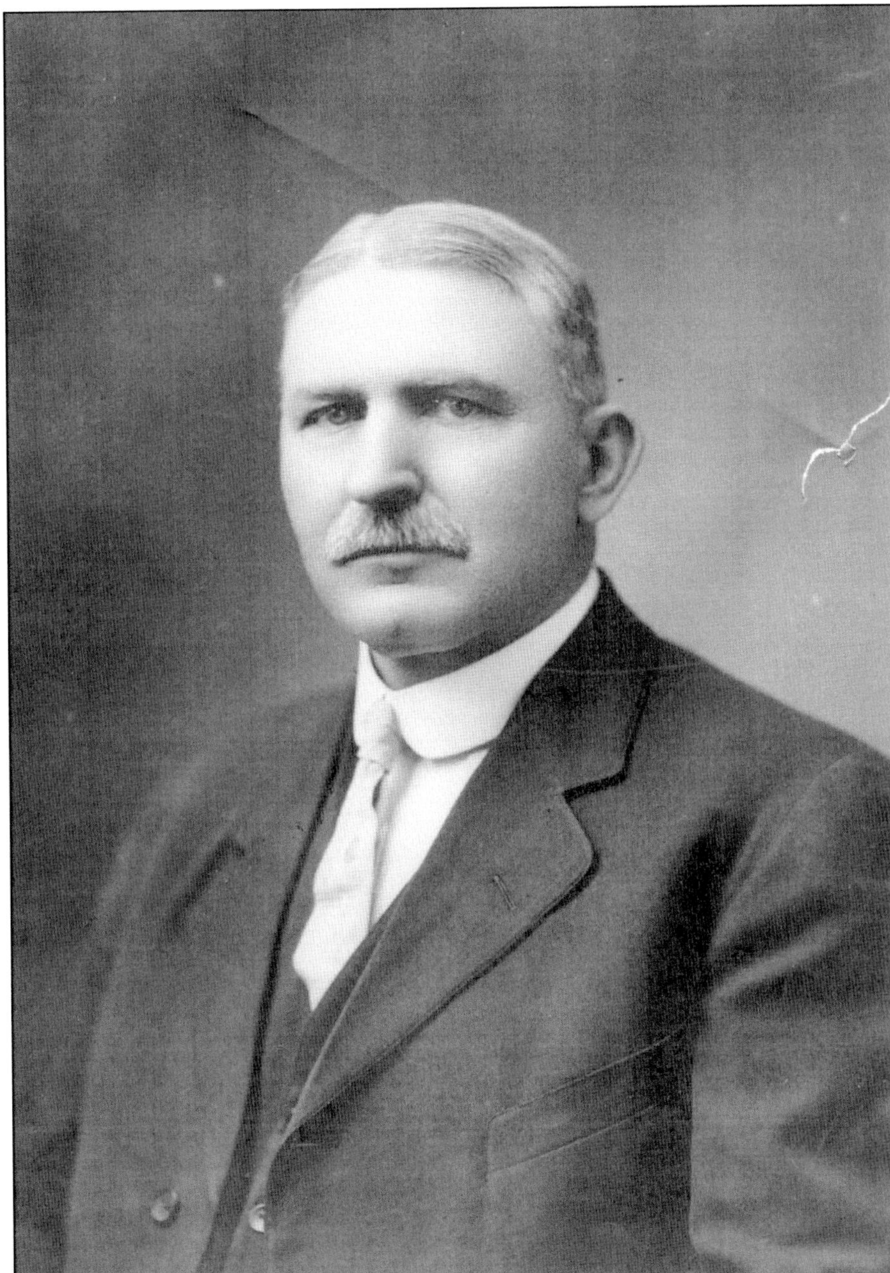

Samuel McAfee was nine years old when his family came to Evans. He attended the school here but quit at age 15 to apprentice as a carpenter. He soon learned that he was not interested in the profession, and he left to work in the printing office at the *Evans Journal*. Over the years, McAfee worked for various newspapers in Denver and Castle Rock and spent two years as manager of the *Sentinel* in Syracuse, Kansas, before returning to Evans permanently in 1889. Immediately upon his return to Evans, McAfee bought the *Evans Journal* and reestablished it as the *Evans Courier*, which remained in business until 1896. McAfee was elected as a trustee to the town in 1890 and was elected mayor three years later. Other offices he held include town clerk, police judge, justice of the peace, and postmaster.

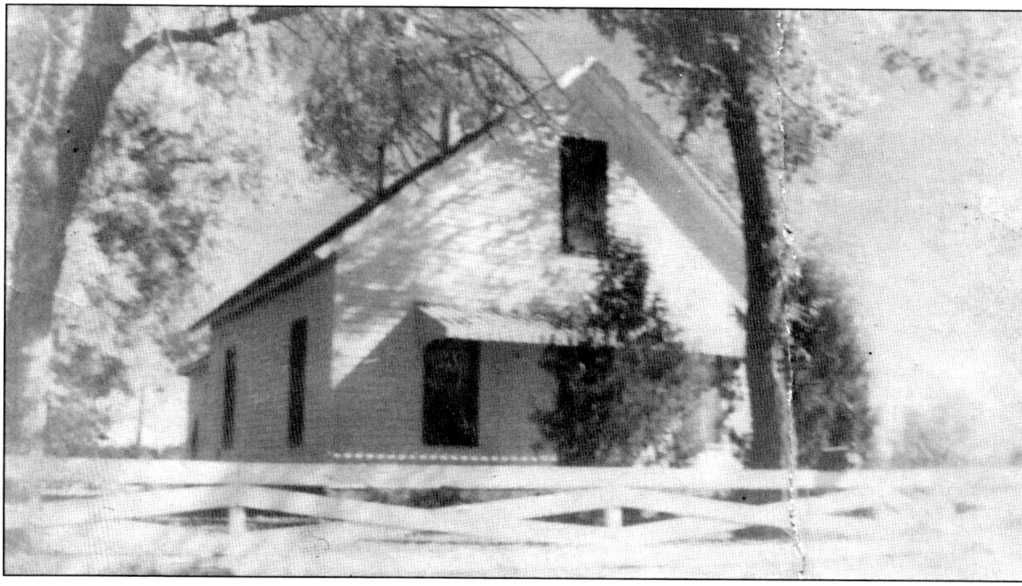

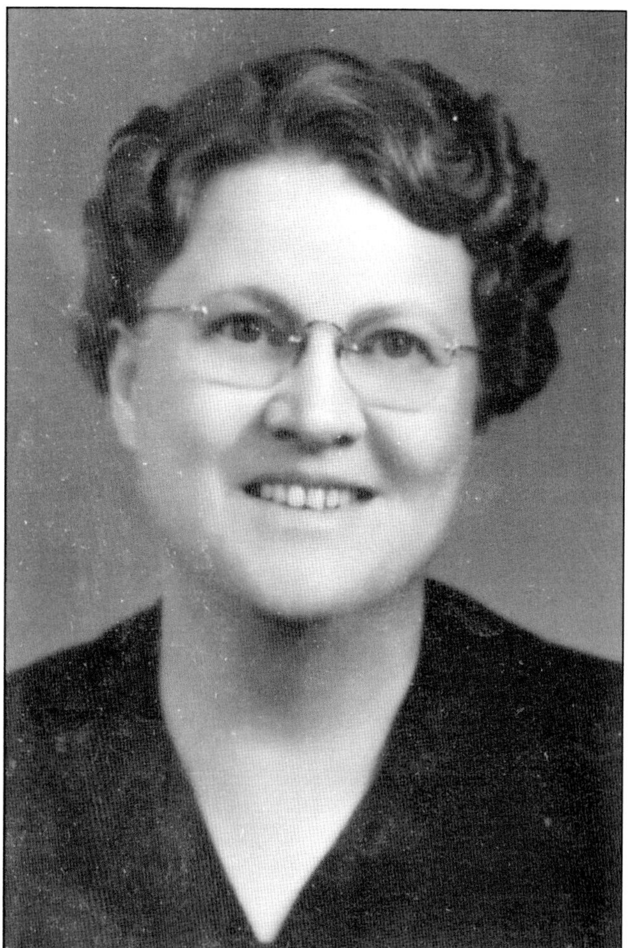

This home, located at 3502 Empire Street in Evans, is where Samuel and Sallie McAfee lived and raised their five children: Harry, Elizabeth, Montgomery, George, and Blair. Later, Jacob Kohler, a lifetime member of the Evans VFW—who was at one time the oldest living Spanish-American War veteran in northern Colorado—lived in this home.

Henrietta Reed was born in Nebraska in 1896 to parents C.H. and A.D. Reed. The Reed family came to Colorado and lived in Windsor for a few years before coming to Evans in 1904 to live on a farm. C.H. traded his farm for an old building in the business district of Evans and remodeled it into a store with a home in the back for the family.

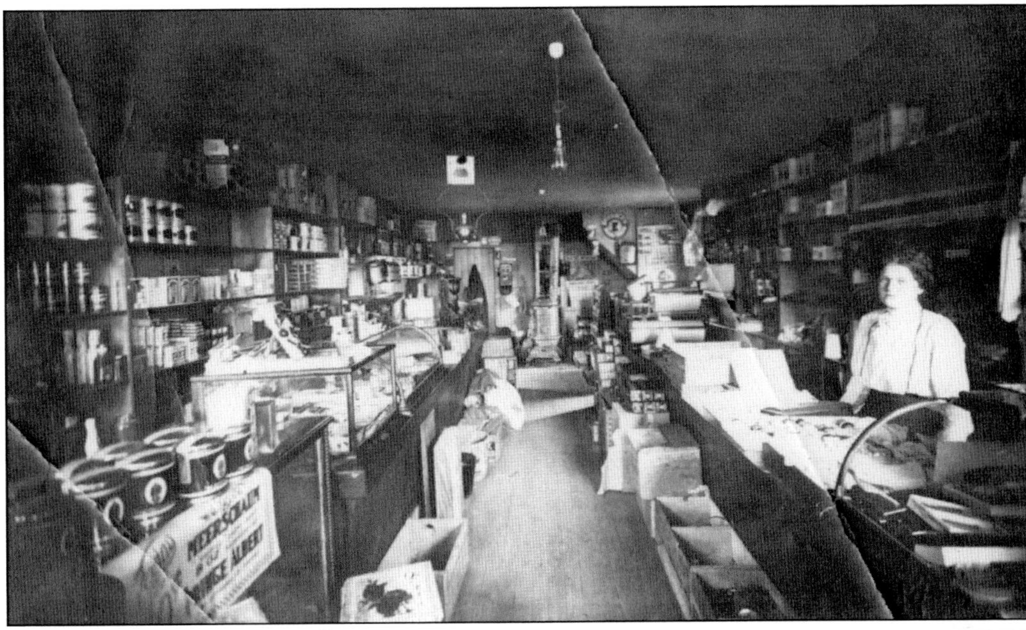

In 1910, C.H. Reed became ill, and he passed away the next year. Henrietta quit school at the age of 15 to run the general store, where she worked until her death in 1950. The store was originally called the C.H. Reed General Merchandise Store but later came to be known as the Evans Mercantile. This photograph shows Henrietta working at the store. (Courtesy of City of Greeley Museums, Permanent Collection, 1991.42.1106S.)

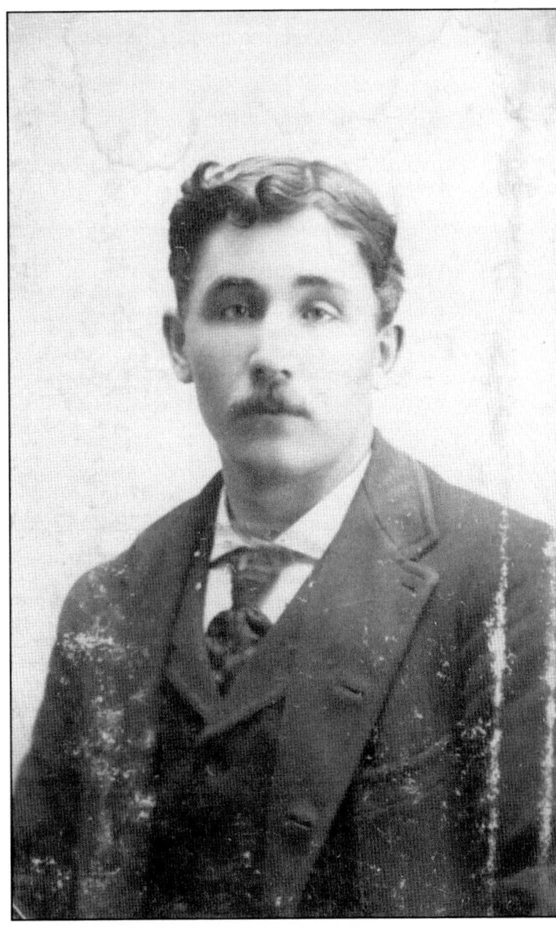

Henry Averill was born in Warren, Vermont, on April 4, 1876. Henry attended the public schools in Vermont but finished his education at a seminary in Montpelier, graduating in 1898. He then headed west to attend Denver Medical School, graduating in 1907. Dr. Averill worked in the mountain towns of Eagle and Idaho Springs and had his own medical practice in Denver.

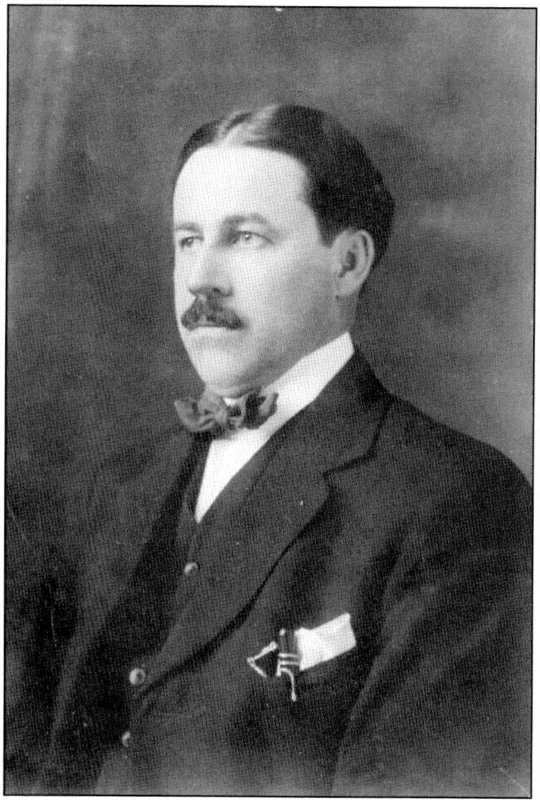

In 1913, Henry Averill left Denver to attend more medical classes at the University of Chicago. After completion of his courses, Dr. Averill once again headed to Colorado, settling in Evans and opening a medical practice in town. He met Henrietta Reed, and the couple was married on March 30, 1918.

Henry Averill was awarded this diploma from the City and County Hospital of Denver in 1906 for completing courses in general medical surgery and the study of nervous and mental diseases. During his career, Dr. Averill was a member of several medical associations, including the American Medical Association, the Colorado Medical Society, and the Weld County Medical Society.

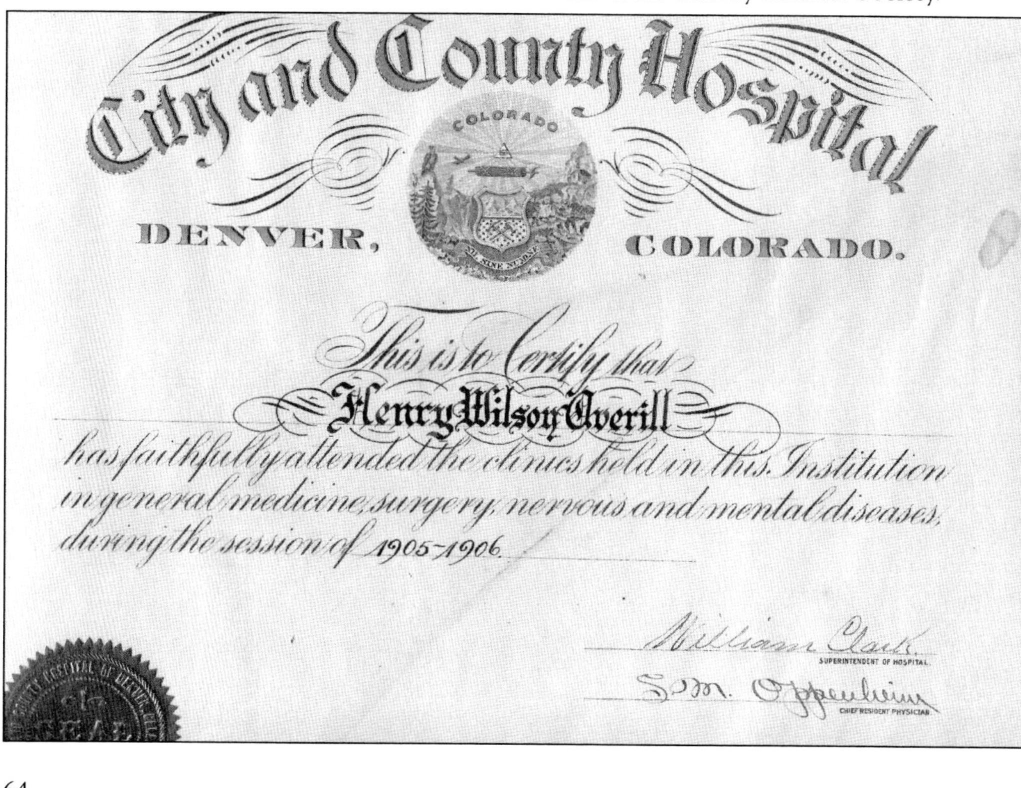

City and County Hospital

DENVER, COLORADO.

This is to Certify that

Henry Wilson Averill

has faithfully attended the clinics held in this Institution in general medicine, surgery, nervous and mental diseases, during the session of 1905-1906.

William Clark
SUPERINTENDENT OF HOSPITAL.

S. M. Oppenheim
CHIEF RESIDENT PHYSICIAN.

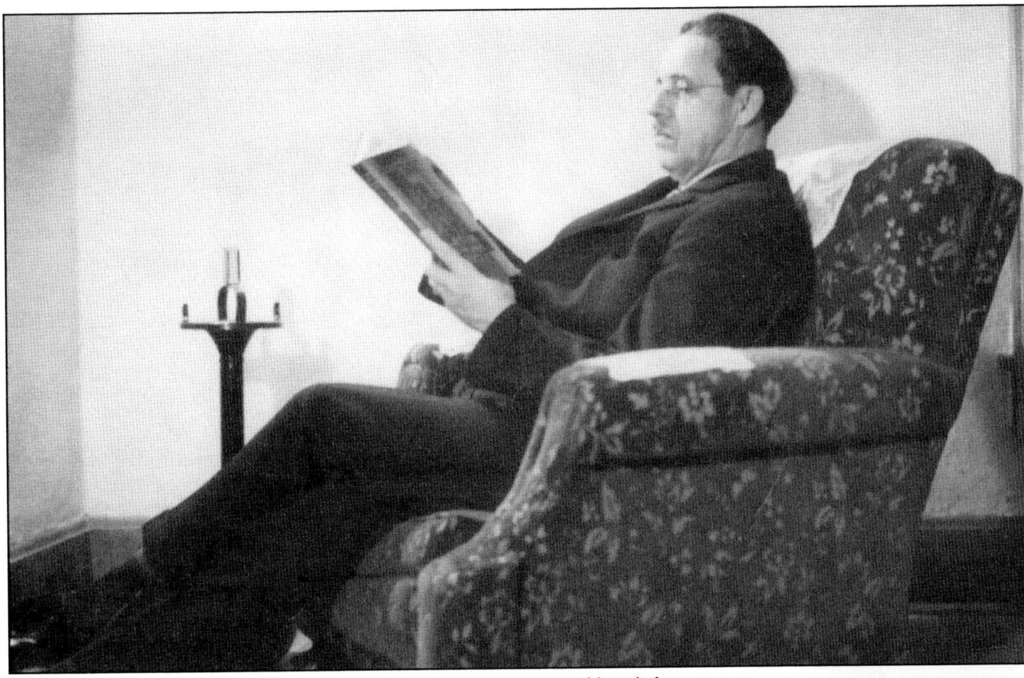

Dr. Averill practiced medicine in Evans for the rest of his life. He was a liked and respected doctor, treating the community, delivering babies, and offering comfort to those who sought his care. This undated photograph shows Dr. Henry Averill enjoying a relaxing moment at home in Evans.

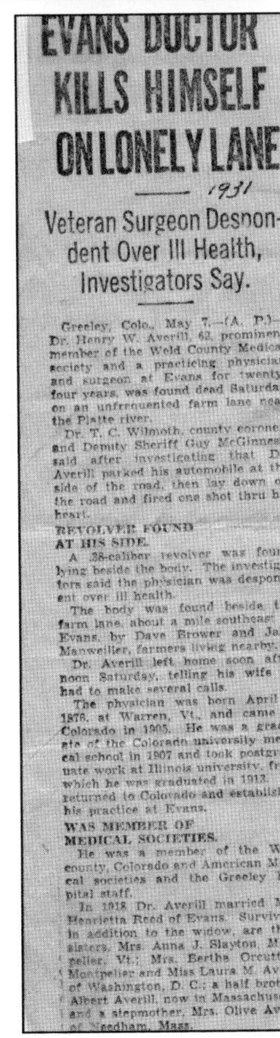

EVANS DOCTOR KILLS HIMSELF ON LONELY LANE

1931

Veteran Surgeon Despondent Over Ill Health, Investigators Say.

Greeley, Colo., May 7.—(A. P.)—Dr. Henry W. Averill, 62, prominent member of the Weld County Medical society and a practicing physician and surgeon at Evans for twenty-four years, was found dead Saturday on an unfrequented farm lane near the Platte river.

Dr. T. C. Wilmoth, county coroner, and Deputy Sheriff Guy McGinness, said after investigating that Dr. Averill parked his automobile at the side of the road, then lay down on the road and fired one shot thru his heart.

REVOLVER FOUND AT HIS SIDE.

A .38-caliber revolver was found lying beside the body. The investigators said the physician was despondent over ill health.

The body was found beside the farm lane, about a mile southeast of Evans, by Dave Brower and Jake Manweiller, farmers living nearby.

Dr. Averill left home soon afte[r] noon Saturday, telling his wife h[e] had to make several calls.

The physician was born April [illegible] 1876, at Warren, Vt., and came t[o] Colorado in 1905. He was a gradu[ate] of the Colorado university med[i]cal school in 1907 and took postgrad[u]ate work at Illinois university, fro[m] which he was graduated in 1913. H[e] returned to Colorado and establishe[d] his practice at Evans.

WAS MEMBER OF MEDICAL SOCIETIES.

He was a member of the We[ld] county, Colorado and American Med[i]cal societies and the Greeley ho[s]pital staff.

In 1918 Dr. Averill married Mi[ss] Henrietta Reed of Evans. Survivin[g] in addition to the widow, are thr[ee] sisters, Mrs. Anna J. Slayton, Mon[t]pelier, Vt.; Mrs. Bertha Orcutt [of] Montpelier and Miss Laura M. Aver[ill] of Washington, D. C.; a half brothe[r] Albert Averill, now in Massachuset[ts] and a stepmother, Mrs. Olive Aver[ill] of Needham, Mass.

In May 1931, tragedy struck the Averill family. Henry had apparently found out bad news about his state of health and, perhaps because seeing so much pain and heartache in the medical profession over the years, took his own life on a country road outside of Greeley.

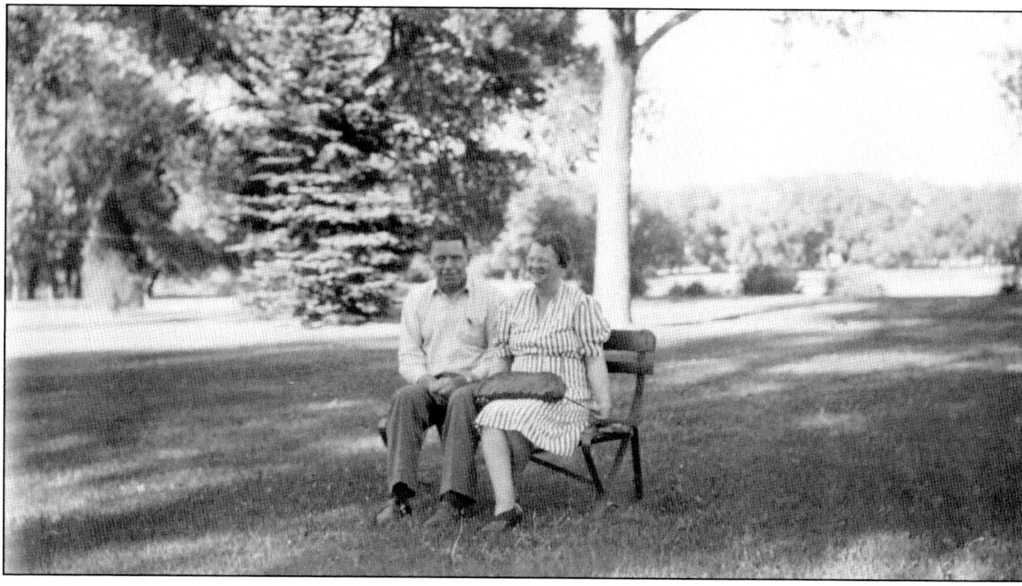

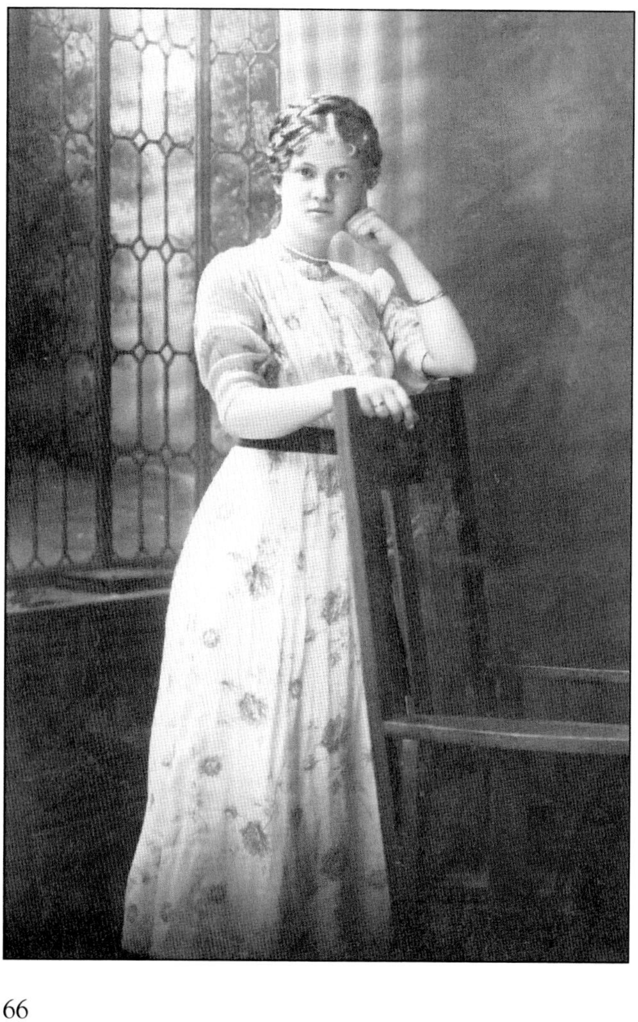

After the death of her husband, Henrietta Averill continued to live in Evans and run the Evans Mercantile. In the 1940s, she married a neighbor by the name of Maurice Maloney, who worked as a painter in the building industry. Maurice had not been married before, and along with his sister, he lived with and cared for his mother.

Henrietta's younger sister, Barbara Reed, was born in Nebraska in 1900. She attended school in Evans and later attended the Colorado State Teachers College, graduating in 1918 with a bachelor's degree in pedagogy. She taught in Uncompahgre in Montrose County, where she met her future husband, Chester Wiggins. They were married on October 12, 1921, in Weld County.

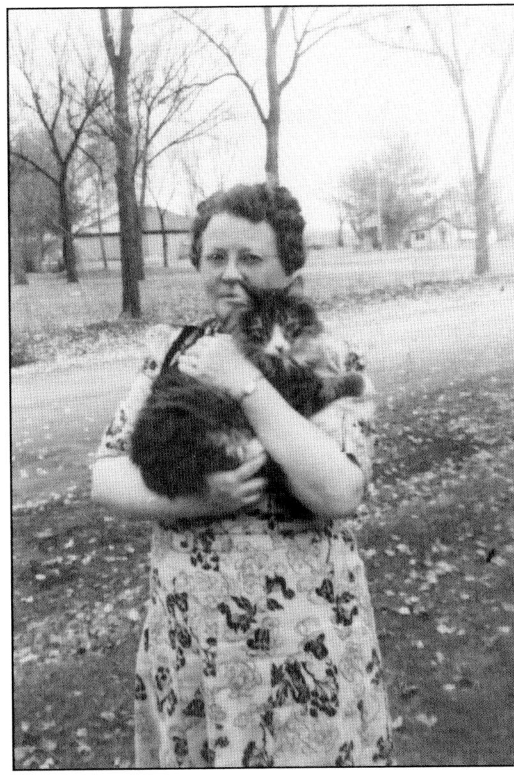

Chester and Barbara Wiggins had been living in Arizona during the 1920s while Chester worked as a coal mine operator. After the death of Dr. Averill, they moved back to Colorado with their young son and lived with Henrietta at 628 Boulder Street in Evans. They remained in Colorado until 1948, when they relocated to Wyoming. These two photographs of Henrietta (right) and Barbara (below) show the sisters posing with Henrietta's pet cat Sefur at their home in Evans sometime in the 1930s or 1940s.

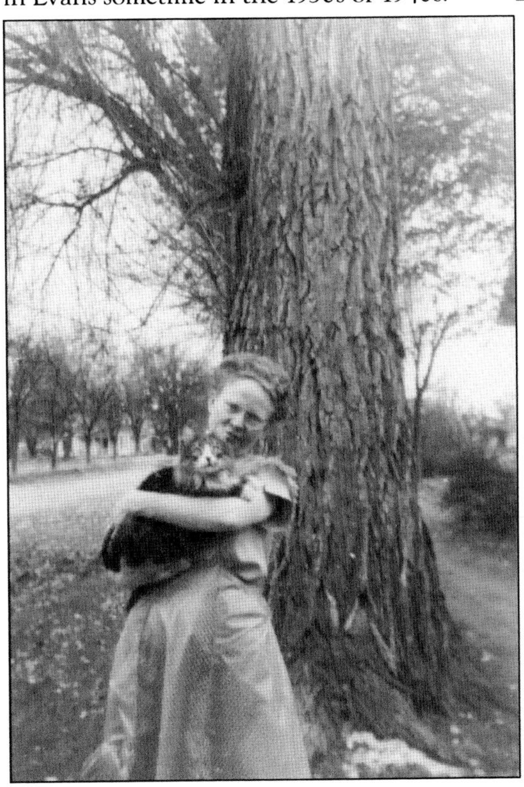

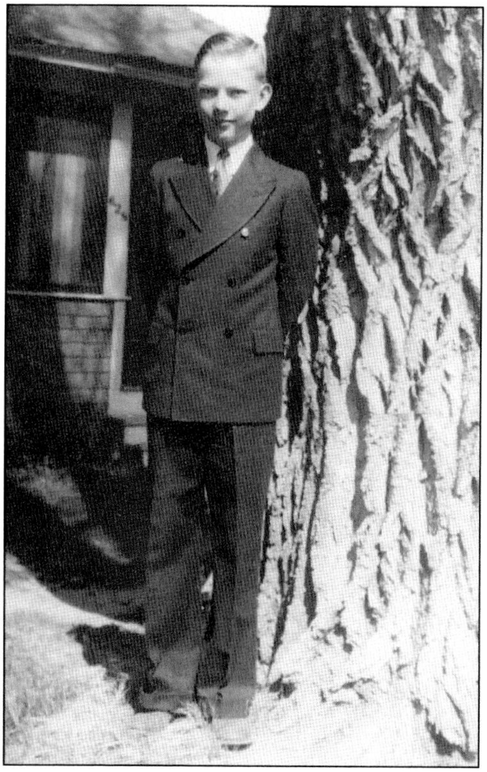

Evans was once home to one of the framers of the Peace Corps. Warren Wiggins, the only son of Barbara and Chester Wiggins, was born in Arizona in 1923. Warren graduated from the Evans and Greeley schools and later attended college at the University of Colorado and Colorado State.

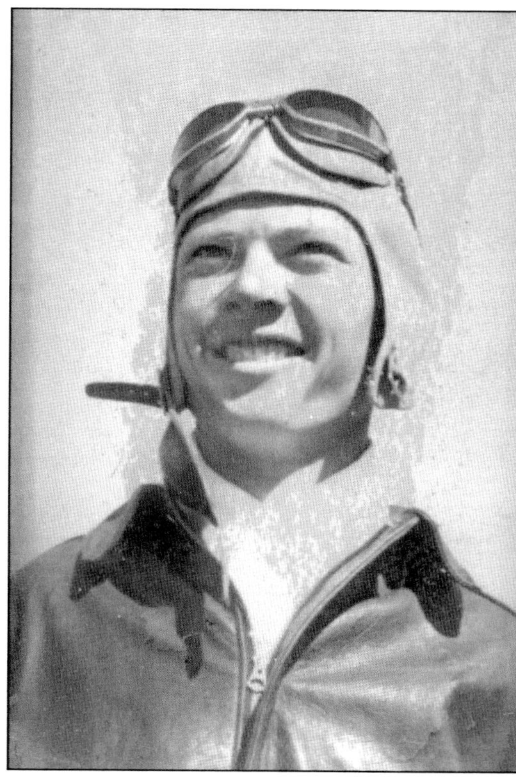

Warren Wiggins left the University of Colorado to serve in the Army Air Forces during World War II. He flew transport planes in the China-India-Burma theater and received a Distinguished Flying Cross. After his service, Warren returned to Colorado to complete his education at Colorado State. He worked as a twin-engine instructor for the Army in New Mexico and Texas before returning to school, earning a degree in economics from Harvard in 1949.

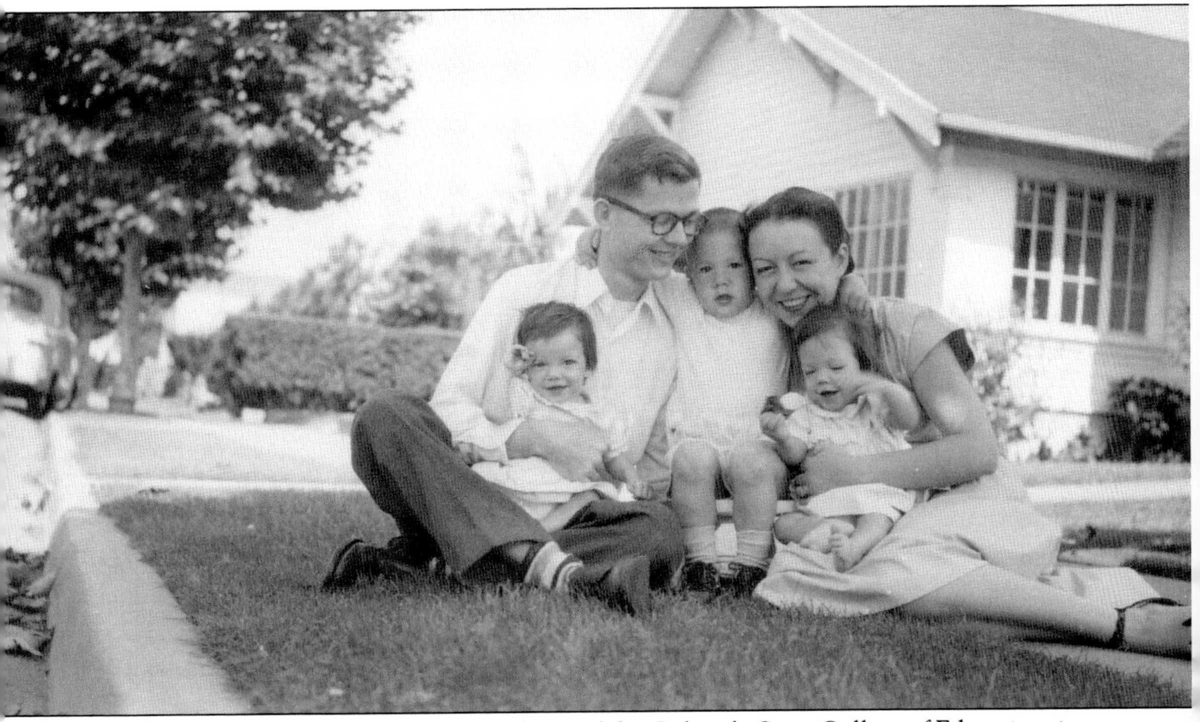

Warren Wiggins married Edna Abell, a graduate of the Colorado State College of Education, in Greeley. They had four children. The Wiggins family lived all over the world, because Warren worked as a foreign policy advisor for the International Cooperation Administration of the federal government, which administered foreign assistance and coordinated nonmilitary security programs. This job took the Wiggins family to Norway, several locations in Western Europe, the Philippines, and Bolivia. In 1961, Warren Wiggins authored a paper called "The Towering Task," which laid out the groundwork for an extensive foreign aid program. When Sergeant Shriver, brother-in-law to President Kennedy, came across the paper, he knew that it was the model he was looking for to put Kennedy's campaign promises of dynamic foreign policy into action. "The Towering Task" was the philosophical document that led to the creation of the Peace Corps in 1961. Shriver served as the first president of the organization, and Wiggins served as deputy director until 1967, when he left to form the nonprofit organization Trans Century, which ran job centers and remedial education programs in needy areas.

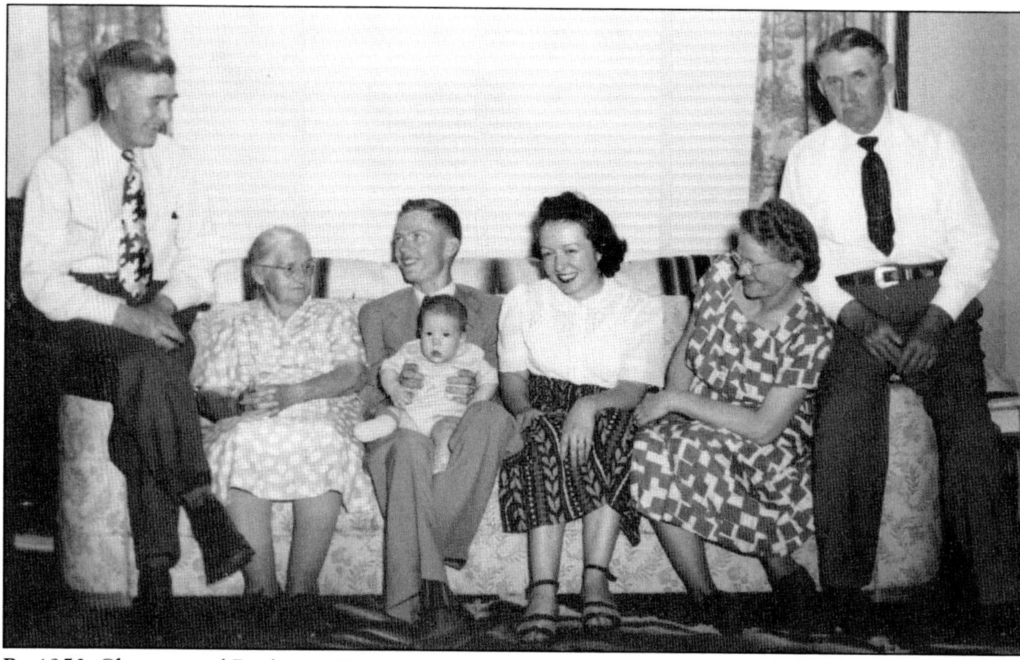

By 1950, Chester and Barbara Wiggins moved to San Bruno, California. This family photograph was taken when Warren and Edna visited them. It appears to be shortly after the birth of their first child. From left to right are two unidentified people, Warren Wiggins, an unidentified child, Edna Wiggins, Barbara Wiggins, and Chester Wiggins.

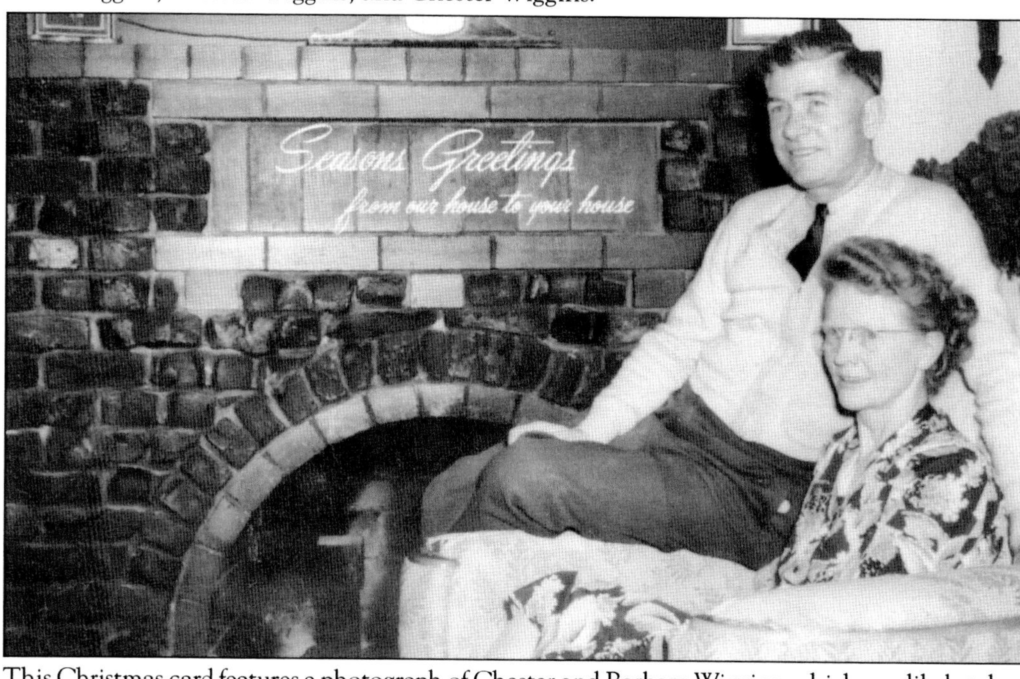


This Christmas card features a photograph of Chester and Barbara Wiggins, which was likely taken at their home in California in the 1950s. By the early 1960s, rather than settle into retirement, the Wigginses left their California home to set out on their next adventure, which would lead them to South America.

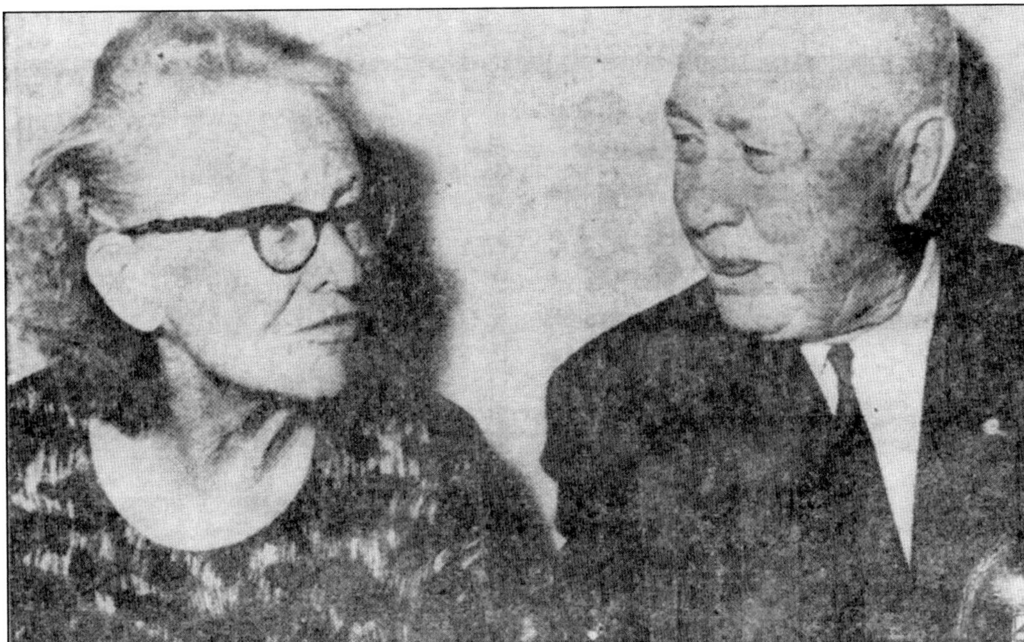

**OLDEST PEACE CORPS PAIR**—Chester N. Wiggins, 67, and his wife, Barbara, 65, reminisce at San Bruno, Calif., home near San Francisco Monday. They have returned from Peru, where they worked for two years in the Peace Corps. Oldest in the corps, they served in slum area of Arequipa. (AP Wirephoto)

Chester's background as a foreman in the construction and mining industries and Barbara's as a teacher perfectly suited them to join the Peace Corps program that their son helped to create. They served in Arequipa, Peru, a city badly damaged by earthquakes in 1958 and 1960. Chester supervised the construction of the Juan F. Kenedi School and Barbara taught nursery school classes to the local children.

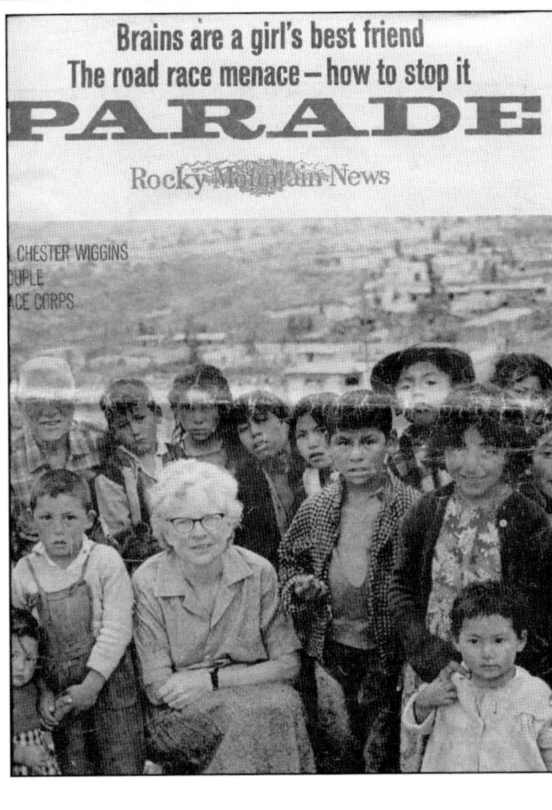


The August 4, 1961, issue of *Parade*, a special edition of the *Rocky Mountain News*, featured a story about Chester and Barbara Wiggins, who were at that time the oldest couple (though not the oldest members) in the Peace Corps. In the article, Barbara stated, "Who wants to retire when you can use your time to help someone else? The people in Peru will never forget the Peace Corps."

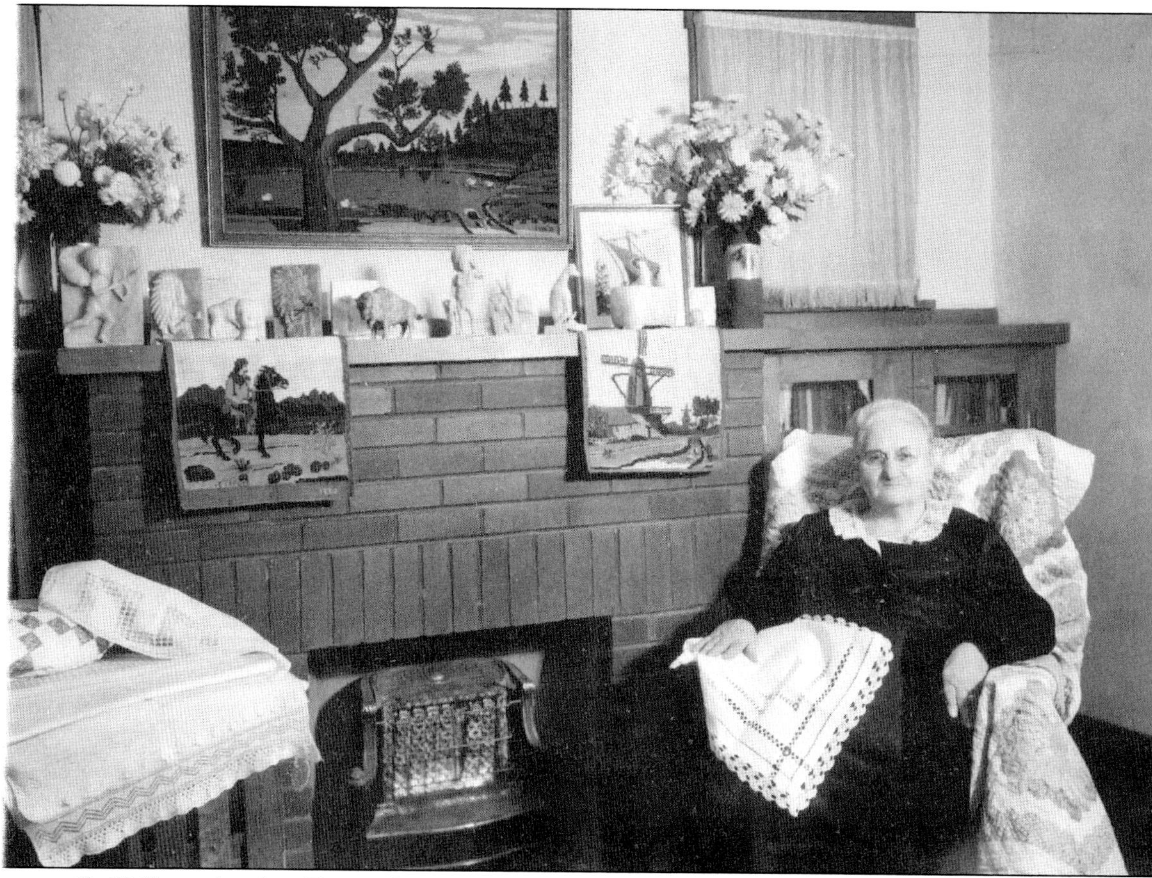

Ila Holloway lived on Empire Street in Evans during the 1920s. She was a skilled crafter, creating carved figurines, embroidery, and hand-knit lace. Ila grew up in Iowa and came to Colorado as a young woman. She lived with her husband, James, and their three children in Table Rock, Colorado, in El Paso County before permanently settling in the Evans and Greeley area. A hand-knit lace table runner made by Ila will be placed on permanent display at the Riverside Library and Cultural Center in late 2014.

# Three

# A Century of Learning

## Going to School in Evans

The people of Evans have always put a great value on the importance of schools in their community. From the establishment of School District 15 when the town was barely starting out to the founding of the normal school by Reverend Todd and even to the present day, schools have been at the center of civic and social life in Evans.

There have been four public school buildings in Evans. The first, simply known as the Evans School, was built in 1874 and served students from first grade through high school. By 1908, the district decided that high school students would be better served attending classes in Greeley, where there were more funds and resources available to them. The school continued to serve elementary and middle school students until it was torn down in 1927 to build a larger, more modern building. Students attended classes held in homes and public buildings around town in the interim. In 1929, the second Evans School, later renamed Chappelow, was open to students. By the 1950s, there was a growing desire on the part of Evans residents to bring students back from Greeley and open a high school. Chappelow West, a combined junior and senior high school, was opened in 1953.

Like many small and rural schools across the nation, the Evans school district faced pressures reorganize in the 1960s. In Evans, as was often the case in smaller districts, teacher salaries, school facilities, equipment, and resources were not up to par with those of larger districts. The superintendent of District 15 felt that it was a good idea to join District 6. The community was divided—some people wanted to join District 6 because they believed that a larger district could offer their students better opportunities. Others wanted to hold onto the schools because of a sense of community pride and to retain local control. After much deliberation, the Greeley school board voted 3-2 to close the Evans schools. Residents fought the decision in court, but ultimately, the battle to keep School District 15 in business was lost, and the district was dissolved in 1965.

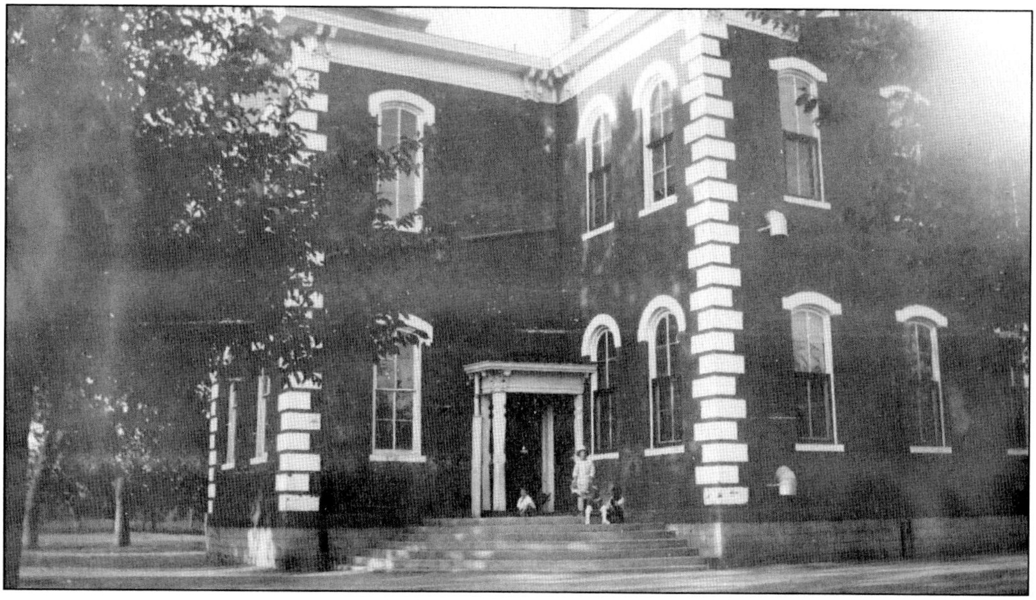

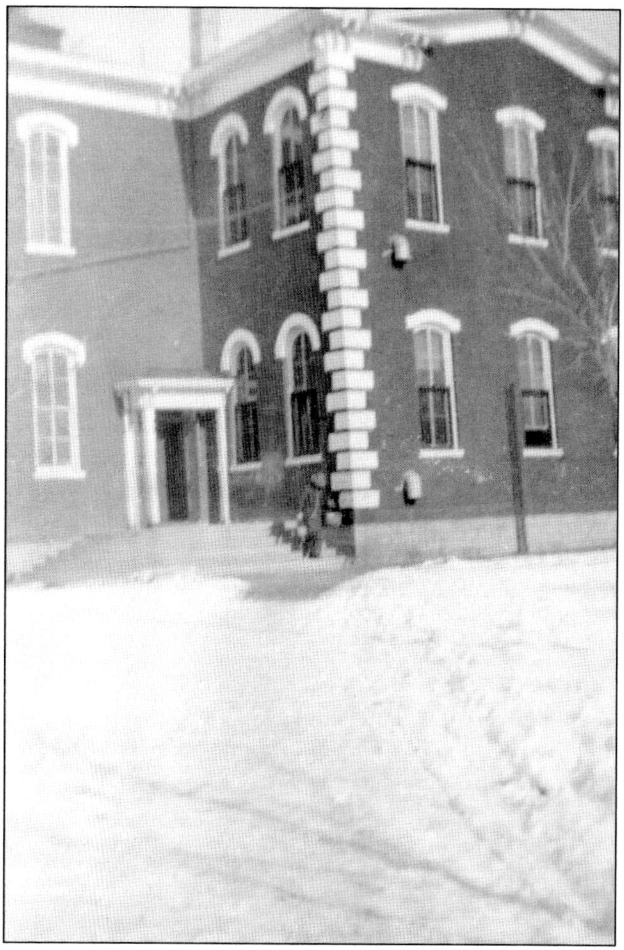

Education was important to the early settlers of Evans. School District 15 was established on January 24, 1870, just two months after the town was founded. The newly formed district took in all of Sections 19, 20, 29, and 30 in Township 5, Range 65 West, which covered a large section of farmland surrounding Evans.

Though the school district was established right away, it took a while for the town to get enough money and resources together to build a proper school building. Classes were held in private homes, churches, and public buildings until the first permanent school was built in 1874. This beautiful two-story brick building was arguably the nicest building in town for many years and was considered quite modern for its time.

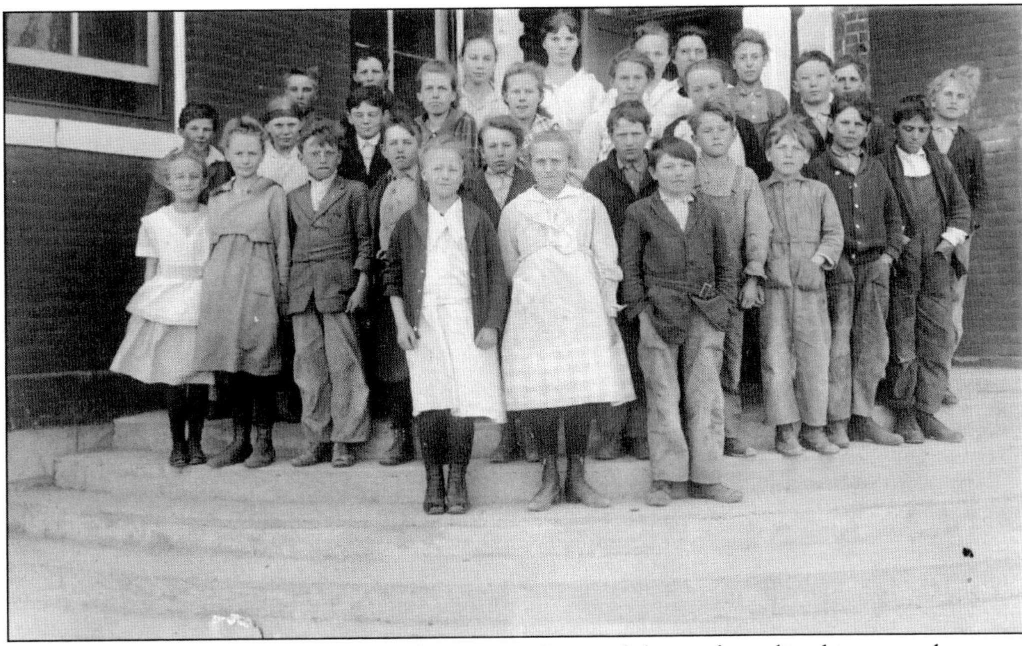

Evans schools served students from a large area. Some of the students lived in town, but many others lived on farms surrounding the town. In 1880, Evans was still very small, with a population of less than 200, but the school was larger due to the students from the countryside near town.

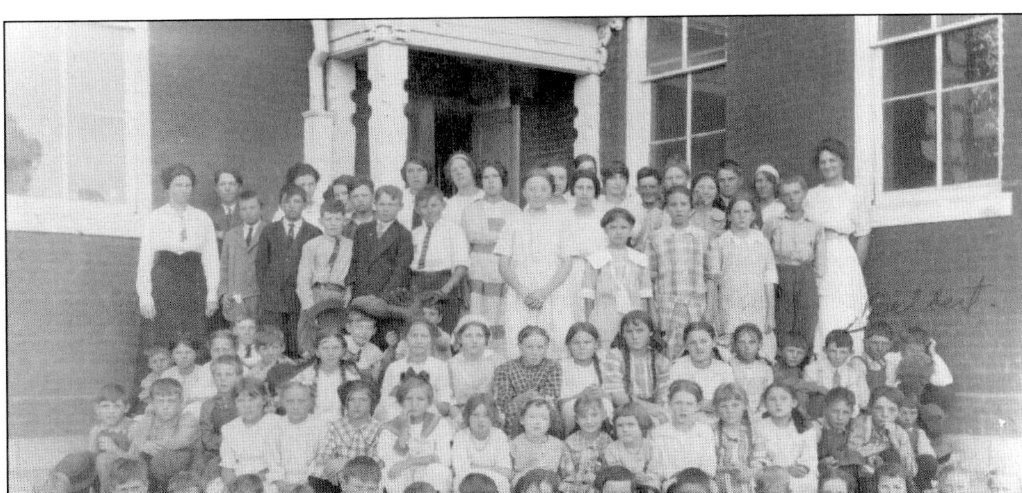


This undated photograph is of the entire student body and teachers of the Evans School around the late 1800s. The students range in age from very young to junior high or high school age. Two of the elementary school students are identified as Evelyn and Delbert.

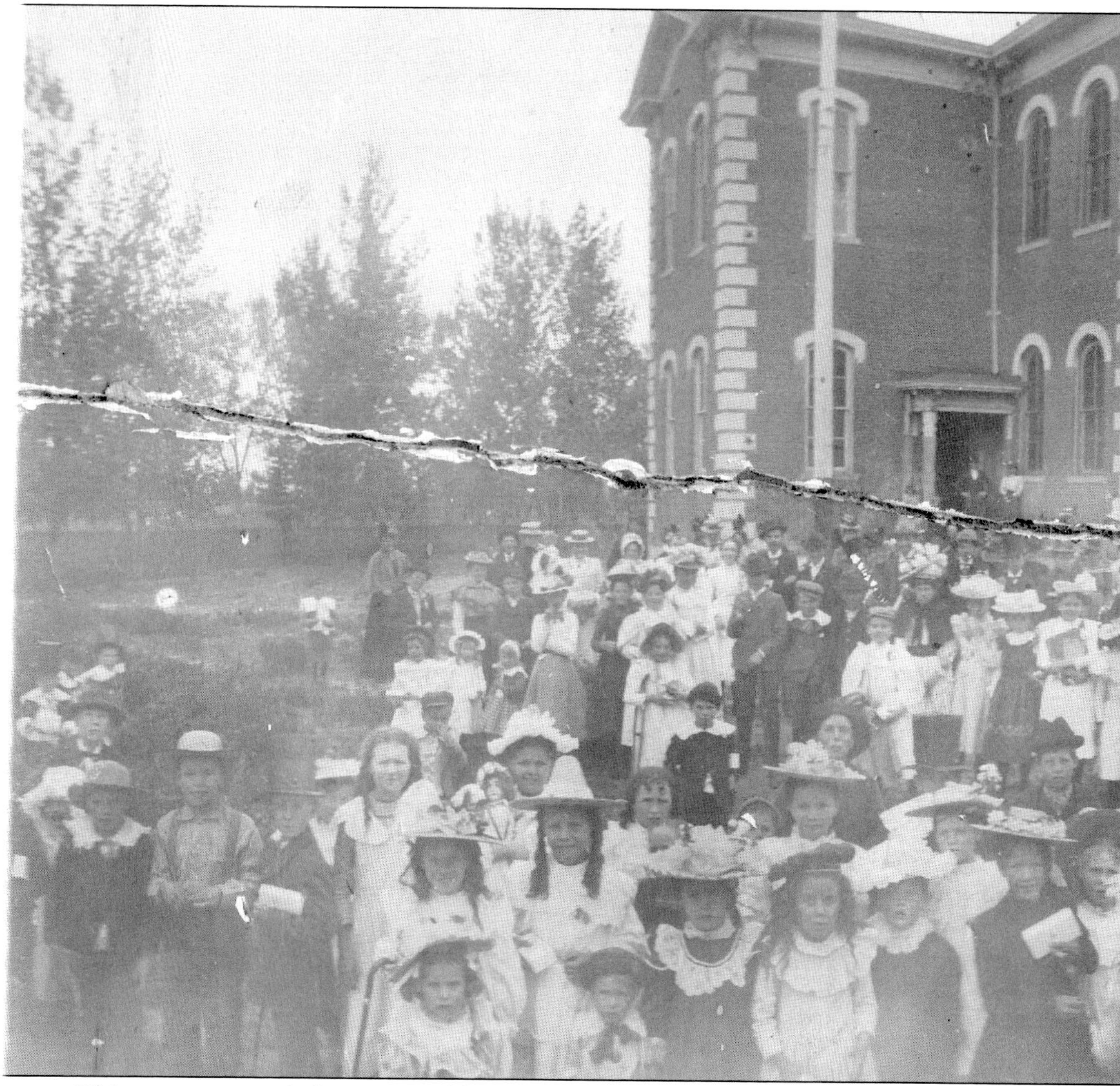

This panoramic north-facing view of the Evans School was taken in 1903. It is apparent that there is a celebration of some sort happening. There are parents standing to the side of the crowd on the right side of the picture. Some of the women appear to be holding programs. The schoolchildren are dressed more elaborately that they normally would have been for a regular day at school.

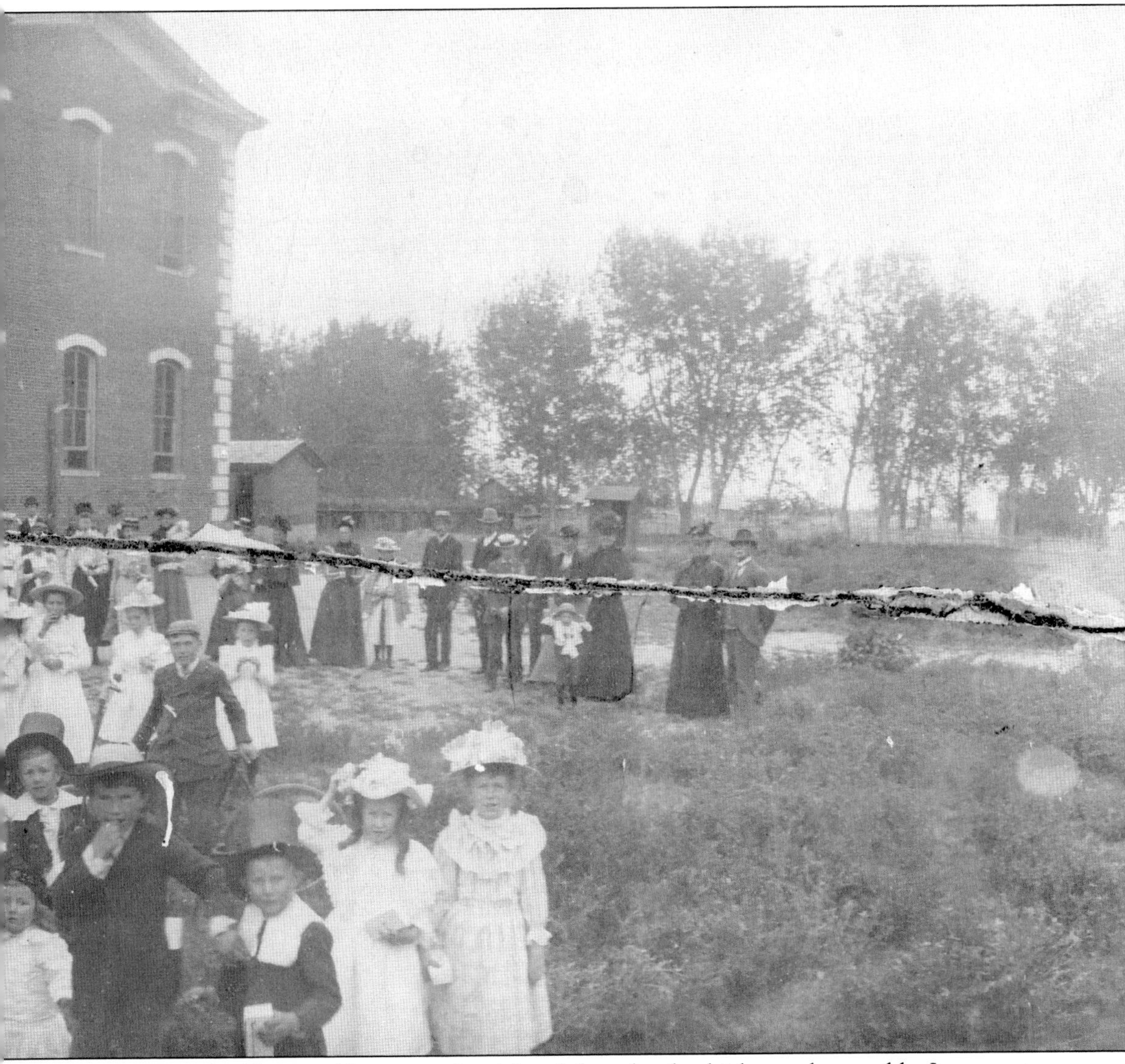

There is an outbuilding visible just to the right of the school, which may be a stable. It was not at all uncommon for schools in the country or small towns to have a horse stable, because some children would ride their horses to school, as there was no bus service until much later.

# Third

# Annual Announcement

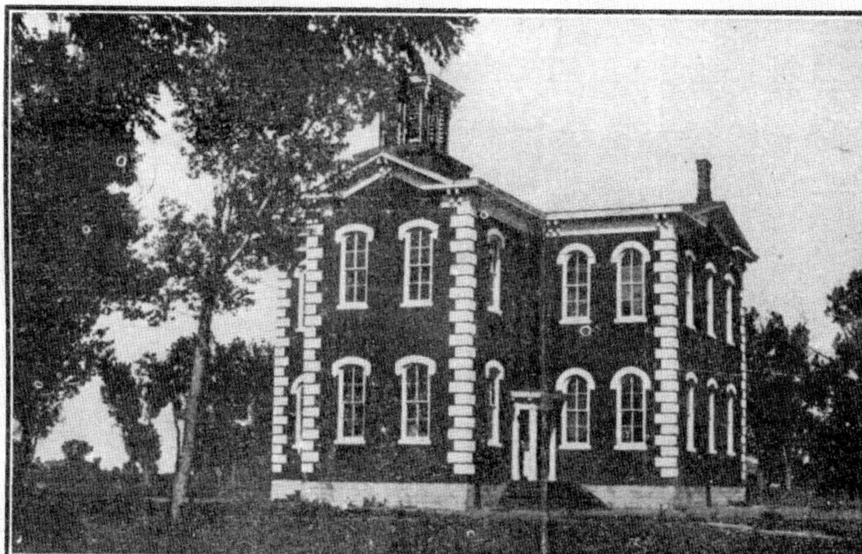

MAIN BUILDING

## The Evans Public Schools

Evans, Colorado

For the Term of 1910-11

*Issued by order of the Board of Education*
*August 1910*

This is the 1903 annual announcement for the Evans School, printed by School District 15. The pamphlet contains information about the town of Evans and its school, including a list of courses for the high school students. There is also a small business directory and advertisements for a lot of the businesses in town. The school likely sold advertising space in the annual announcement to help raise money for the school. Several of the businesses were mainstays in Evans, such as Behrens Lumber, Al Weinhold's Feed and Coal, Young's Hall, and The Pioneer.

This list shows the high school courses offered at the Evans School in 1903. Note the emphasis on history, math, Latin, and literature. These subjects make up what is considered a "classical education." Between approximately 1890 and 1920, John Dewey's educational philosophy, known as Progressive Education, was becoming increasingly popular across the country. The child-centered, explorative methods of Dewey were never fully embraced in rural or small-town schools.

## *High School Course of Study*

FIRST YEAR.

| First Half | Second Half |
|---|---|
| Hist.-Ancient | Hist.-Ancient |
| English | English |
| Latin | Latin |
| Algebra | Algebra |
| *Zoology | *Botany |
| *Physical Geography | *Bookkeeping |

SECOND YEAR.

| | |
|---|---|
| *Plane Geometry | *Plane Geometry |
| *Latin | *Latin |
| English | English |
| Algebra | Plane Geometry |
| History-Mediaeval | History Modern |
| *Zoology | *Botany |
| *Arithmetc | *Bookkeeping |
| | *Elective |

Pupils may choose not to exceed five full studies, at the discretion of the superintendent.

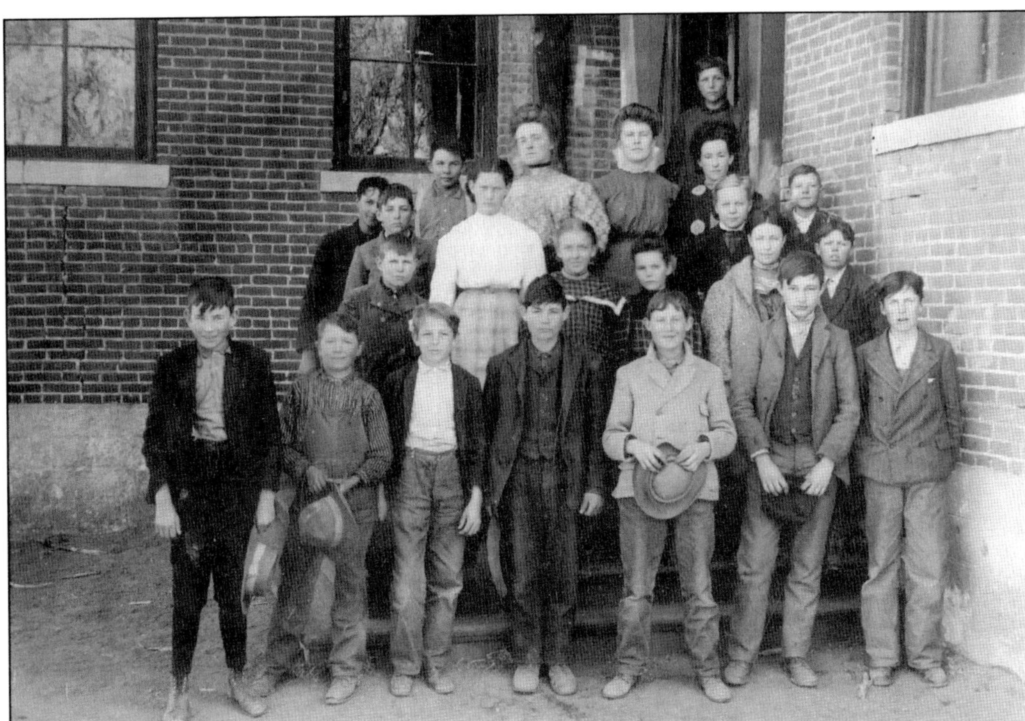

These are the Evans School junior high school students from the 1903–1904 school year. They are shown here with their teachers, who are standing in the back row. These students would be some of the last to be able to attend high school in Evans, as the high school courses were discontinued in 1908, after which time students finished their schooling in Greeley.

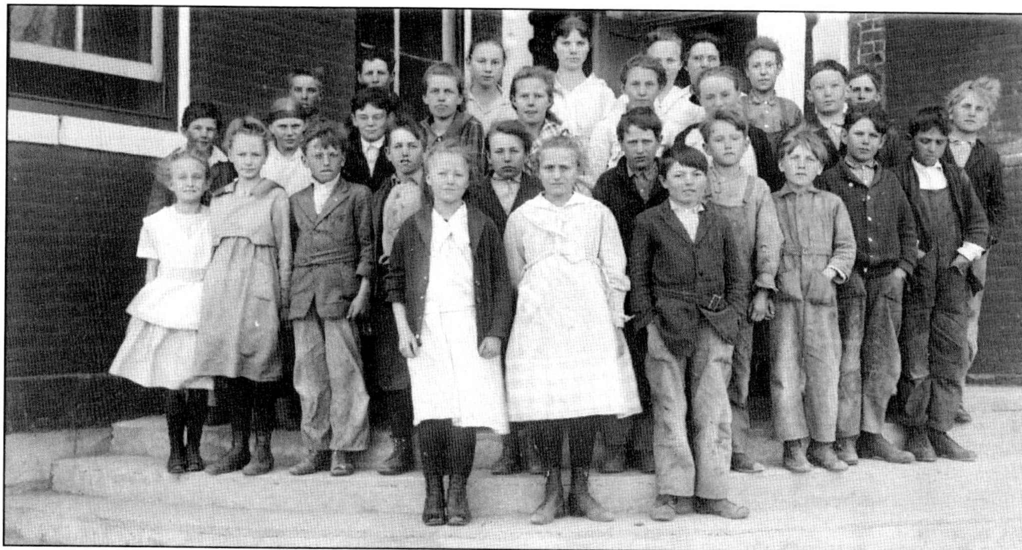

In the first decades of the 20th century, educators debated the merits of Progressive Education, and rural schools were facing widespread closures and consolidations. As one of the larger schools in the area at the time, the Evans School was spared consolidation, but it was no doubt subjected to intense scrutiny, as nearly all small-town and country schools were during this period.

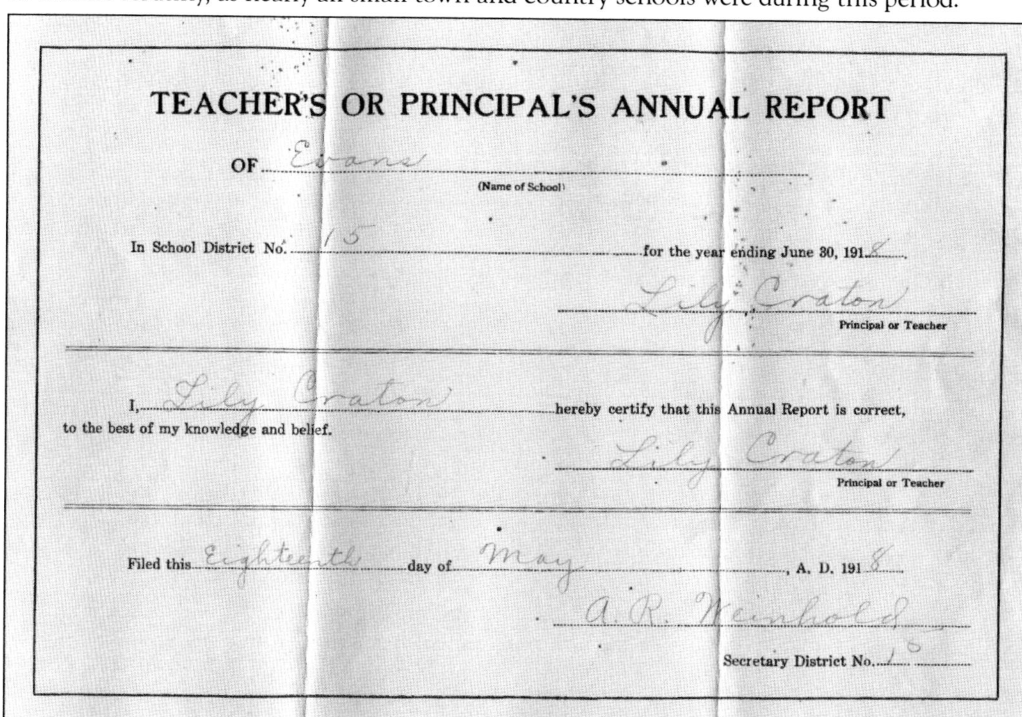

**TEACHER'S OR PRINCIPAL'S ANNUAL REPORT**

OF Evans
(Name of School)

In School District No. 15 for the year ending June 30, 1918

Lily Craton
Principal or Teacher

I, Lily Craton hereby certify that this Annual Report is correct, to the best of my knowledge and belief.

Lily Craton
Principal or Teacher

Filed this Eighteenth day of May, A. D. 1918

A. R. Weinhold
Secretary District No. 15

This booklet is the teacher's or principal's annual report of School District 15 from 1918. It is signed by Albert R. Weinhold Sr., who was the secretary of the district and owner of the feed and coal store in Evans. The annual report contained information that was useful in helping the school board make decisions, such as enrollment, attendance records, teachers' salary, and financial records of the school.

Loretto Lane Chappelow was one of the most loved and respected teachers in Evans for many years. The school was later named after Chappelow, and several different places around Evans today bear her name. She taught at schools in Sunrise, Wyoming; Muskogee, Oklahoma; and the Colorado towns of Edwards, Canon City, Ordway, and Bracewell before coming to Evans in 1922.

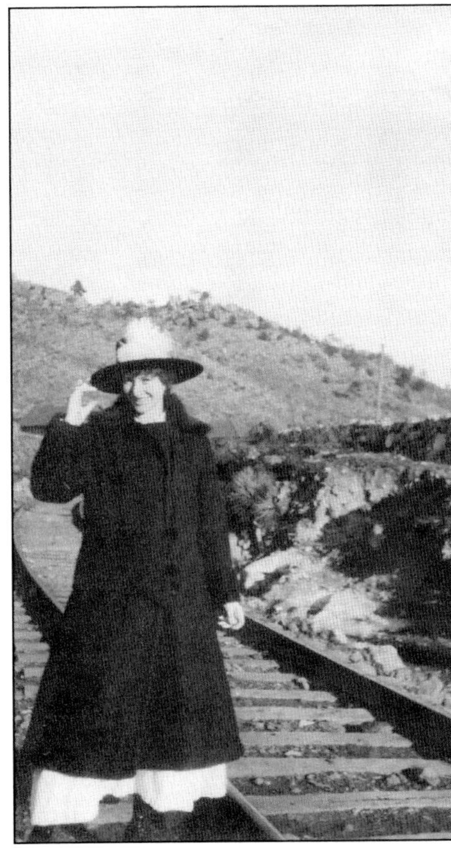

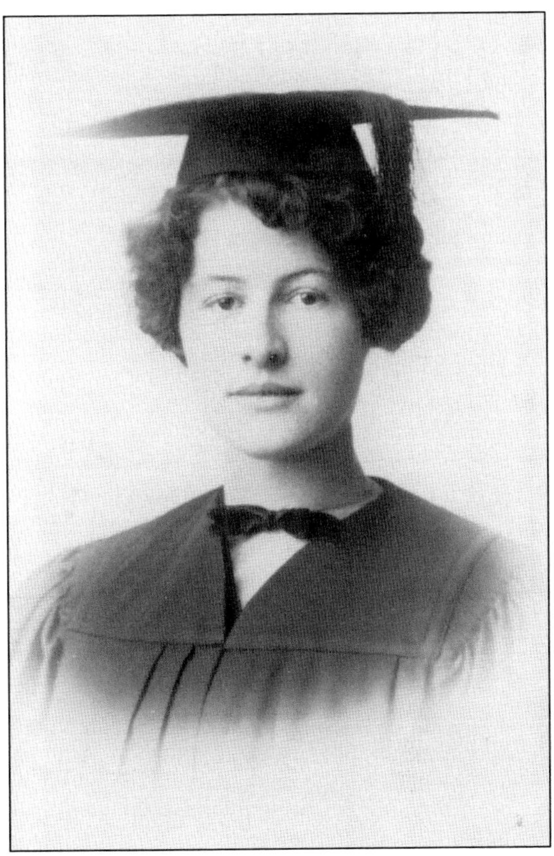

Loretto Lane was born in Leadville in 1893. Her family later moved to Canon City, where she graduated as valedictorian of her class. She later attended the Colorado Teachers College in Greeley. This photograph was taken when Loretto was a second-year college student in 1914.

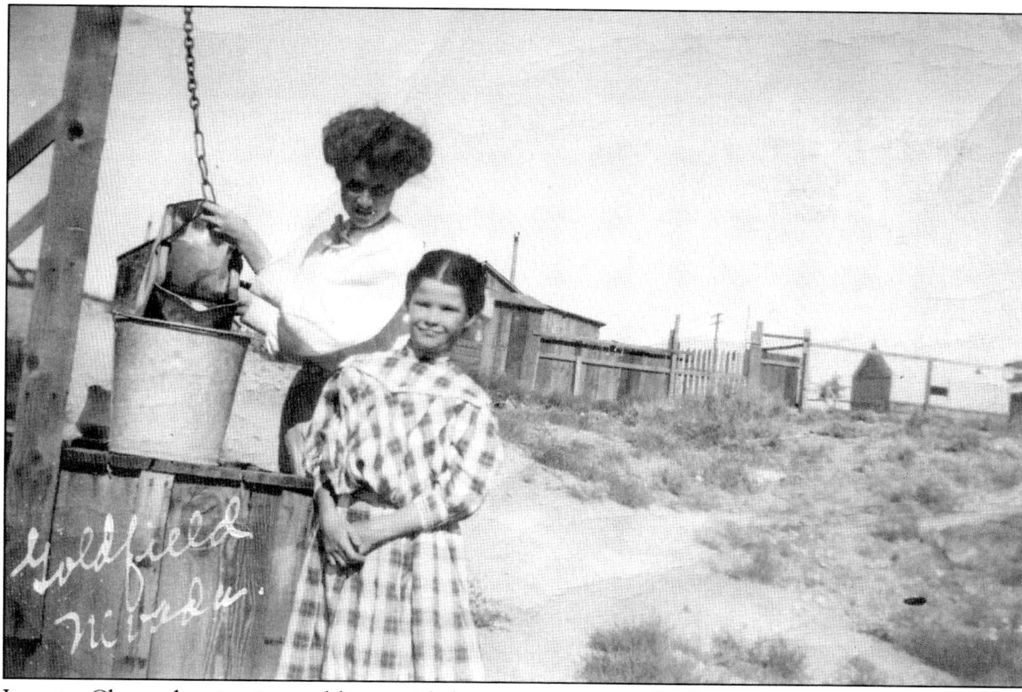


Loretto Chappelow is pictured here with her younger sister Ruth Lane pumping water at their home near Canon City in the 1900s. Their mother, Annie, and Ruth both moved to Greeley in the 1930s, and they lived with Loretto and her husband for a number of years.

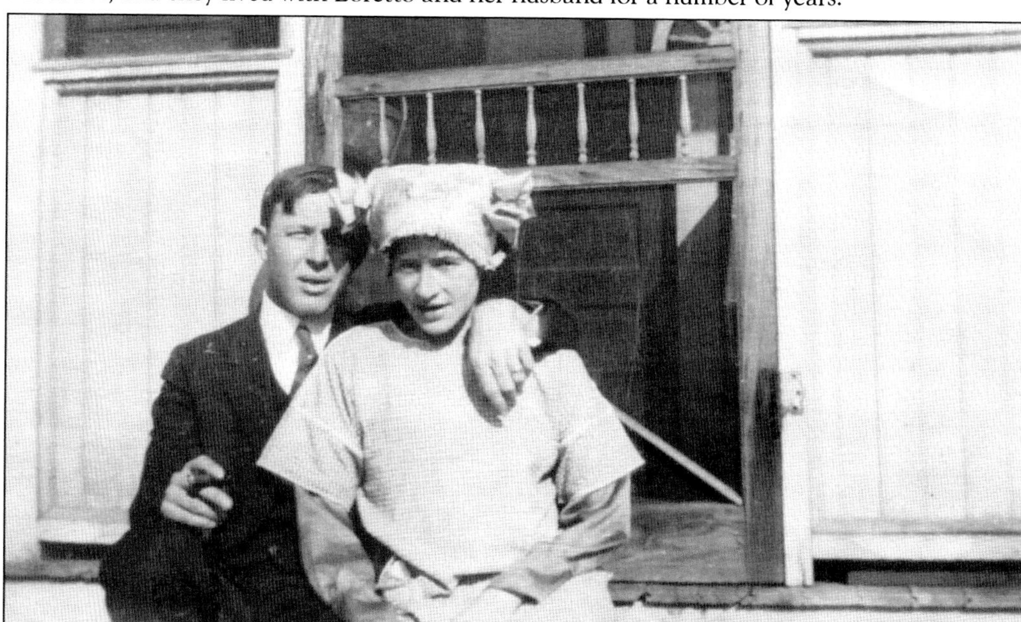

This photograph, taken sometime in the early to mid-1910s, shows Earl Chappelow and Loretto Lane enjoying a day together while the couple was dating. The pair likely met in Greeley when Loretto was attending school at the Colorado State College of Education. They were married on December 2, 1917, in Greeley, Colorado.

Earl Chappelow was originally from Kansas but moved to Greeley with his parents as a young child. Earl and his father both worked as blacksmiths in Greeley. Early city directories show that Earl was working at the A.A. Blacksmith and Shop in Greeley, but by 1930, he was the proprietor of his own business.

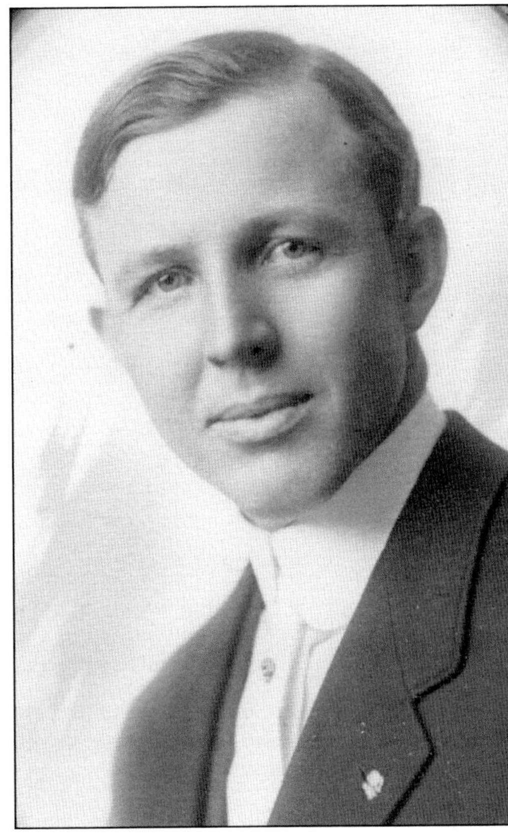

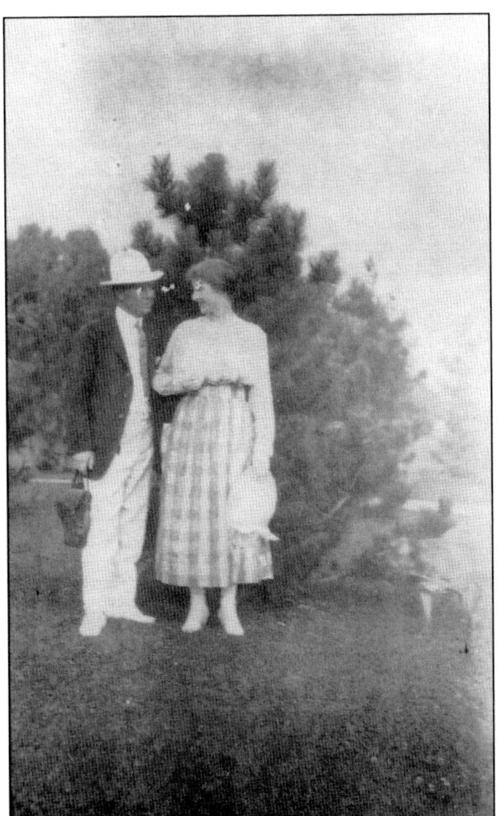

One story often told by Loretto Chappelow and her students is the time that the children "put one over" on their teacher. On a particularly windy day, the class told her that they had to evacuate the school because the building was not safe. Being new to the school, she figured that it was the standard procedure, so she had the children line up and led them outside. Once outside, the students erupted in laughter, giddy that they had fooled their teacher.

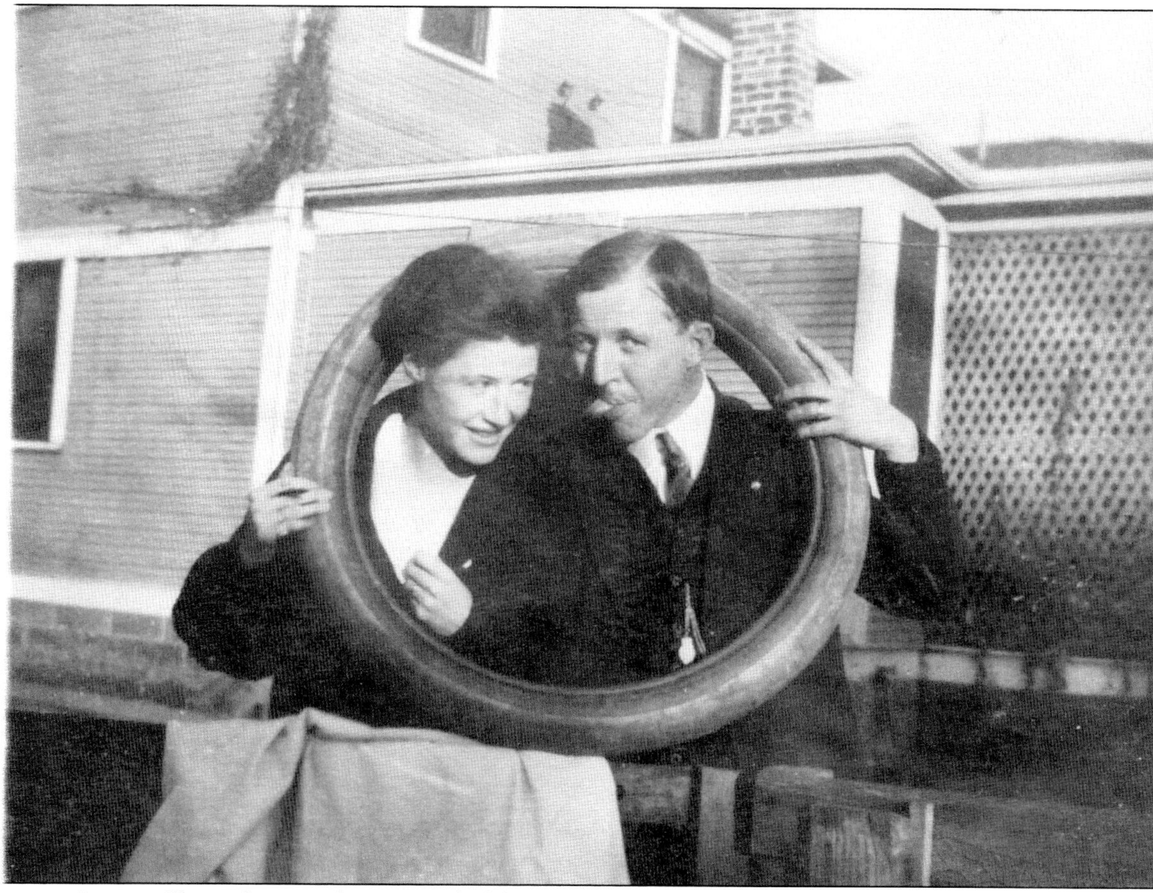

Loretto Chappelow was the principal of the Evans School for the last 20 years before her retirement in 1958. Even after she officially retired, she volunteered as the school librarian for another 22 years. When the class of 1955 at Evans High School dedicated their yearbook to Loretto Chappelow, they asked her to explain her love of teaching. She responded by explaining, "I do not believe that I can make it clear to an outsider the pleasure I have had in teaching. I have worked in other fields, but I would rather earn my living by teaching than in any other way. Teaching is not merely a life work, a profession, an occupation, a struggle; but it is a love to work with and for children. Teaching is also an art so great and difficult to master that a person can spend a long life at it without much more than realizing his limitations and mistakes and his distance from the ideal."

A letter titled "Tribute to a Great Lady" was read on the local radio on Good Friday, 1956, and also on March 29, 1965. The letter praises Loretto Chappelow's kindness, understanding, and dedication to her students. She left a legacy in Evans best described in the letter: "Hardly a day goes by without meeting someone who has been greatly benefited by a kind work or deed from our great lady, Loretto Chappelow." In 1965, Chappelow was awarded the Pro Ecclesia et Pontifice medal, the highest honor the Vatican can bestow upon a lay person. After her death in 1970, the Chappelow School Parent Teacher Council commissioned a portrait of her. The newspaper clipping with the portrait shows the unveiling of the painting by Leo Michaud, a longtime Evans School board member and friend of Loretto Chappelow.

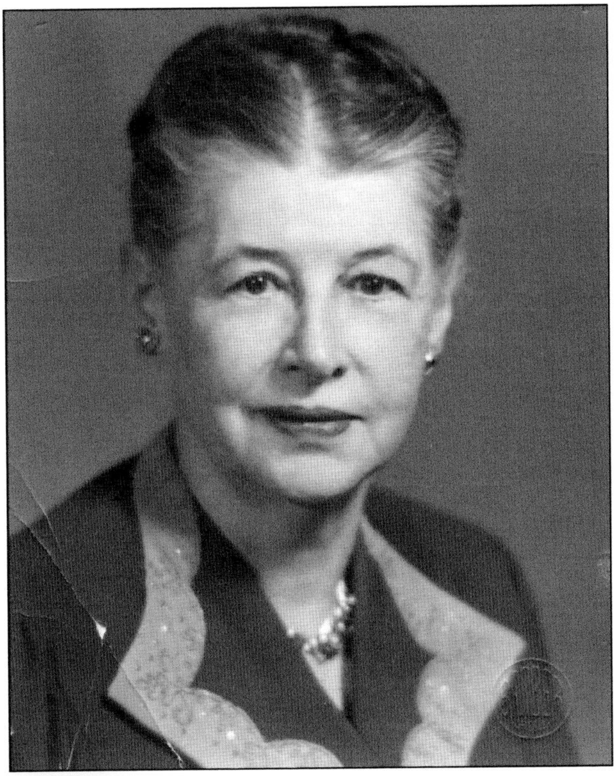

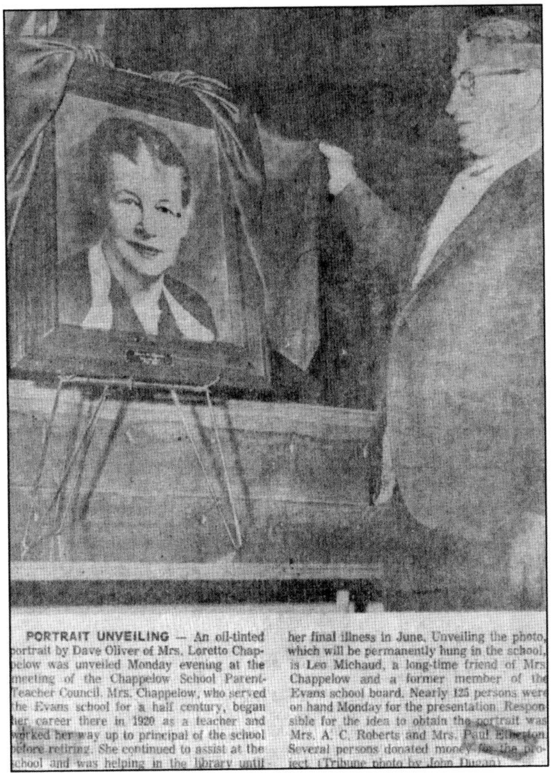

**PORTRAIT UNVEILING** — An oil-tinted portrait by Dave Oliver of Mrs. Loretto Chappelow was unveiled Monday evening at the meeting of the Chappelow School Parent-Teacher Council. Mrs. Chappelow, who served the Evans school for a half century, began her career there in 1920 as a teacher and worked her way up to principal of the school before retiring. She continued to assist at the school and was helping in the library until her final illness in June. Unveiling the photo, which will be permanently hung in the school, is Leo Michaud, a long-time friend of Mrs. Chappelow and a former member of the Evans school board. Nearly 125 persons were on hand Monday for the presentation. Responsible for the idea to obtain the portrait was Mrs. A. C. Roberts and Mrs. Paul [illegible]. Several persons donated money for the project. (Tribune photo by John Dugan)

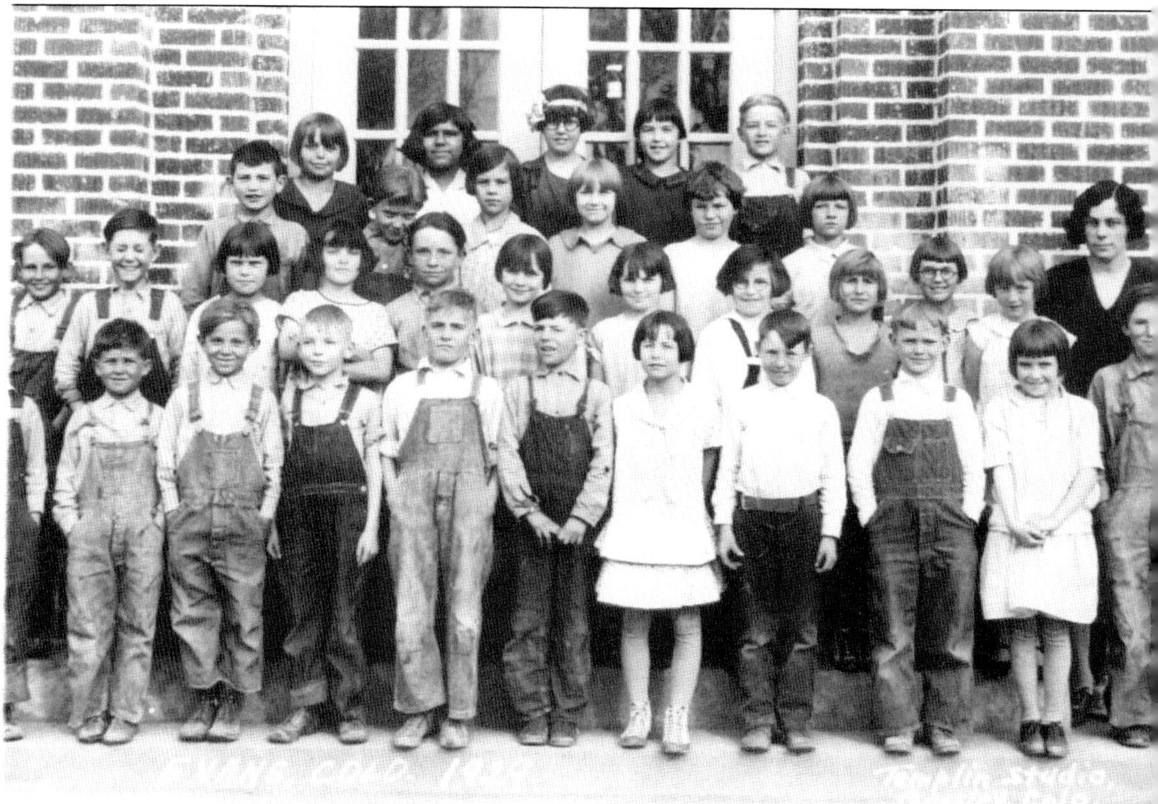


The third-grade students in this combined third- and fourth-grade picture were the first class of students to begin their education in the first grade at the newly built Evans School in the fall of 1927. When they graduated from Evans after the ninth grade in the spring of 1944, they became the first students to attend all nine years of school in this building.

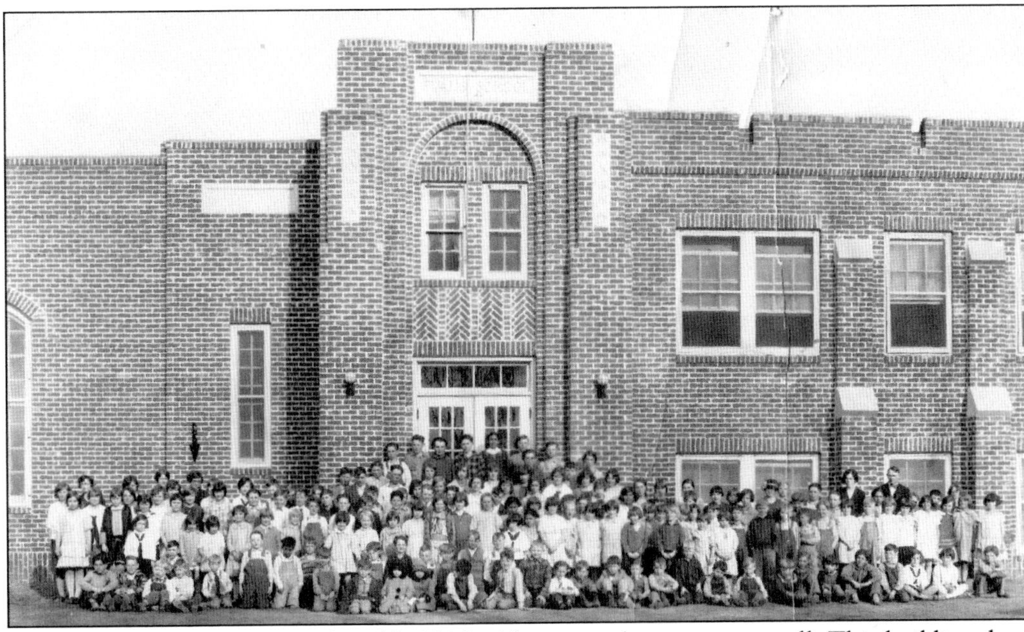

As the town began to grow, the old 1874 building soon became too small. This building, later renamed the Chappelow School, was built in 1927. There was a short period of time between the demolition of the old building and the opening of the new one, so school classes were held at Young's Hall. This picture of the school was taken around 1930, when Chester Hatch was the principal.

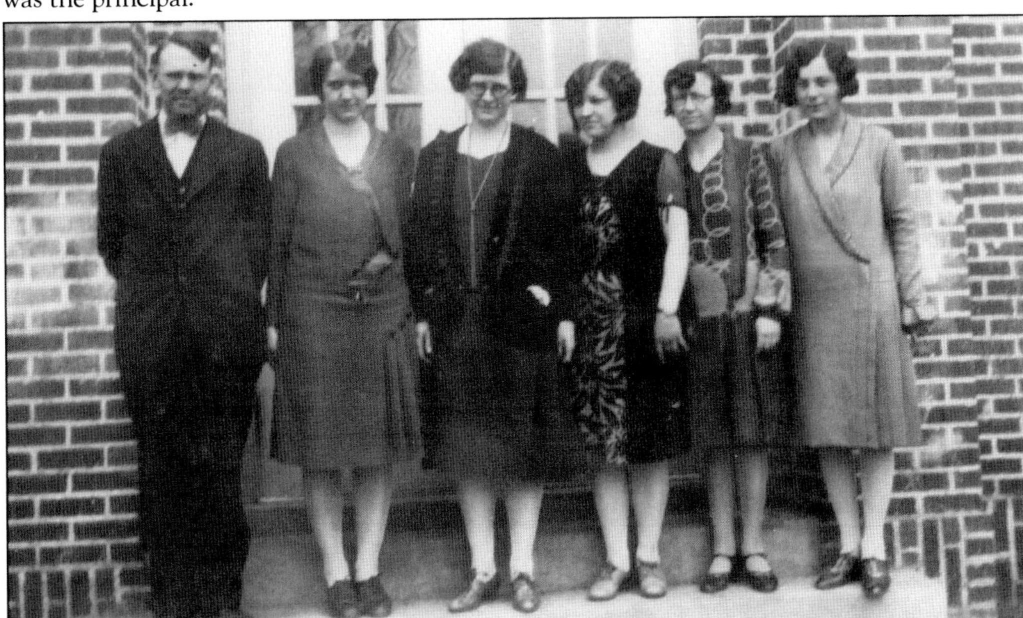

The teachers who taught at the Evans School over the years were loved and respected by the students and the community alike. Several of them, including Loretto Chappelow and Veda Fuerstock, taught in Evans for the rest of their careers. The teachers, from left to right, are Chester Hatch (principal), Helen Bissell, Loretto Chappelow, Mary Hill, Veda Fuerstock, and Gertrude Briscoe.

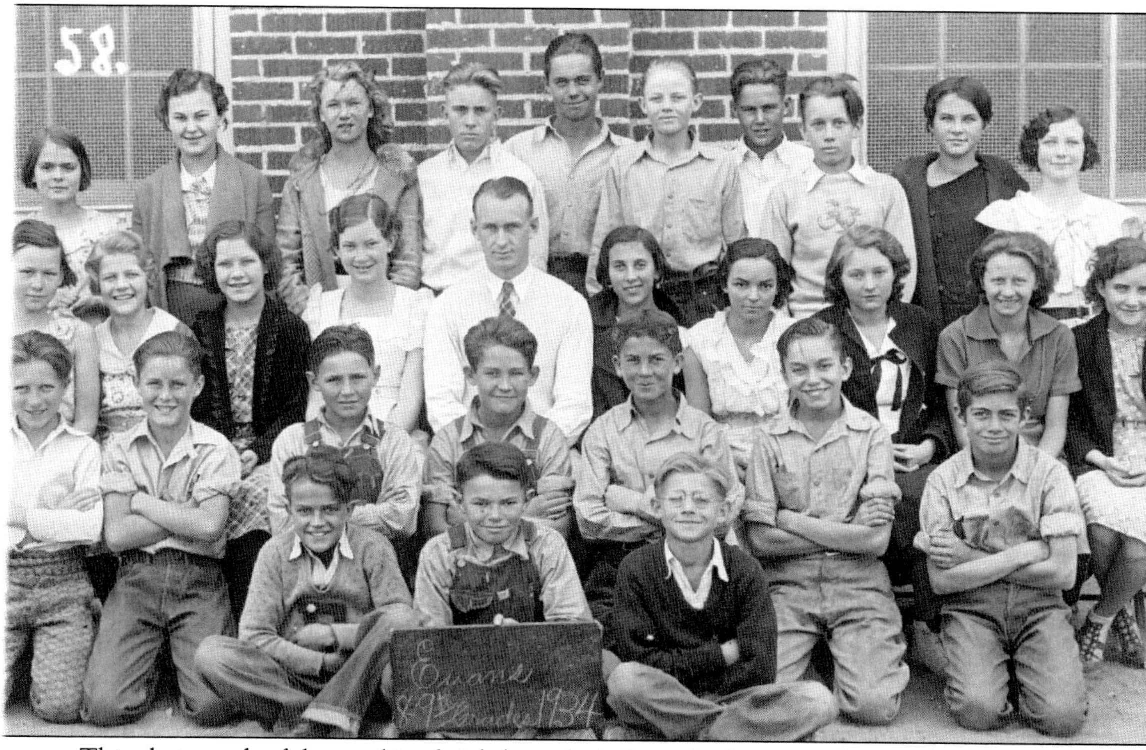


This photograph of the combined eighth- and ninth-grade class was taken on the steps in front of the school in 1934. Their teacher, Chester Hatch, is seated at the center of the photograph. Hatch was also the principal of the Evans School during the 1930s.

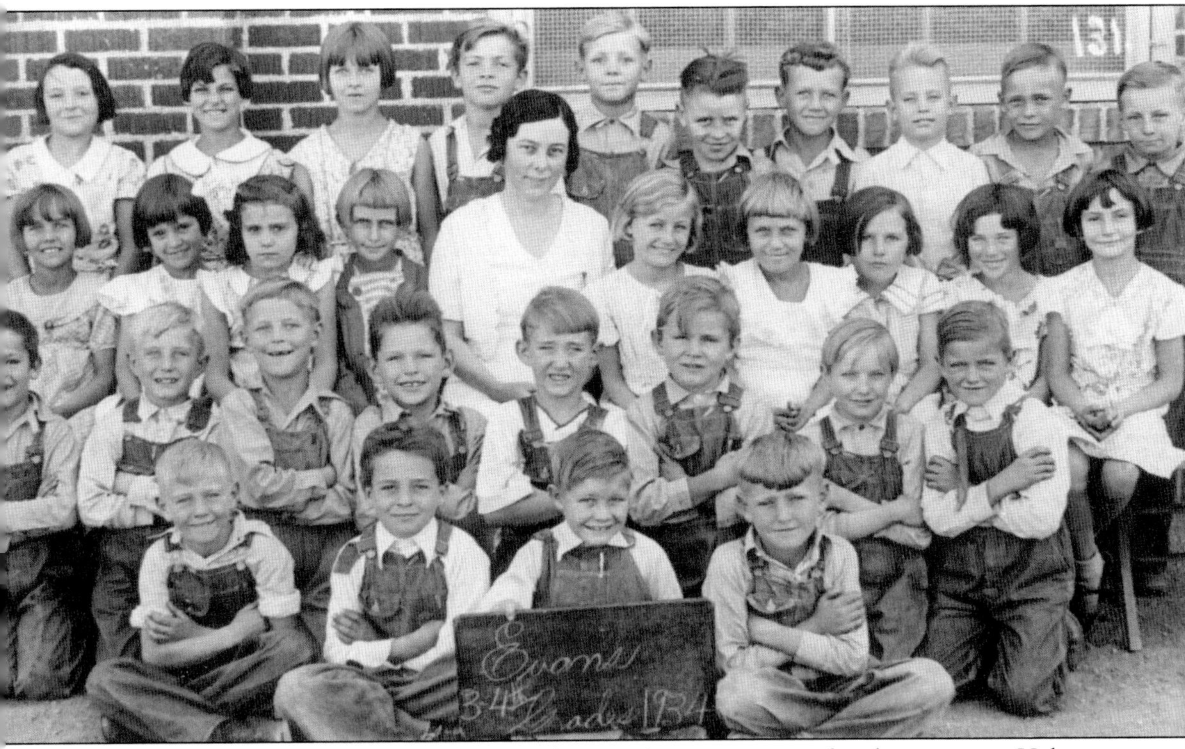


Many of the children in this 1934 photograph came from prominent families in town. Helen Overman's father started the volunteer fire department in the 1920s, Marilyn Bly was the granddaughter of Joseph and Minnie Kinsinger, and the Durr and Fugate families lived in Evans for a long time and were active in many organizations. From left to right are (first row) unidentified, Paul Roth, Ralph Vanbuskert, and Everett Meyer; (second row) five unidentified youths, Bill Rickard, unidentified, and Floyd Ruth; (third row) unidentified, Doris Roberts, Margie Durr, Marilyn Jo Bly, Gertrude Briscoe, Lorraine Meyer, Violet Wiese, two unidentified youths, and Helen Overman; (fourth row) Margie Mitchell, Ruth Fugate, three unidentified youths, Ralph Farquer, ? Lott, two unidentified youths, and Jimmy "James" Adamson.

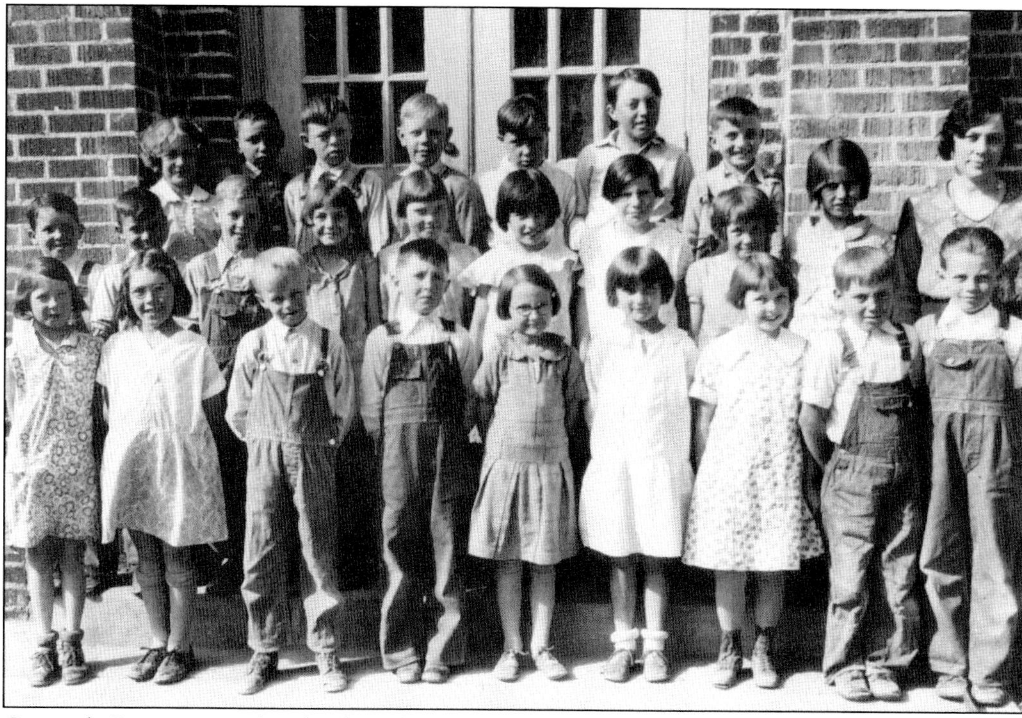

Gertrude Briscoe was the third- and fourth-grade teacher in Evans for many years. She was originally from Oklahoma and lived in Illinois, North Carolina, and Texas before coming to Colorado in 1913. She graduated from high school at Rocky Fort and then attended the Colorado State Teachers College in Greeley.

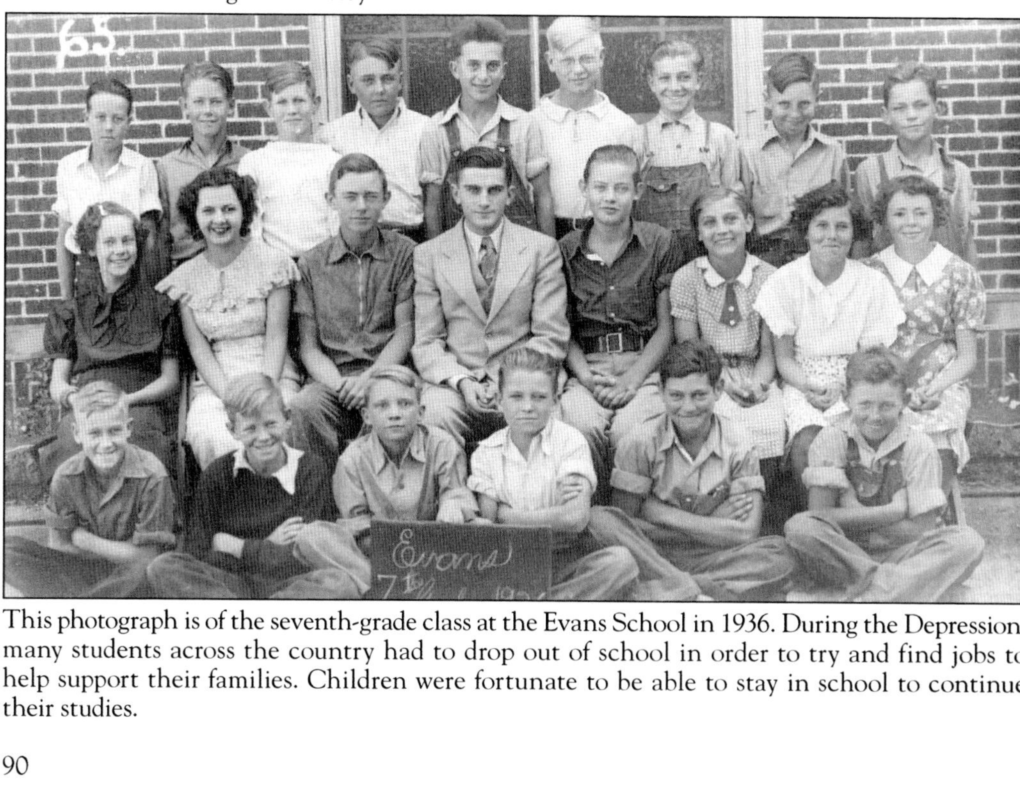


This photograph is of the seventh-grade class at the Evans School in 1936. During the Depression, many students across the country had to drop out of school in order to try and find jobs to help support their families. Children were fortunate to be able to stay in school to continue their studies.

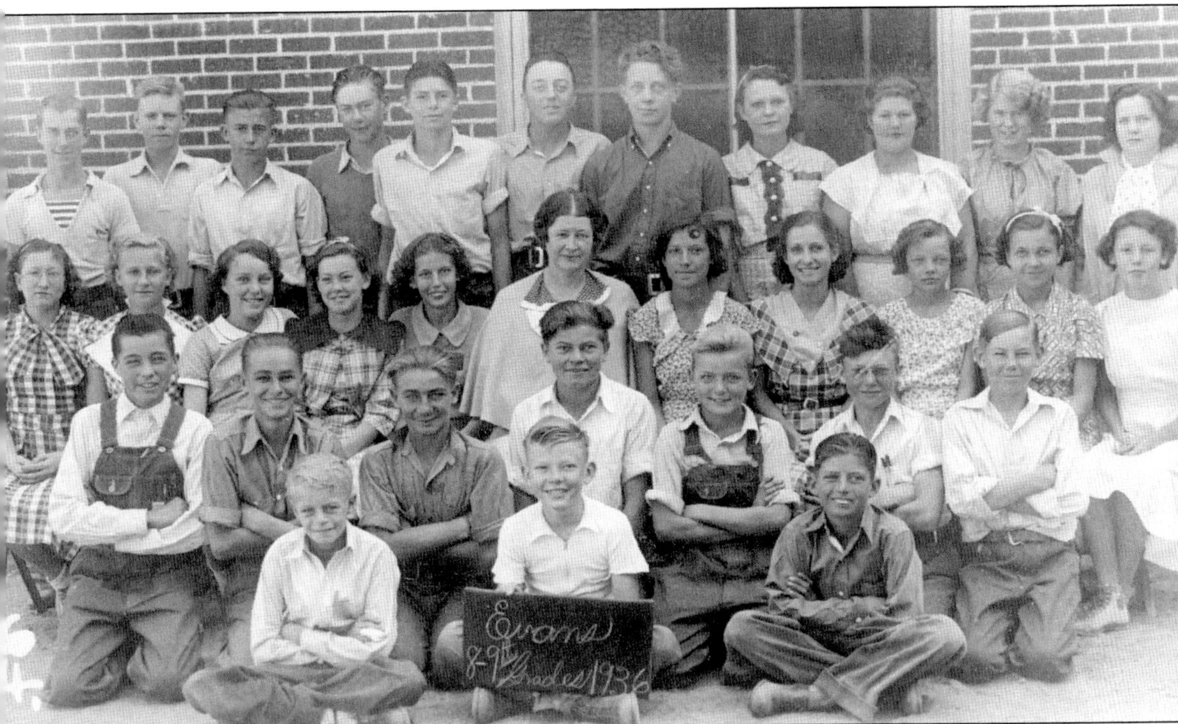


Pictured here is the combined eighth- and ninth-grade class of 1936. Pictured from left to right, are (front row) John Maloney, Warren Wiggins, and Ralph Roliurett; (second row) Charles Graham, Adolf Miller, Raymond Jorquer, Alvin Heimbigner, Alice Gephardt, and Sam Hoff; (third row) Clara Dwiggins, Frances Carlson, Darlene Guek, Pauline Frederick, unidentified, Jewel Hicks, Loretto Chappelow, unidentified, Trene Ellis, Evelyn Griffin, Lourdes Boon, and Epionne Jordan; (fourth row) Lewis Moran, Alvin Magnuson, Les Donily, unidentified, Dean Carmichael, Earl Mitchell, William Griffin, Helen Durr, Dorothy Lyons, Esther Cleaver, and Grace Ireland.

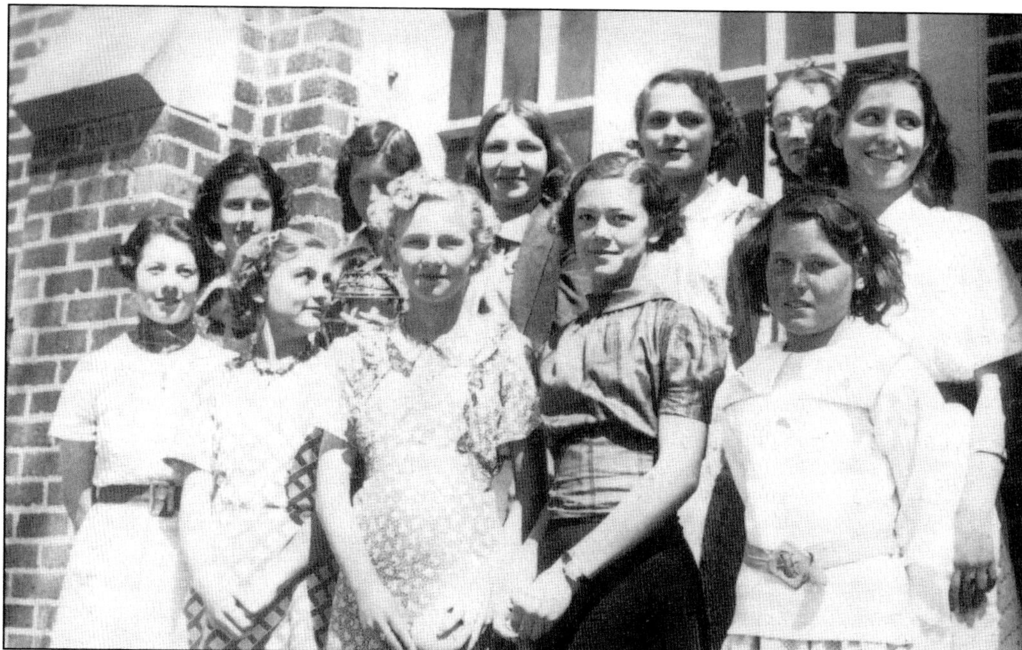

Though small, the Evans School had sporting opportunities for boys and girls. Pictured here is the girls' baseball team in 1937. From left to right are (first row) unidentified teacher, unidentified student, Frances Carlson, Pauline Frederick, and Anna Ruth; (second row) Jewel Hicks, two unidentified girls, Helen Durr, Clara Dwiggins, and Ilya Gephardt.

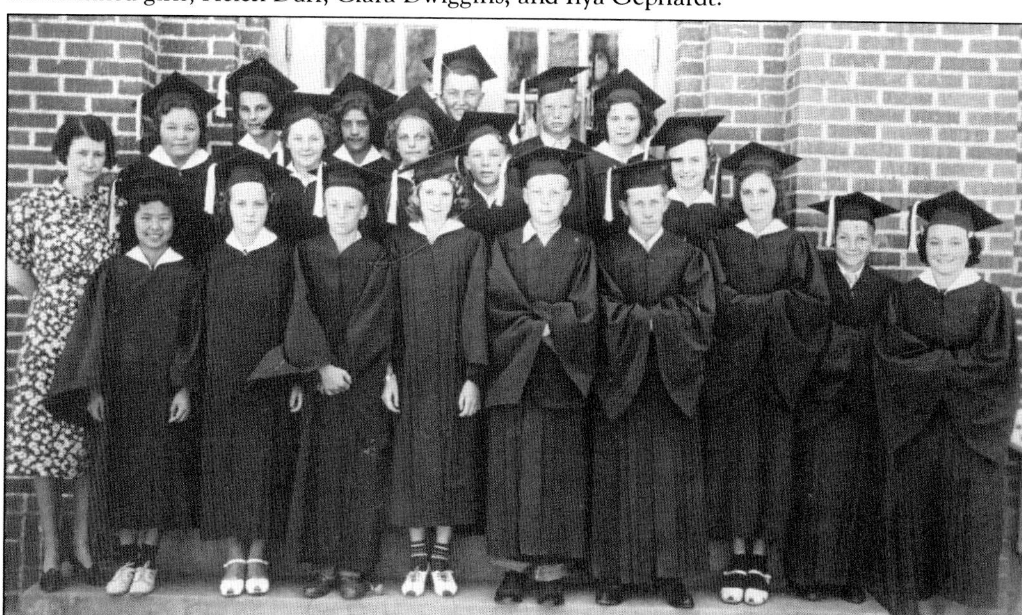

Loretto Chappelow is shown here with her ninth-grade graduation students in 1940. From left to right are (first row) Norma Berryman, Mabel Ishiguro, Amy Fairchild, Jimmy Adamson, Shirley Roberts, Glen Bauder, Lloyd Armstrong, Phyllis Nickerson, Roy Early, and Margie Mitchell; (second row) Chappelow, Donna Lee Rathbun, Ruth Fugate, Mary Kirkpatrick, Shirley Armstrong, Elaine Rhemer, Roy Mitchell, Wesley Kirkpatrick, Melvin Bauder, and Margie Durr.

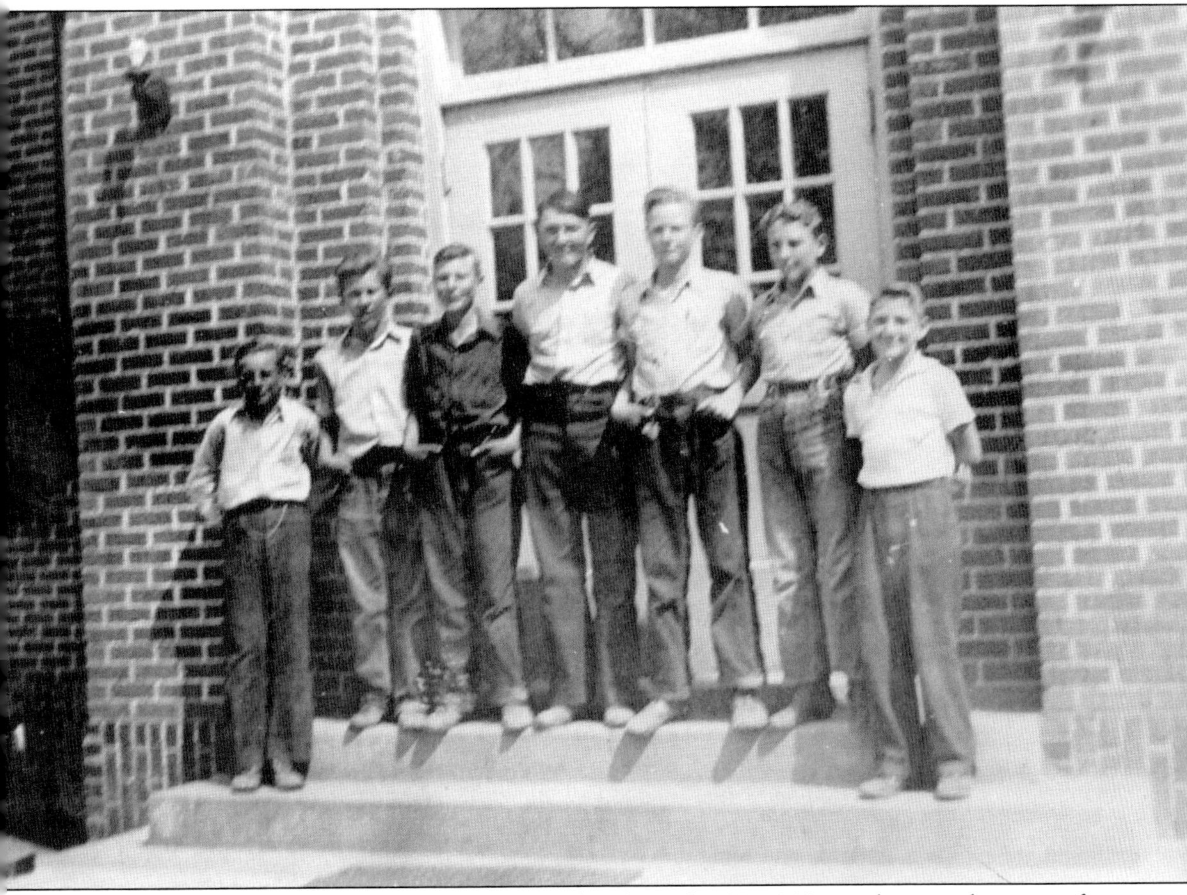

This photograph is of the ninth-grade boys of the class of 1939–1940 standing on the steps of the school. Evans schools only went to the ninth grade between 1908 and 1958 because it simply was not cost effective to keep students in the district. After ninth grade, Evans students could attend high school in Greeley, with the Evans school district paying tuition. The boys, from left to right, are Jim Adamson, Floyd Armstrong, Glenn Bauder, Roy Mitchell, Melvin Bauder, Wesley Kirkpatrick, and Ray Early.

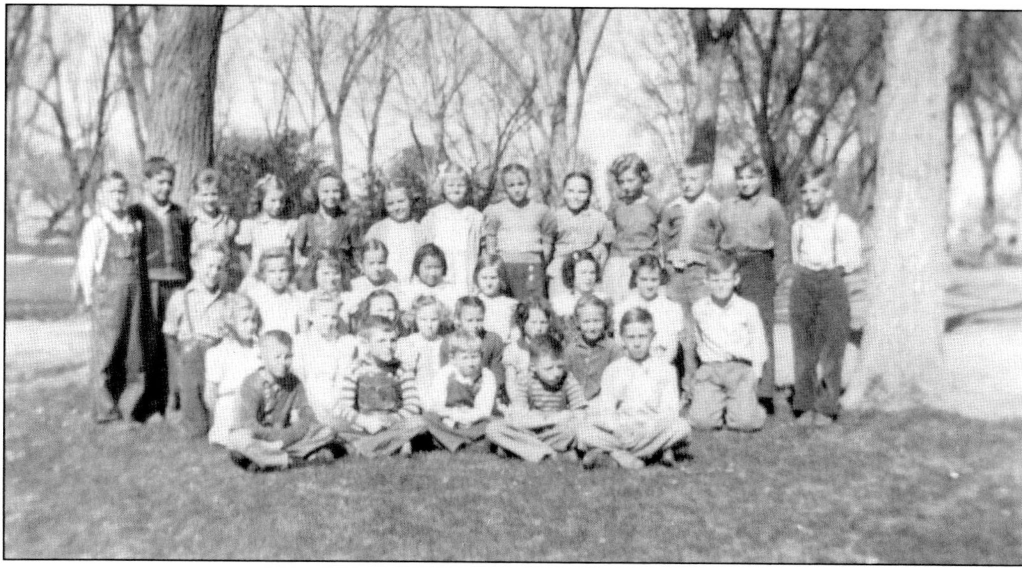

During World War II, everybody was encouraged to participate in the war effort. Schoolchildren like these third- and fourth-grade students in 1943 were encouraged to ration and help out in the family Victory Garden. Boys may have collected scrap metal, and girls may have knitted socks for the soldiers. It was believed that everyone, no matter age or ability, could do something to help out with the war effort.

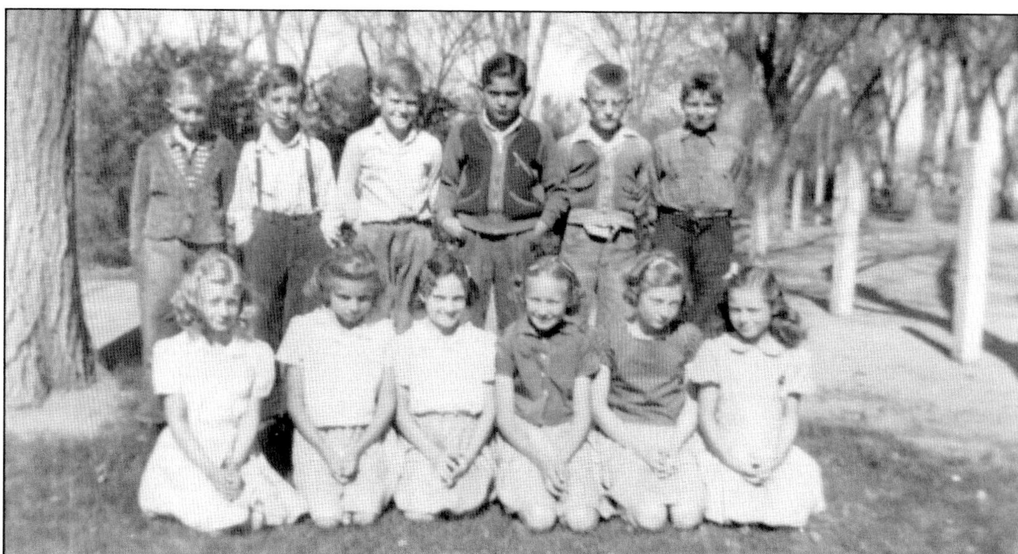

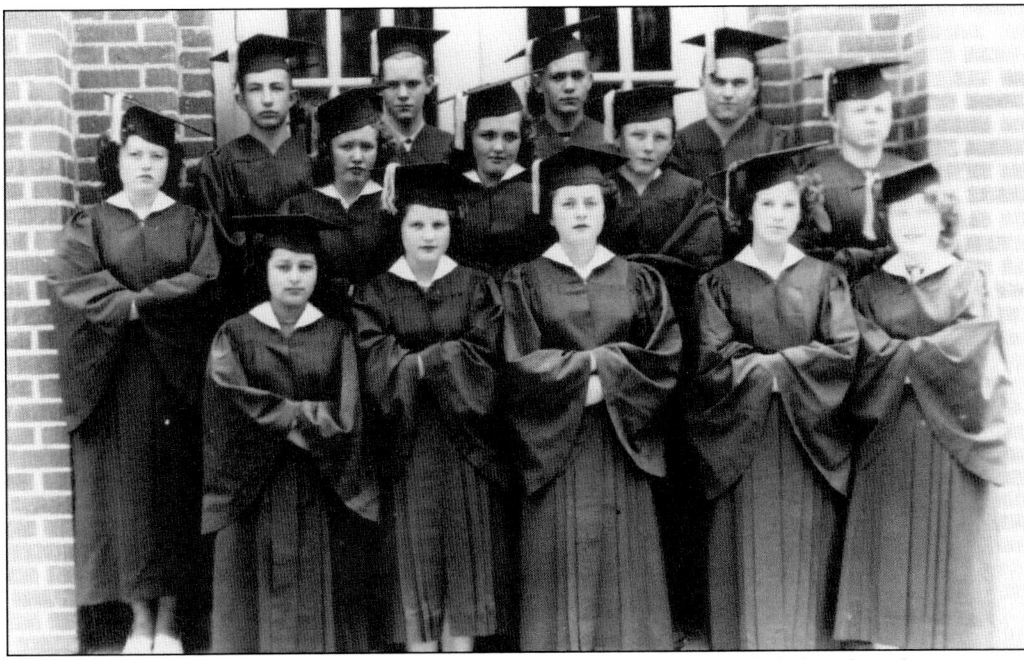

Evans did not have a high school until 1953, so Evans students attended their last three years at Greeley High. This is the ninth-grade graduation of 1948. From left to right are (first row) Rose Marie Jarueque, Norma Romhild, Elsie Bierig, Rumy Morey, and June Tryner; (second row) Jo Ann Forrester, Twila Rathbun, Ruth Judd, Don Windecker, and Bill Green; (third row) Orice Turner, Alen Trenary, Bob Durr, and Carleton Shaw.

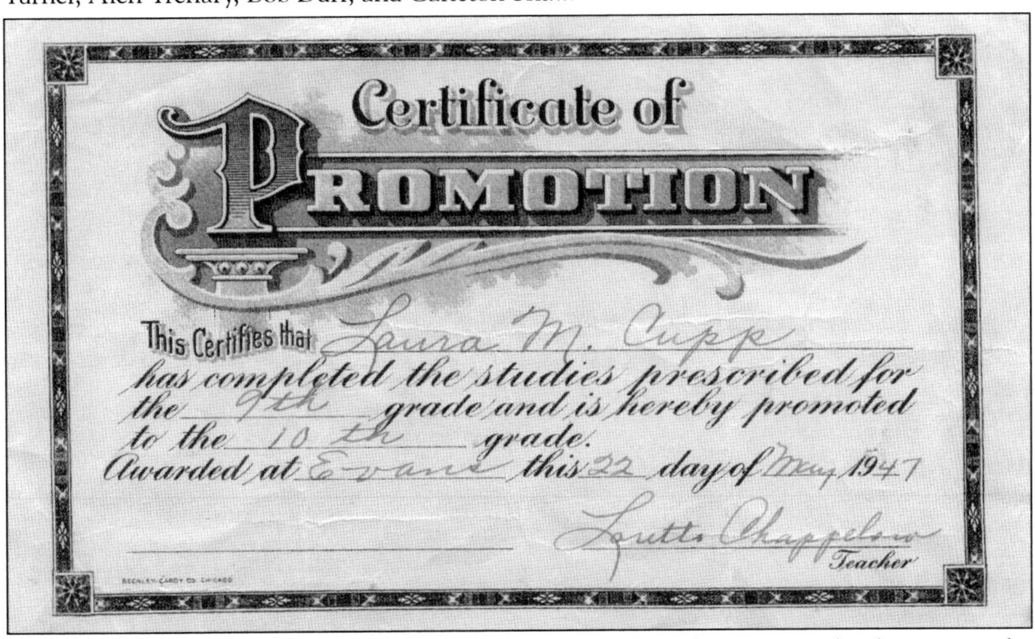

Certificate of
PROMOTION

This Certifies that Laura M. Cupp
has completed the studies prescribed for
the 9th grade and is hereby promoted
to the 10 th grade.
Awarded at Evans this 22 day of May 1947

Loretto Chappelow
Teacher

On May 22, 1947, Laura M. Cupp was promoted to the 10th grade, meaning that her time at the Evans School was over and she would be able to attend high school in Greeley in the fall. Loretto Chappelow, who no doubt sent many students off from Evans with a firm foundation and best wishes, signed her certificate.

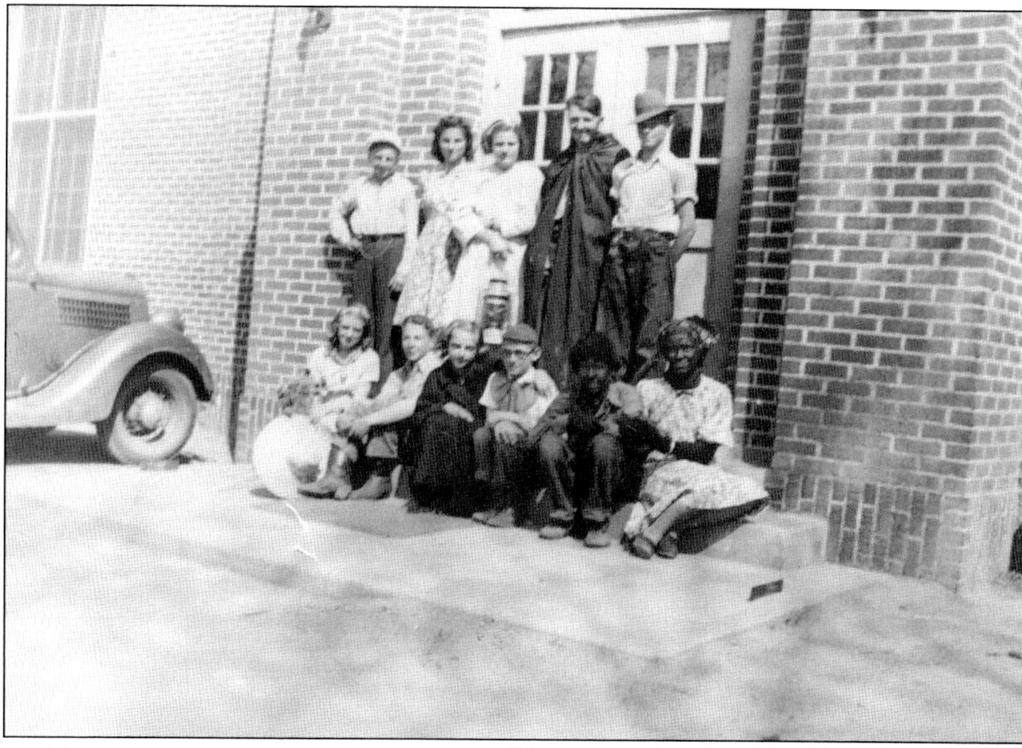

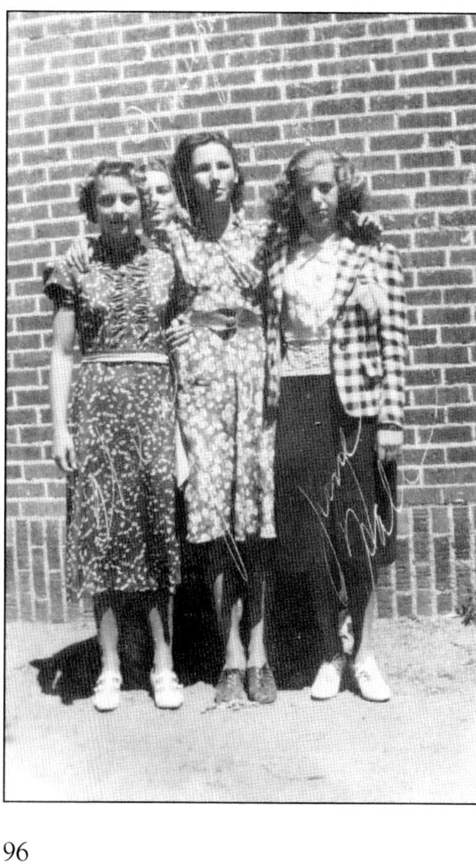

This group of students performed Mabel Conkin Allyn's 1937 play titled *Mystery at World's End.* The owner of the original photograph identified the cast and their characters as follows: Jim A. as Montan, Ruth F. as Laura, unidentified as Benetha, Ray M. as Cale, Melvin B., Shirley R., Wesley R. as Lanney, Elaine R. as Minnie, Ray E. as Eddly, Glenn B. as Tom, and Norma as Pansy.

Here, a group of friends poses outside the Evans School in 1937 or 1938. The girls are, from left to right, Thelma Durr, Lavonne Jordan, June Hall, and unidentified. This photograph was taken during their ninth-grade year, marking their last year in Evans School District 15.

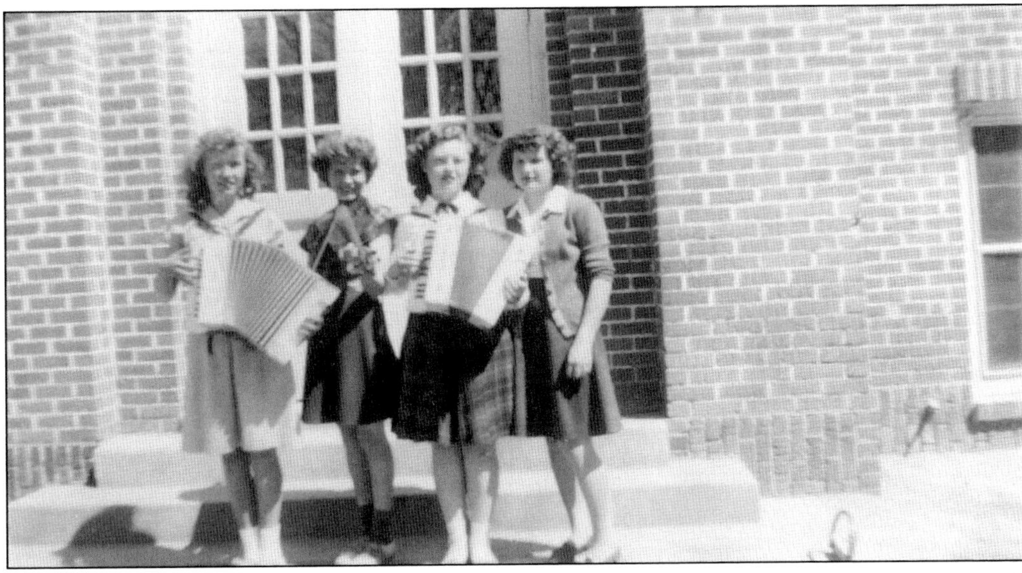

This is the group that performed all of the music for the ninth-grade class play of 1948, *What a Family*. From left to right are Twila Rathbun (accordion), Ruby Morey (violin), Jo Ann Forrester (accordion), and Norma Romhild (vocals).

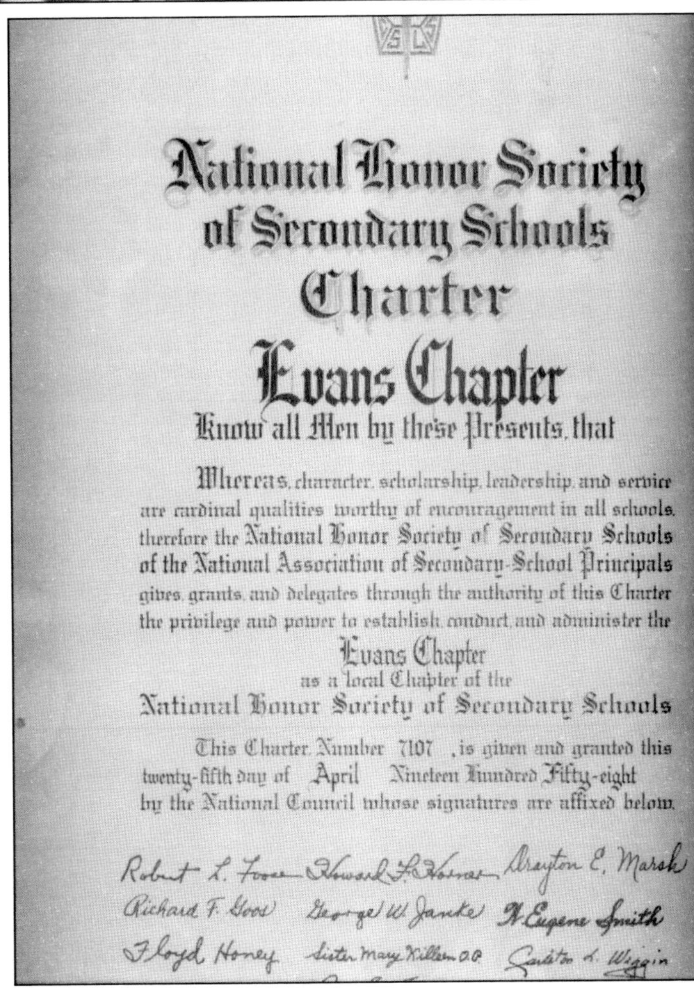

National Honor Society
of Secondary Schools
Charter
Evans Chapter
Know all Men by these Presents, that

Whereas, character, scholarship, leadership, and service are cardinal qualities worthy of encouragement in all schools, therefore the National Honor Society of Secondary Schools of the National Association of Secondary-School Principals gives, grants, and delegates through the authority of this Charter the privilege and power to establish, conduct, and administer the

Evans Chapter
as a local Chapter of the
National Honor Society of Secondary Schools

This Charter, Number 7107, is given and granted this twenty-fifth day of April Nineteen Hundred Fifty-eight by the National Council whose signatures are affixed below.

The National Honor Society was founded in 1921 by the National Association of Secondary School Principals to honor high-achieving high school students with recognition, scholarships, and other awards. The Evans Chapter of the National Honor Society was officially formed on April 29, 1958. For the next seven years, the Evans NHS Chapter recognized many outstanding students who had progressed through the years at School District 15.

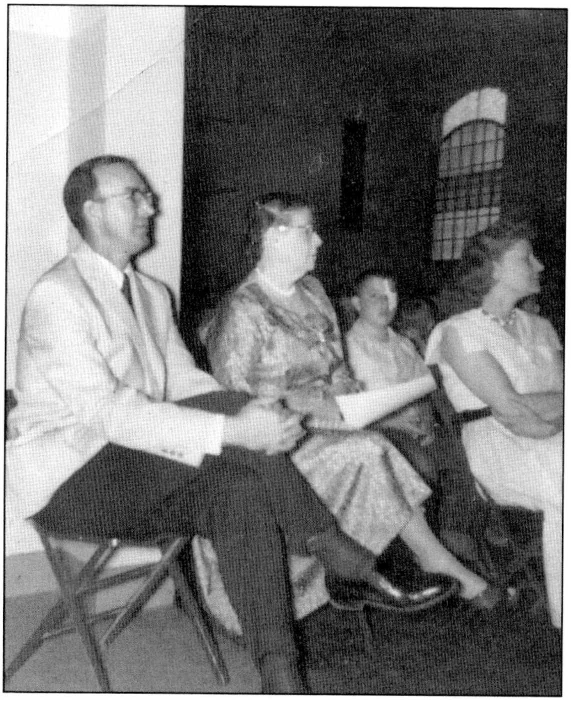

Don Bennett was the superintendent of School District 15 for nearly a decade. He was born in Missouri and attended high school and college in Kansas. In 1942, he married his wife, Abigail Bishop Bennett, and shortly thereafter entered the Army. He fought at the Battle of the Bulge and was awarded the Bronze Star for his heroism. After the war, Bennett returned to college at Kansas Wesleyan to finish his degree and later came to Colorado to attend the Colorado State College of Education, earning a master's degree in 1952. He had volunteered at the Evans School while attending CSCE, and in July 1954, he became superintendent of the Evans Schools. When consolidation with Greeley became inevitable, Bennett drew up the merger contract between the two districts. He is seen here at an awards ceremony at the Chappelow School.

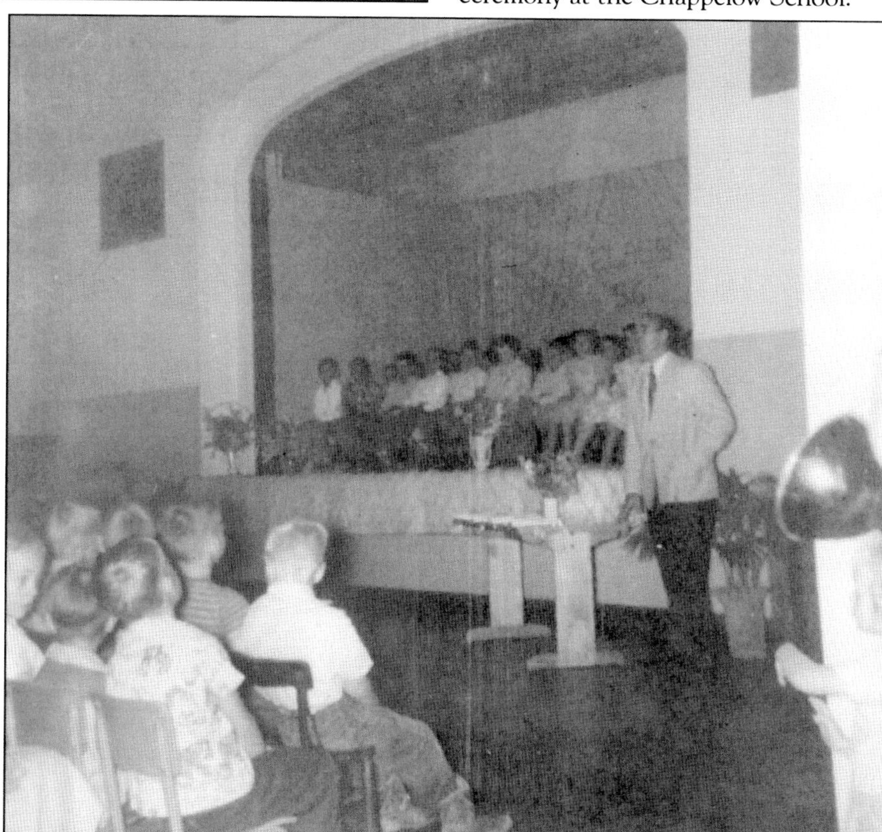

EVANS SCHOOL DISTRICT #15

D E D I C A T I O N

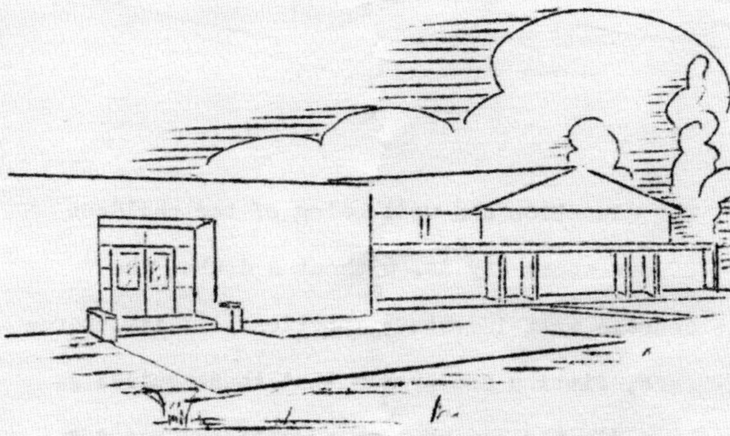

EVANS HIGH SCHOOL AUDITORIUM

November 20, 1957

8:00 P M

A dedication ceremony for School District 15 took place at the high school auditorium on November 20, 1957. According to Supt. Don Bennett, "The education and well-being of the children of our community is, without a doubt, the schools most important function. It is, therefore, fitting and proper that these buildings be dedicated to a better educational program to serve the youth of our community, forever keeping in mind the importance of the child today and the service that he must give to the world tomorrow." The ceremony included music, presentations from the principals of the high school and elementary school (Loretto Chappelow was the principal of the elementary school in 1957), and performances by the junior high and high school music groups. Refreshments were served at the grade school building after the ceremony.

CONGRATULATIONS!!

Joan White
Carole Riddle
Gisela Palok
Patty Karst

EVANS ECHO

HOMECOMING QUEEN CANDIDATES

Evans High School    October, 1958    Page 1

# HOMECOMING PLANS PROGRESS

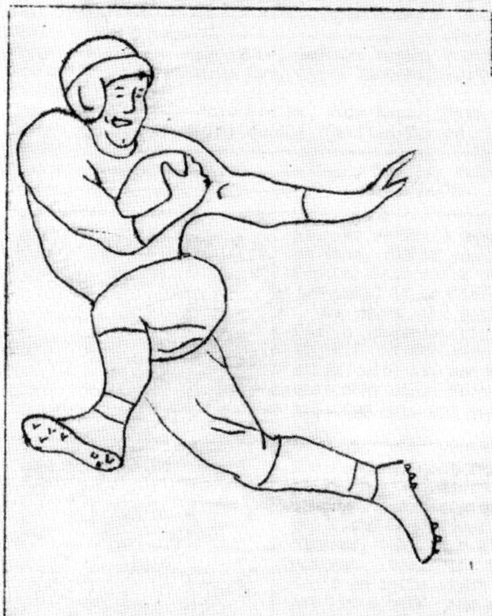

Big things are happening behind the scenes at Evans High. Plans are under way for a big homecoming celebration Friday, October 10.

The Student Council has preparations in full swing and from news picked up by this reporter it sounds like it will be the best celebration yet.

Mead will be the opponent at the football game beginning at 1:30 P. M. Half time activities will be presented by the Pep Club, with some lucky girl being crowned Queen of the festivities. A picnic for students and alumni will be held in the evening. The climax to the day will be a dance held in the Grade School gym.

Plan your day so that you can attend each event. Make this the best Home Coming ever!!

## M.Y.F. RETREAT

You've heard of some animals storing food in preparation for the winter months; the Evans Methodist Youth Fellowship used this same idea by making plans for the winter and spring activities schedule. That was the purpose of the M.Y.F. Retreat, September 26th and 27th held at the Valhalla Cabins, in Estes Park, Colorado. There were 13 members, 6 sponsors and 1 dog in all. After driving and getting settled, the majority of the morning ning Sunday evening fellowship services.

After everyone's stomach's were settled from noon's chow time, a few members attempted a challenging feat. That was to climb the mountain behind our luxurious cabins. Mountain climbing really brings on the appetite, so everyone made sure they were back on time for a big supper of hot dogs, B-O's and all the trimmings.

The conclusive decisions of activities for the future 8 months were discussed at the evening fel- ication service and a very impressive candlelight ceremony.

Mr. Bennett and Mr. Seela volunteered to make breakfast for us that morning while we went to the morning sunrise service to a site where the boys erected a cross on the side of a mountain. Breakfast consisted of pancakes and bacon and mmmm- very good since the members didn't have much K.P. that morning.

We hurriedly left our memorable sites behind at a little after noon, but the memories of the fun and

The Evans High School had a student-run newspaper called the *Evans Echo*, which was published once a month during the regular school year. Special editions for important school events, like prom or graduation, were also sometimes published. The paper was written by students on the newspaper committee and typed, mimeographed, and distributed to all the students at the school. The *Echo* covered events important to students: dances, sporting events, contests, stories written by students, and some lighthearted gossip. This October 1958 issue of the *Echo* discusses the plans for homecoming week, which included the traditional football game, a halftime show performed by the Pep Club, a student and alumni picnic at the high school, and a dance in the school gymnasium.

By the 1950s, the Evans School District had grown so much that additions had to be made to the old buildings. The high school received a new, state-of-the-art gymnasium with full-sized courts and plenty of audience seating. The elementary school had a new wing built to the north side of the old building, which included several classrooms.

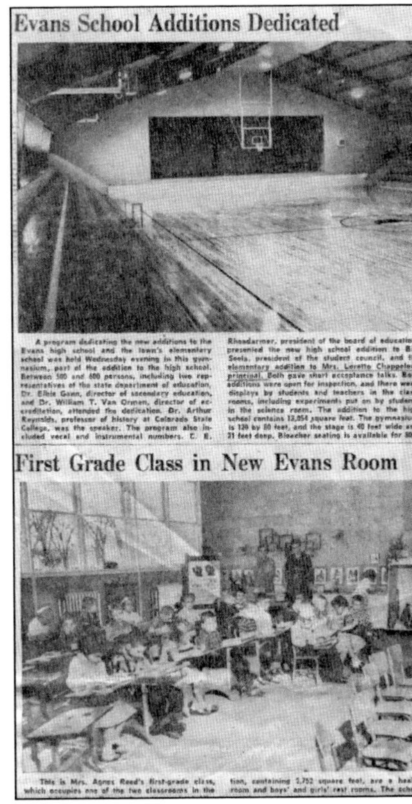

**Evans School Additions Dedicated**

A program dedicating the new additions to the Evans high school and the town's elementary school was held Wednesday evening in this gymnasium, part of the addition to the high school. Between 500 and 600 persons, including two representatives of the state department of education, Dr. Elbie Gann, director of secondary education, and Dr. William T. Van Ornmen, director of accreditation, attended the dedication. Dr. Arthur Reynolds, professor of history at Colorado State College, was the speaker. The program also included vocal and instrumental numbers. C. E. Rhoadarmer, president of the board of education, presented the new high school addition to Bill Seels, president of the student council, and the elementary addition to Mrs. Loretto Chappelow, principal. Both gave short acceptance talks. Both additions were open for inspection, and there were displays by students and teachers in the classrooms, including experiments put on by students in the science room. The addition to the high school contains 12,054 square feet. The gymnasium is 120 by 80 feet, and the stage is 40 feet wide and 21 feet deep. Bleacher seating is available for 800.

**First Grade Class in New Evans Room**

This is Mrs. Agnes Reed's first-grade class, which occupies one of the two classrooms in the tion, containing 1,752 square feet, are a health room and boys' and girls' rest rooms. The school

This graduation announcement from the early 1960s has a line drawing of the Evans High School. While this building no longer serves as a school for the Greeley-Evans School District, it may be recognizable as the Envision Center on the corner of Eleventh Avenue and Thirty-seventh Street.

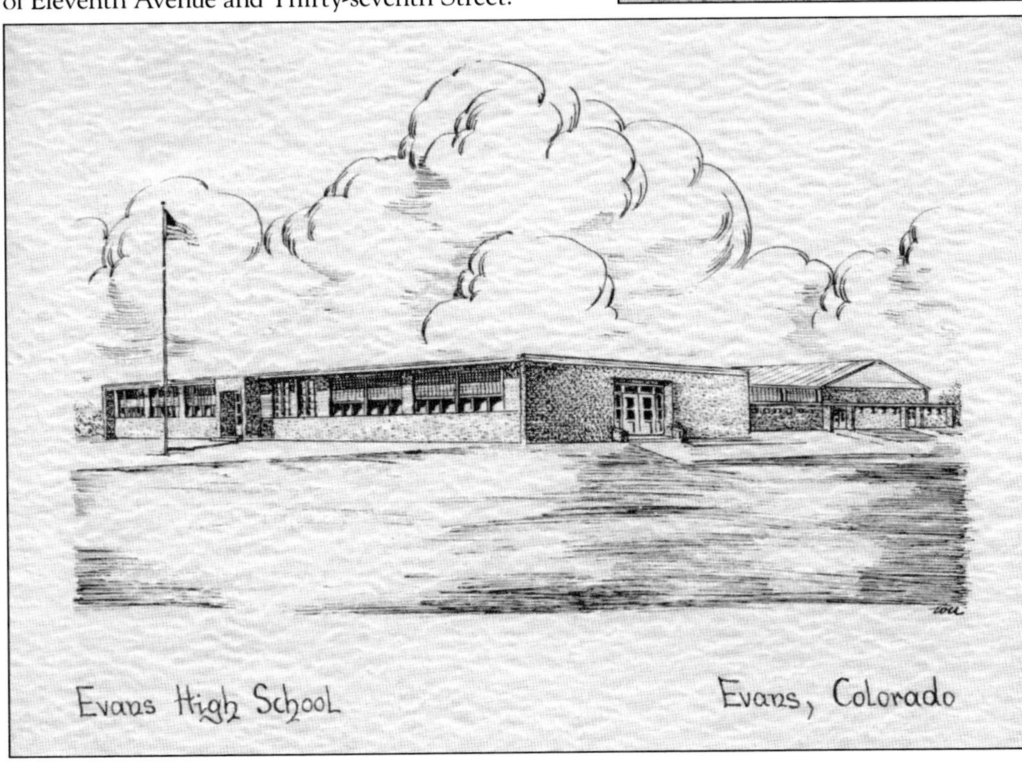

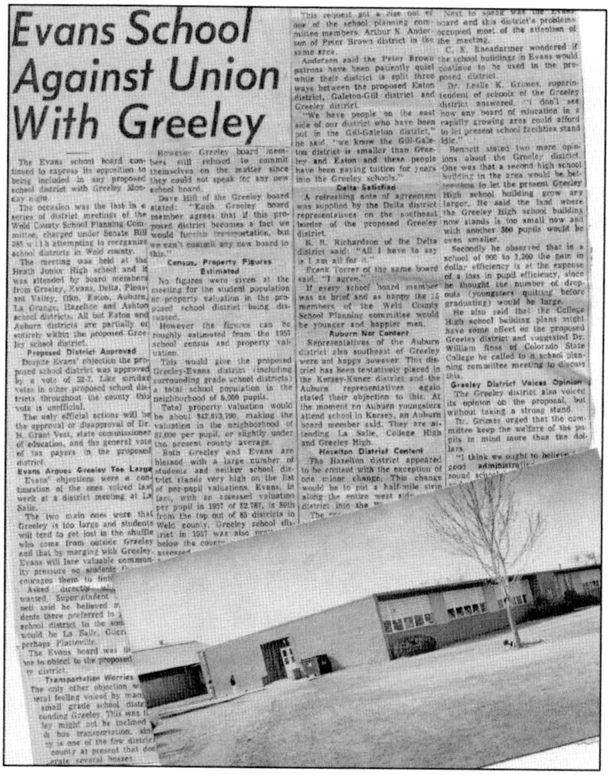

# Evans School Against Union With Greeley

The Evans school board continued to express its opposition to being included in any proposed school district with Greeley Monday night.

The occasion was the last in a series of district meetings of the Weld County School Planning Committee, charged under Senate Bill 385 with attempting to reorganize school districts in Weld county.

The meeting was held at the Heath Junior High school and it was attended by board members from Greeley, Evans, Delta, Pleasant Valley, Olin, Eaton, Auburn, La Grange, Hazelton and Ashton school districts. All but Eaton and Auburn districts are partially or entirely within the proposed Greeley school district.

**Proposed District Approved**

Despite Evans' objection the proposed school district was approved by a vote of 22-7. Like similar votes in other proposed school districts throughout the county this vote is unofficial.

The only official actions will be the approval or disapproval of Dr. H. Grant Vest, state commissioner of education, and the general vote of tax payers in the proposed district.

**Evans Argues Greeley Too Large**

Evans' objections were a continuation of the ones voiced last week at a district meeting at La Salle.

The two main ones were that Greeley is too large and students will tend to get lost in the shuffle who come from outside Greeley and that by merging with Greeley, Evans will lose valuable community pressure on students th... courages them to fini...

Asked directly ... wanted, Superintendent ... nett said he believed ... dents there preferred to ... school district to the sou... would be La Salle, Gilcr... perhaps Platteville.

The Evans board was th... ne to object to the proposed ... y district.

**Transportation Worries**

The only other objection w... neral feeling voiced by man... small grade school distr... ounding Greeley. This was ... ley might not be inclined ... h bus transportation, sin... y is one of the few distric... county at present that doe... erate several busses.

However Greeley board members still refused to commit themselves on the matter since they could not speak for any new school board.

Dave Hill of the Greeley board stated: "Each Greeley board member agrees that if this proposed district becomes a fact we would furnish transportation, but we can't commit any new board to this."

**Census, Property Figures Estimated**

No figures were given at the meeting for the student population or property valuation in the proposed school district being discussed.

However the figures can be roughly estimated from the 1957 school census and property valuation.

This would give the proposed Greeley-Evans district (including surrounding grade school districts) a total school population in the neighborhood of 6,000 pupils.

Total property valuation would be about $42,673,790, making the valuation in the neighborhood of $7,000 per pupil, or slightly under the present county average.

Both Greeley and Evans are blessed with a large number of students and neither school district stands very high on the list of per-pupil valuations. Evans, in fact, with an assessed valuation per pupil in 1957 of $2,787, is 80th from the top out of 83 districts in Weld county. Greeley school district in 1957 was also ... below the count... assessed...

This request got a rise out of one of the school planning committee members, Arthur K. Anderson of Peter Brown district in the same area.

Anderson said the Peter Brown patrons have been patiently quiet while their district is split three ways between the proposed Eaton district, Galeton-Gill district and Greeley district.

"We have people on the east side of our district who have been put in the Gill-Galeton district," he said, "we know the Gill-Galeton district is smaller than Greeley and Eaton and these people have been paying tuition for years into the Greeley schools."

**Delta Satisfied**

A refreshing note of agreement was supplied by the Delta district representatives on the southeast border of the proposed Greeley district.

B. H. Richardson of the Delta district said: "All I have to say is I am all for it."

Frank Torrer of the same board said, "I agree."

If every school board member was as brief and as happy the 15 members of the Weld County School Planning committee would be younger and happier men.

**Auburn Not Content**

Representatives of the Auburn district also southeast of Greeley were not happy however. This district has been tentatively placed in the Kersey-Kuner district and the Auburn representatives again stated their objection to this. At the moment no Auburn youngsters attend school in Kersey, an Auburn board member said. They are attending La Salle, College High and Greeley High.

**Hazelton District Content**

The Hazelton district appeared to be content with the exception of one minor change. This change would be to put a half-mile strip along the entire west side ... district into the ...

Next to speak was the Evans board and this district's problems occupied most of the attention of the meeting.

C. E. Rhoadarmer wondered if the school buildings in Evans would continue to be used in the proposed district.

Dr. Leslie K. Grimes, superintendent of schools of the Greeley district answered, "I don't see how any board of education in a rapidly growing area could afford to let present school facilities stand idle."

Bennett stated two more opinions about the Greeley district. One was that a second high school building in the area would be better ... to let the present Greeley High school building grow any larger. He said the land where the Greeley High school building now stands is too small now and with another 300 pupils would be even smaller.

Secondly he observed that in a school of 900 to 1,200 the gain in dollar efficiency is at the expense of a loss in pupil efficiency, since he thought the number of drop-outs (youngsters quitting before graduating) would be large.

He also said that the College High school building plans might have some effect on the proposed Greeley district and suggested Dr. William Ross of Colorado State College be called to a school planning committee meeting to discuss this.

**Greeley District Voices Opinion**

The Greeley district also voiced its opinion on the proposal, but without taking a strong stand.

Dr. Grimes urged that the committee keep the welfare of the pupils in mind more than the dollars.

"I think we ought to believe ... good administra... sound school...

School consolidation was one of the most contentious issues during the 1950s and 1960s in rural America, and Evans was no exception. Even though most people acknowledged that there were definite benefits to consolidating with a larger district—more funding, better facilities, and more opportunities—there was still so much left to lose. For small communities centered on school life, the loss of the school was a loss of local identity and pride.

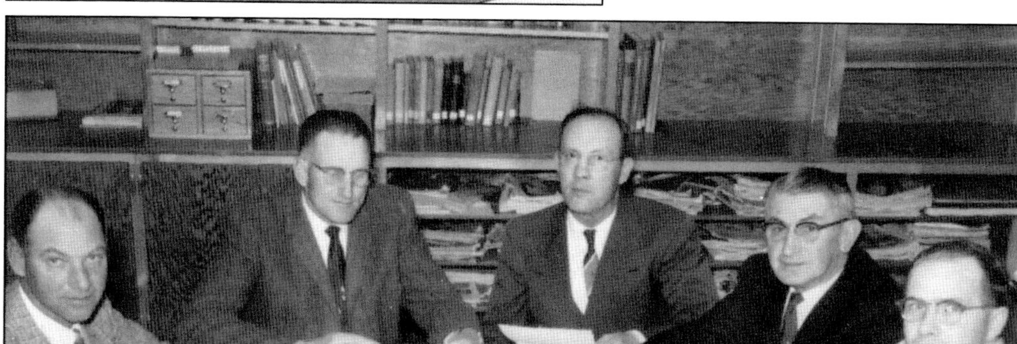

After a long and contentious battle, it was ultimately decided that the students of Evans would be better served by joining the Greeley schools. This is the last school board that served District 15 before it consolidated with Greeley to form Greeley-Evans District 6. From left to right are Ray Arms, Walt Speer, Leo Michaud, Clarence Rhodarmer, and Elvin Crossant.

# *Four*

# For the Good of All
## Church, Charity, and Service

The people of Evans have always been very generous and interested in protecting the well being of others in the community. This is evidenced by fact that there have been so many charitable organizations and service clubs that have thrived here over the years.

The Odd Fellows and Moose Lodge are a couple of the oldest service and fraternal organizations in town, but Evans has a history of charity and service beyond the realm of clubs and organized groups. In the earliest days of the town, residents took it upon themselves to start up a school, holding classes in their own homes and businesses until they could get enough money together for a building. Businessman Henry F. Behrens left a large portion of his estate to the town to set aside for expansion and upkeep of the cemetery. When the town had no way to fight fires that would occasionally break out in homes, businesses, or fields, residents pulled together to establish a firefighting brigade. When there was a need for anything in town, the residents found a way to make it happen.

Churches in Evans, as in many towns, were pillars in the community and their members were engaged in a number of social outreach programs. One of these was the hot lunch program for schoolchildren provided by the Women's Society. There was no cafeteria or kitchen at the Evans school, so the children would walk through the alley from the schoolhouse to the Methodist church to eat meals prepared by the churchwomen.

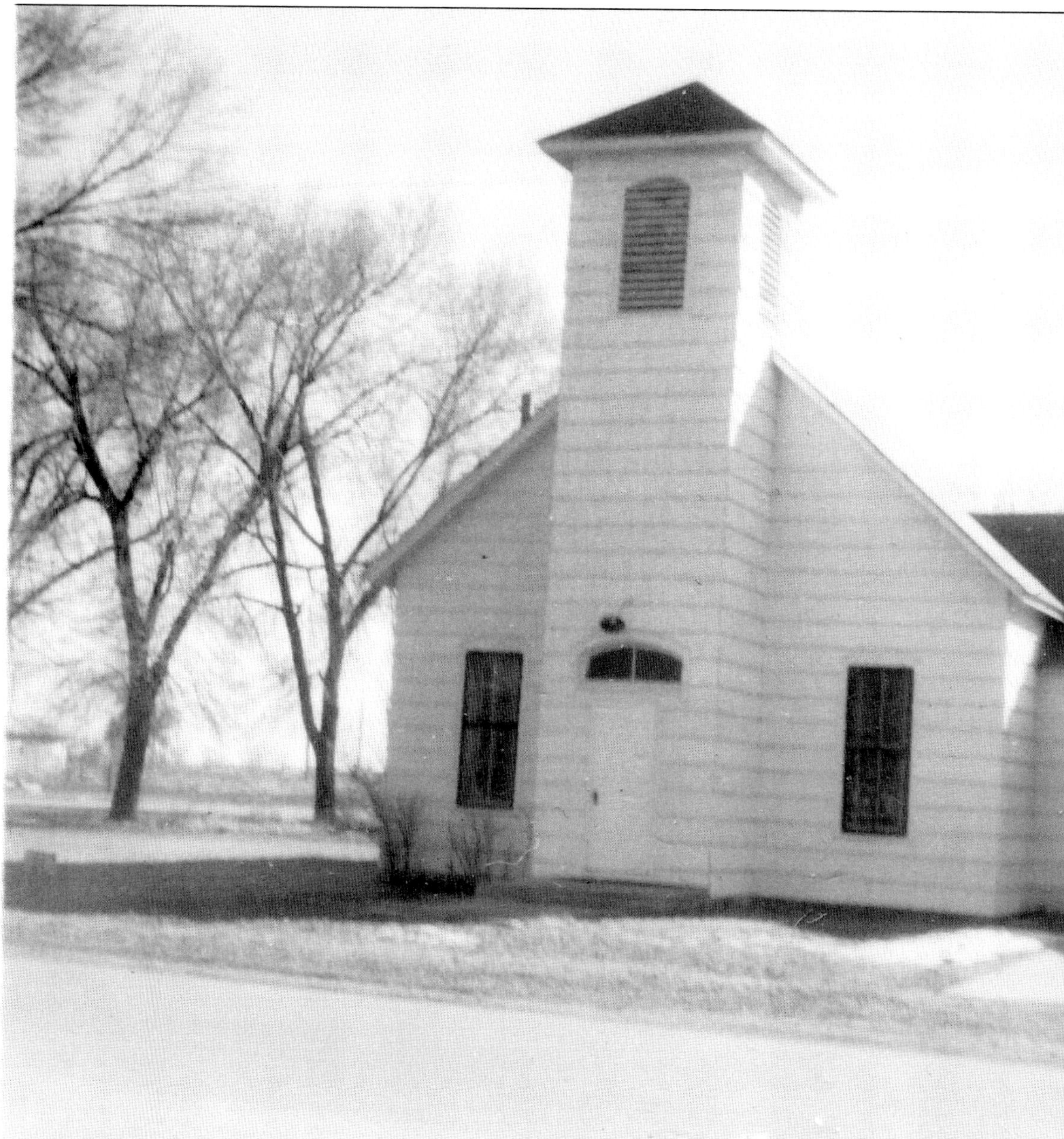

The Evans United Methodist Church is the oldest surviving congregation in town, dating back to 1871, when it was called the Methodist Episcopal church. Though it is the oldest surviving church, membership has always been very small—never exceeding 100 members. Despite this, the Methodist church has been one of the most active by cooking school lunches for students and reaching out and welcoming student pastors from the Iliff School of Theology in Denver. Before the church acquired the building, the congregation met in an old railway coach. The church building was purchased from the United Presbyterian church in 1883 for $850. Additions were made to the building in 1949 and again in 1954 when the Methodist church in Kersey dissolved. The Kersey church was purchased by the Evans congregation and moved to the west side of the original building. The two structures were joined together by a hallway that held a kitchen.

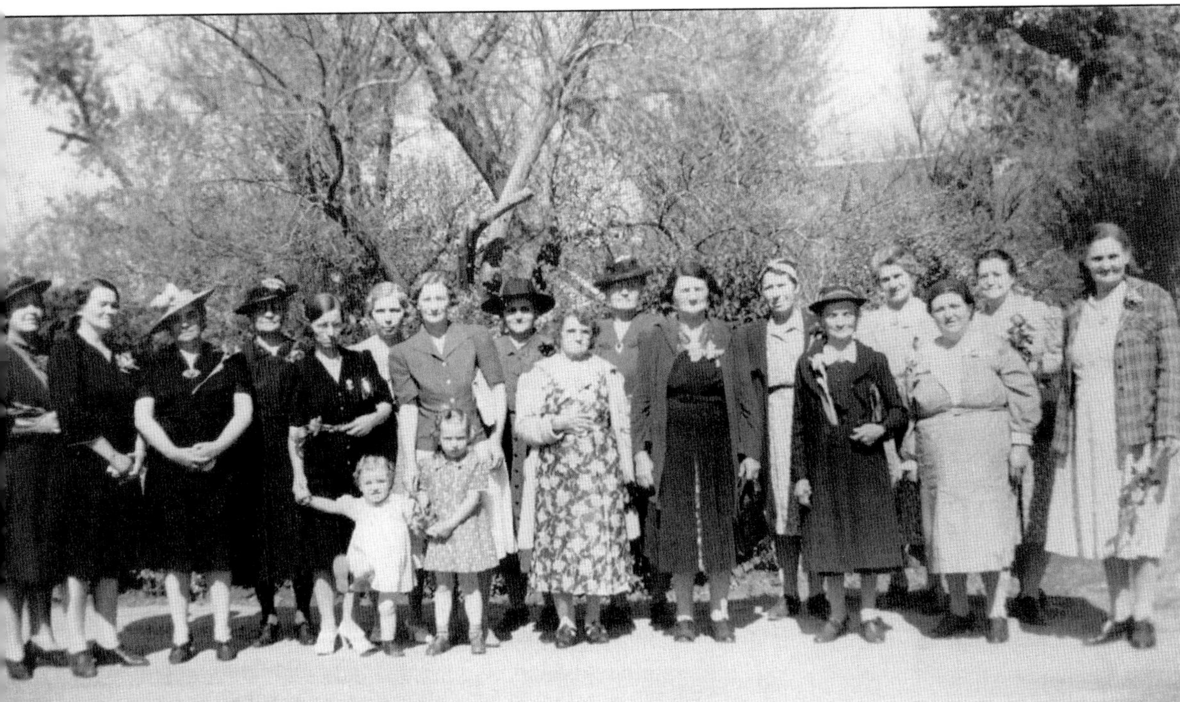

In 1942, war was raging in Europe, the Pacific, and North Africa. Approximately 3.9 million men and women were enlisted in the military—a number that would triple by the end of the war in 1945. Women on the home front formed organizations across the country to support the war effort, often through volunteer work or selling war bonds. A nationwide group of mothers with sons in the war was called Blue Star Mothers. A mother would hang a blue star in the window of her home for each son or daughter that was serving in the war. If the child was killed in the war, the mother would replace the blue star with a gold one. It was a way to show pride for their children's service and sorrow for their loss and signified to other mothers that they had a network of support and people who understood their feelings. This June 1942 photograph shows a group of women from Evans with sons serving in World War II.

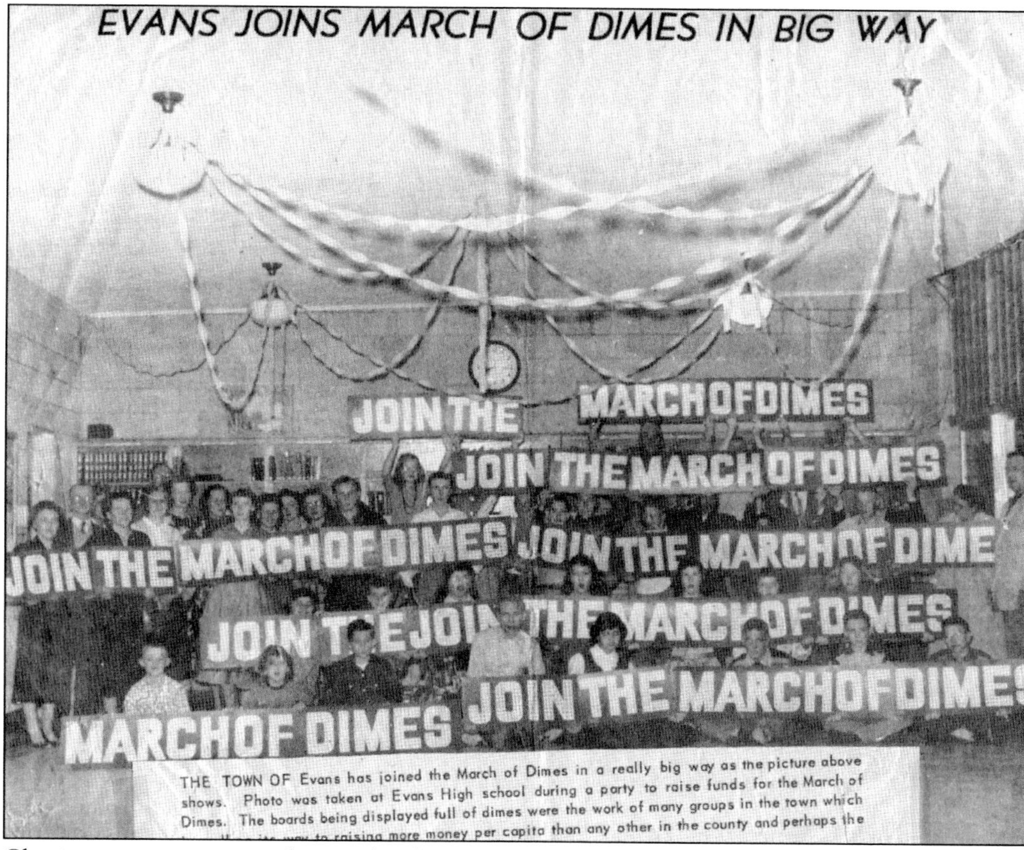


Charity was important to the people of Evans. The March of Dimes was one of the most popular charities in the 1940s and 1950s because its mission to fight polio hit home to many people, as the disease was still all too common at that point in time. Pictured above are students throwing a party in the gymnasium of the high school to raise money for the March of Dimes. The words on the boards they are displaying are spelled out in dimes. Pictured below are the grade school students who sold candy bars to raise money for the organization. According to one newspaper account, the Evans community raised more money for the March of Dimes than any other community in the entire county. The grade school students raised an average of almost $1 per student, which is worth about $9 by today's value.

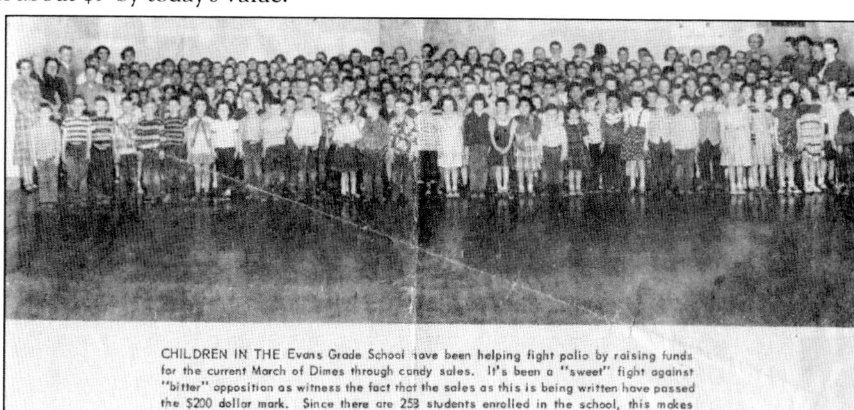

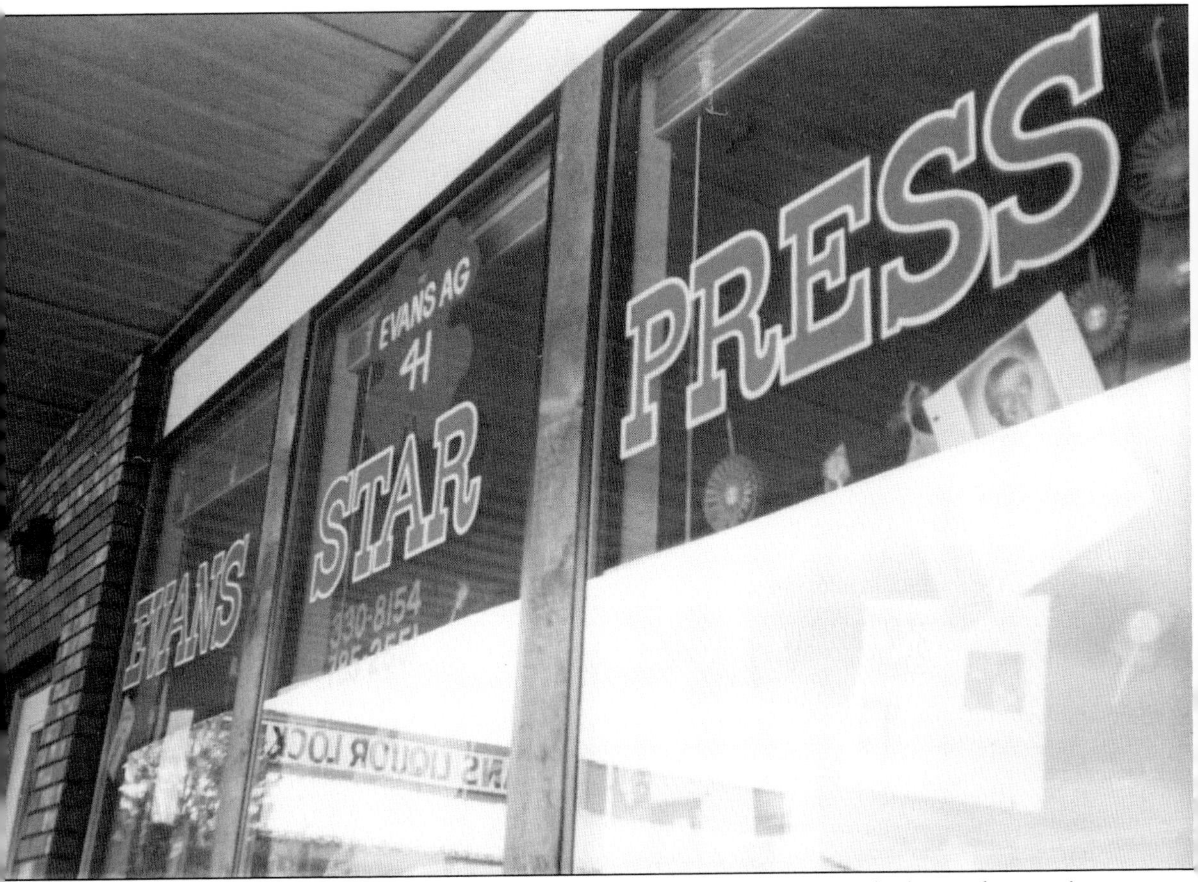


Evans had several newspapers over the years, including the *Evans Express*, which was the town's first newspaper, and the *Evans Journal*, which was published by the early settler Rev. Andrew Calvin Todd. After a nearly 65-year hiatus without a town newspaper, the *Evans Star Press* was launched on May 19, 1983, by Paul and Elizabeth Massey, who also published papers in La Salle and Platteville. A staff of six, comprised of Bill Cissell, Sandra Cissell, Tammy Smith, Al Kalk, Patti Tropp, and Ken "Gus" Peth, worked out of an office on the second floor of the Ramada Inn. The paper was so popular that, by February 1984, the Masseys had to hire more staff, and the *Evans Star Press* moved to the office at the Sundown Center on Eleventh Avenue pictured above. The paper was suspended briefly in 1989 and permanently discontinued in 1995.

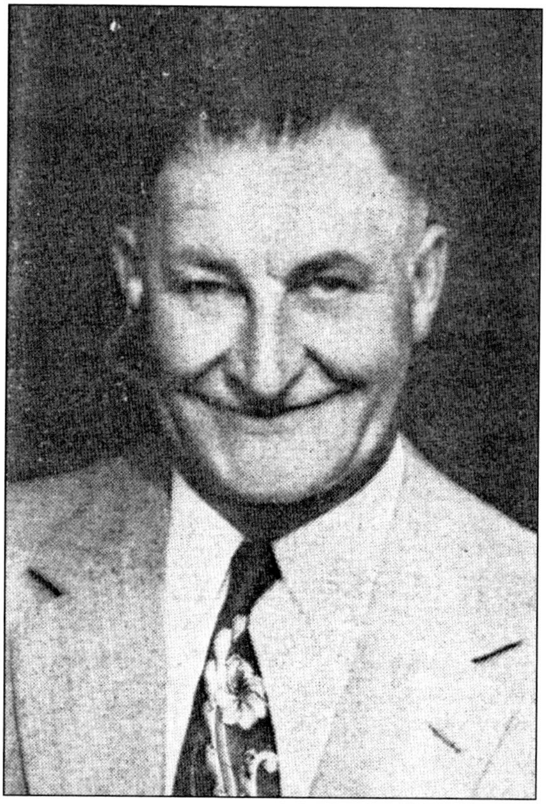

Edward Overman was born in Fort Lupton in 1902. His family moved to Evans when he was three years old, and he attended school here, graduating in 1916. He started the first Evans Volunteer Fire Department in 1922. The department was later reorganized in 1929 and again in 1938. Overman lived in Evans the rest of his life and served as fire chief from 1938 until his passing in 1956.

The Evans Volunteer Fire Department published town directories for a few years. These directories included photographs and history of the department as well as ads, which were sold as a fundraiser for the department. The 1965–1968 directory was dedicated to four members of the department who were retiring after over 20 years of service. They are, from left to right, Walter H. Short, James Fugate, Ray Sneider, and Ralph Doney.

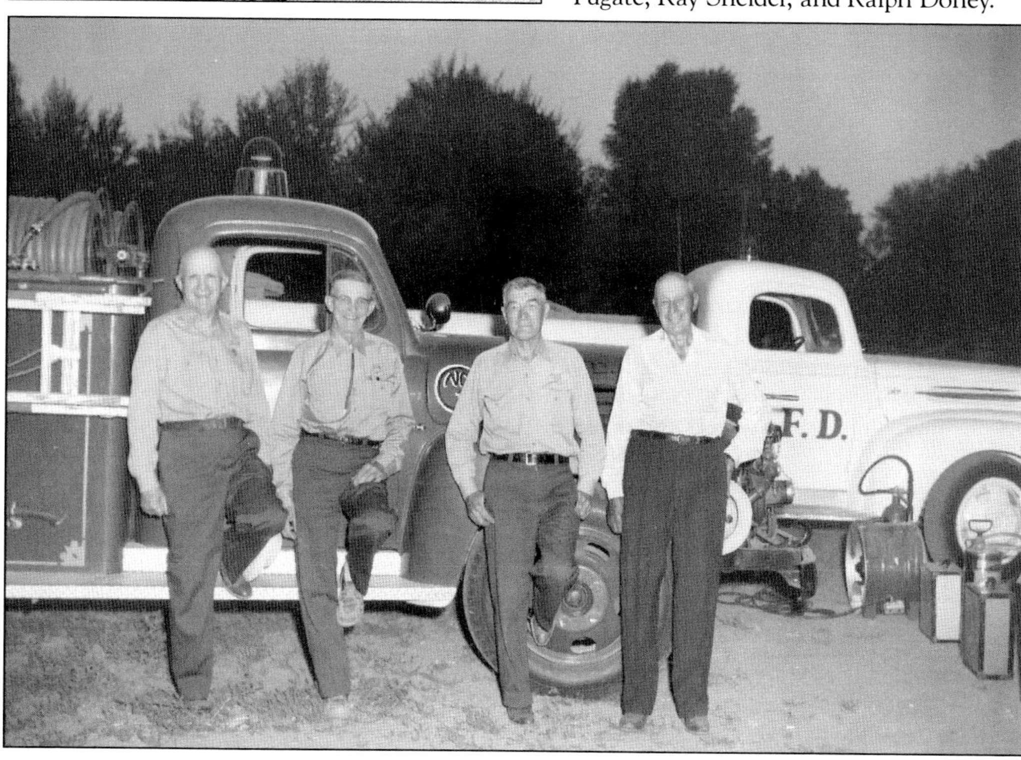

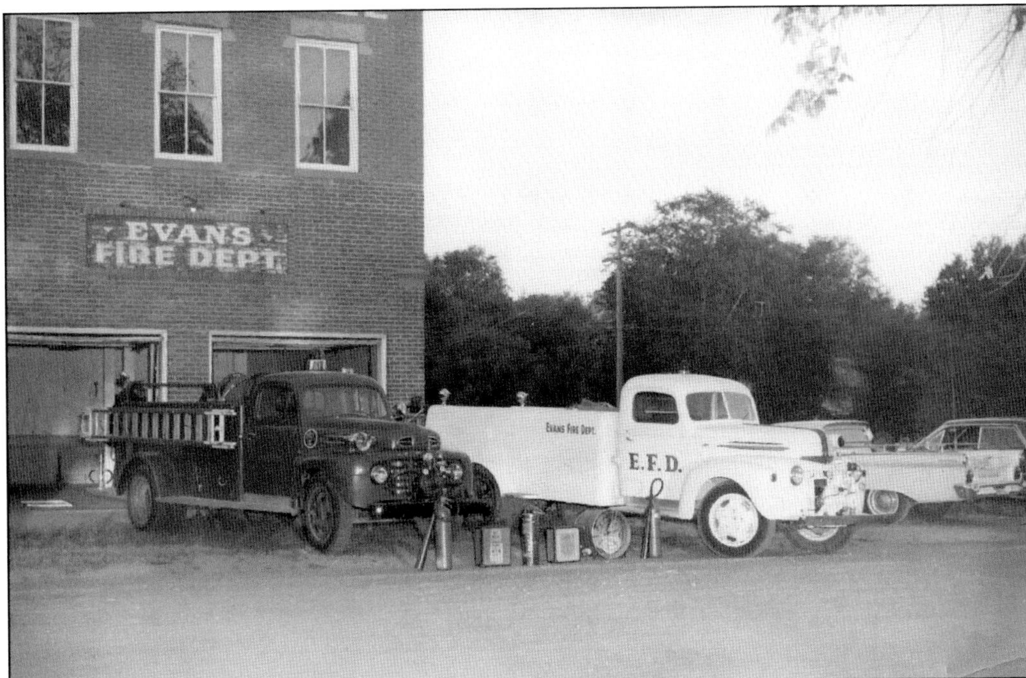


The Evans Volunteer Fire Department used these two fire engines in the 1960s. The truck on the right is a white 1945 Ford with a 350-gallon pumper, and the truck on the left is a red 1949 Ford with a 500-gallon pumper, known as "Old Red."

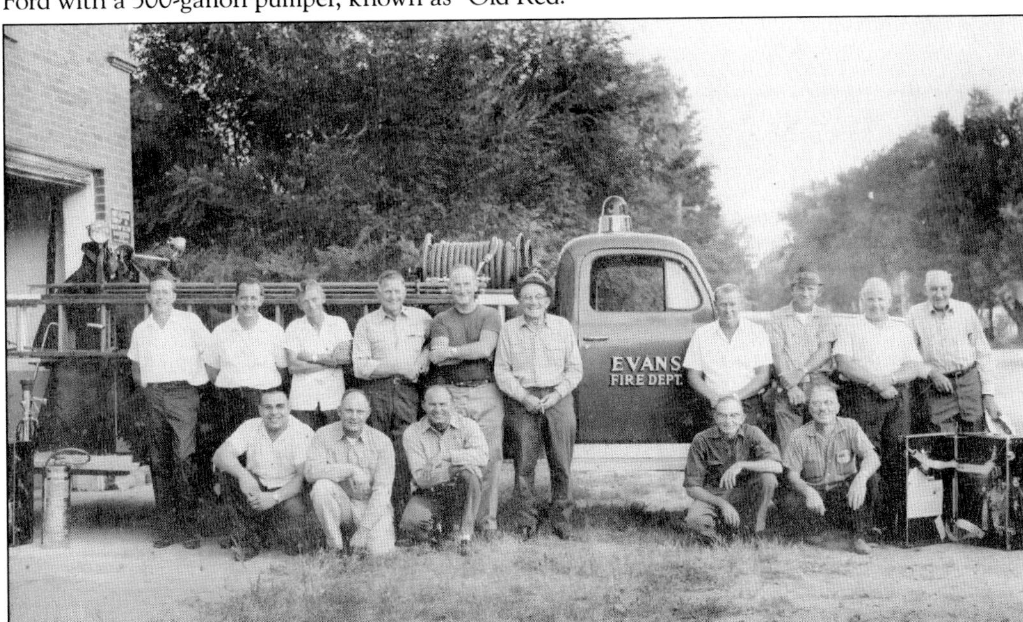


The members of the Evans Volunteer Fire Department are visible here in front of Fire Station No. 1 on Denver Street in 1965. From left to right are (first row) Loyal Weems, Richard Grams, Wilbur Stoll, Laurin Roberts, and E.R. Aplin; (second row) Carl Brown, John May, Harland Clymer, Delon Melby, Edward Huber, Clarence Towns, Leroy Johnson, Joe Crisp, Lloyd Roberts, and Ralph Doney (son of Celia and Jesse Doney).

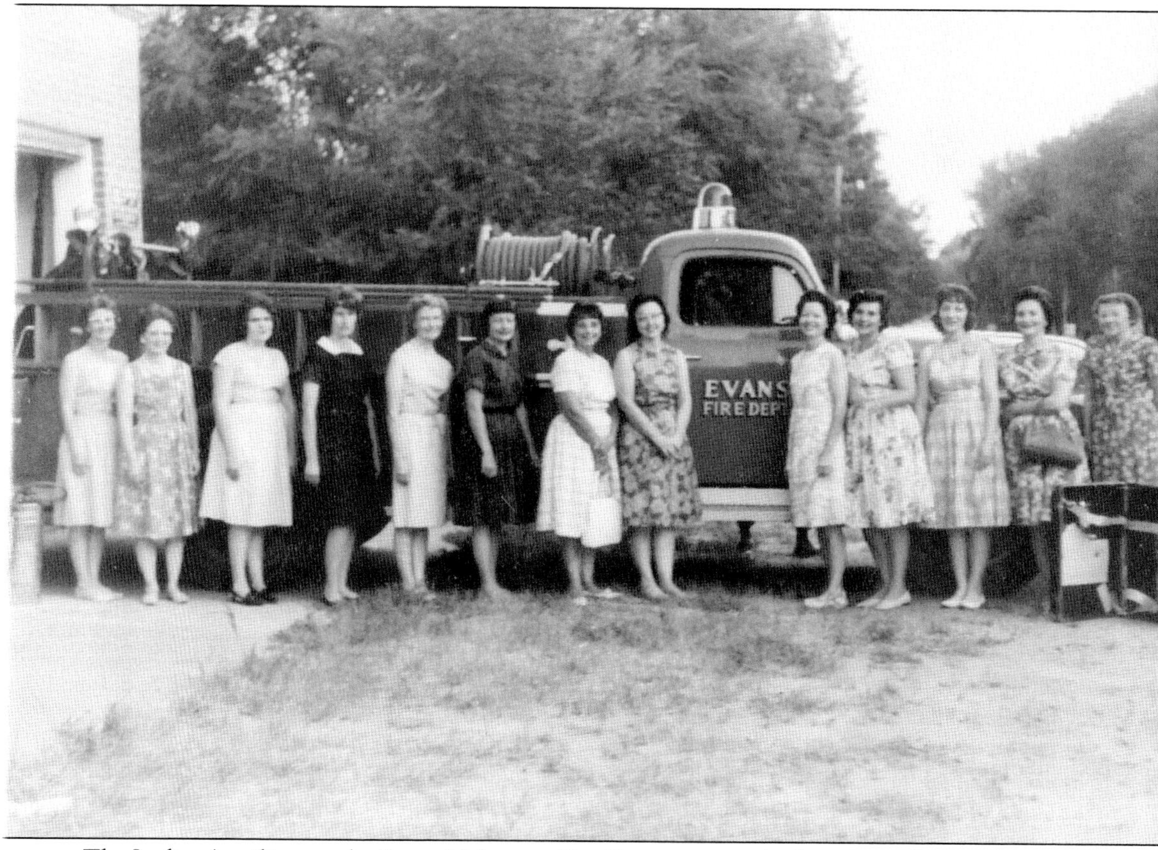


The Ladies Auxiliary to the Evans Volunteer Fire Department, also known as the Sparkettes, was comprised of wives of the volunteer firemen. They had social get-togethers, sometimes with ladies auxiliary groups from other departments. When there was a big fire call, the women would bring food, coffee, water, and other supplies needed to the scene. Though not verified, it has been said that during World War II, many of the men in town were in the military, so some of the women in the auxiliary trained themselves to operate the trucks and equipment and responded to fire calls. The auxiliary continued for many years, providing assistance on calls, and later some members participated in first aid classes at the fire department. The group disbanded sometime in the late 1980s or early 1990s. Pictured here are the Sparkettes in 1965. From left to right are Donna Melby, Velda Roberts, Earlean Weems, Mildred Brown, Bernice Grams, Margaret May, Ida Towns, Hilda Stoll, Frances Clymer, Delores Crisp, Lorraine Johnson, Helen Roberts, and Eva Doney.

# *Five*

# Growth and Change
## Evans Today

Evans has changed considerably from the days of the stagecoaches, railroads, and wild saloons. The city has grown more civically and environmentally minded, thoroughly placing itself among the most up-and-coming modern cities in Colorado. Population-wise, the city has also grown at an exceptional rate. According to a *Greeley Tribune* article from July 10, 2003, "Evans has grown faster, much faster, in fact, than any other Colorado city with more than 10,000 people, according to the latest figures released today from the Census Bureau." The population of Evans increased a whopping 38 percent between 2000 and 2002, beating out the second fastest growing city, Windsor, by over 10 percent. This immense growth has been attributed to commuters who work in Denver, Longmont, and Fort Collins who want to live someplace smaller and quieter. Recent subdivisions on the south and west sides of town—like Cave Creek, Crescent Cove, and Tuscany—are all evidence to this fact.

Along with the growing population, Evans has matured as a city, adding numerous cultural and educational programs as well as entertainment and environmental stewardship. The city has several parks, ball fields, a dog park, hotels and restaurants, a charter school, and new stores. As Evans progresses into the 21st century, it is carrying on the legacy of its original settlers, who prized hard work, entrepreneurship, education, and culture.

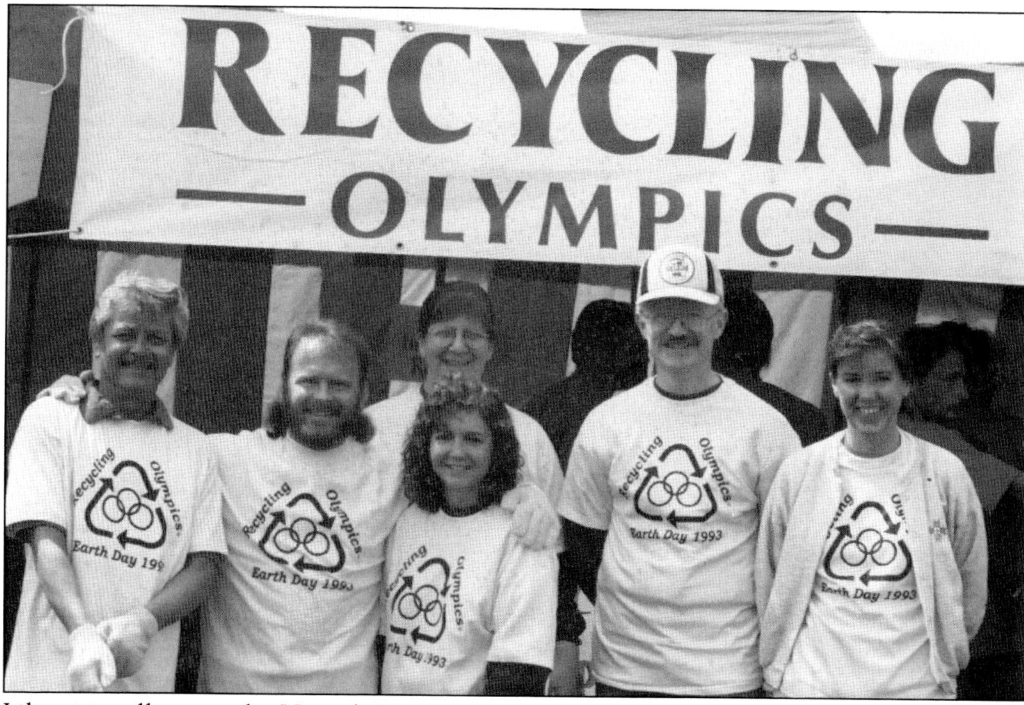


Like cities all across the United States, Evans works to make the city greener, educate the community about environmentally friendly practices, and pique interest in the environment by participating in a number of events. The team visible in this photograph participated in the city's Recycling Olympics competition on Earth Day, April 22, 1993.

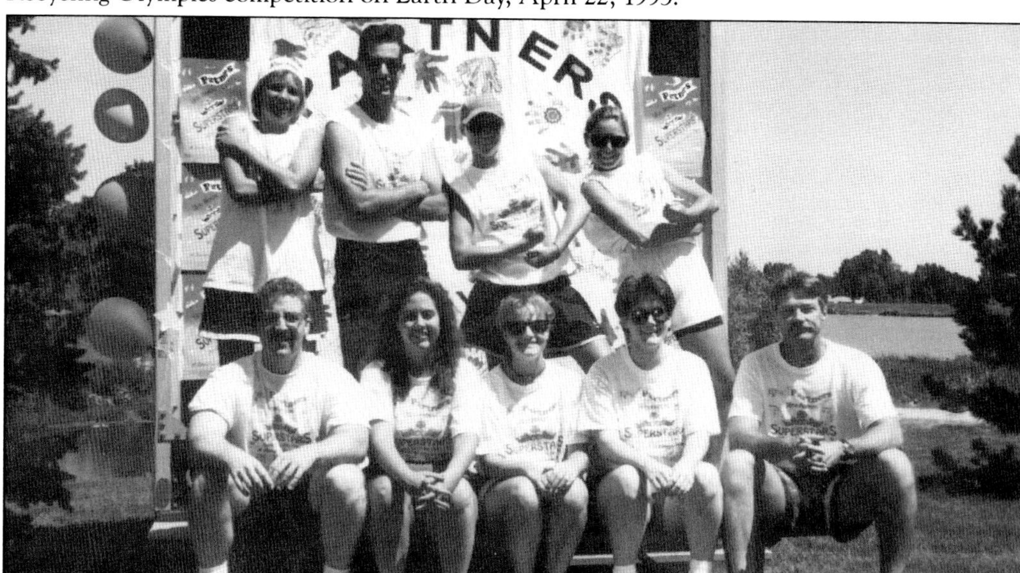

The Partners youth mentorship program has been implemented in Weld County since 1978. One of the biggest fundraisers for Partners is the Partners Superstars Sports Challenge. Participants form teams from different companies and organizations to compete in a variety of athletic activities to raise money for the program. Visible here is a team from Evans that competed in the sports challenge.

This building served as the old Evans town hall. It was located near the intersection of Thirty-ninth and Central Streets, one block north and one block east of the Gerry House Hotel and Young's Hall. In 1976, the city hall was moved to the old Chappelow School building, which was no longer in use.

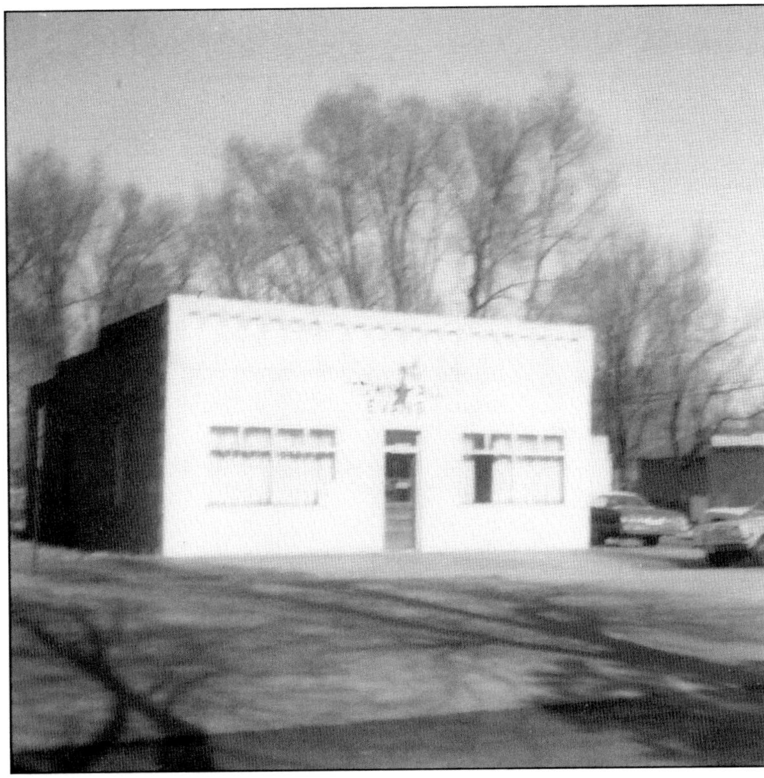

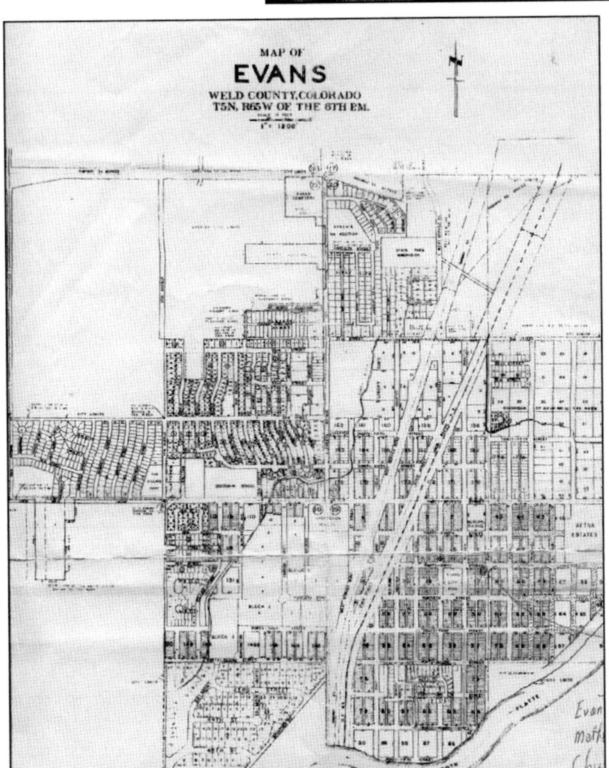


Evans started out as a small settlement to the east of the railroad tracks and west of the South Platte River. Today, Evans stretches east to the river, south nearly to La Salle, north to Highway 34, and west nearly to Milliken. This map shows several subdivisions and commercial developments that were added to the town in the 1960s and 1970s.

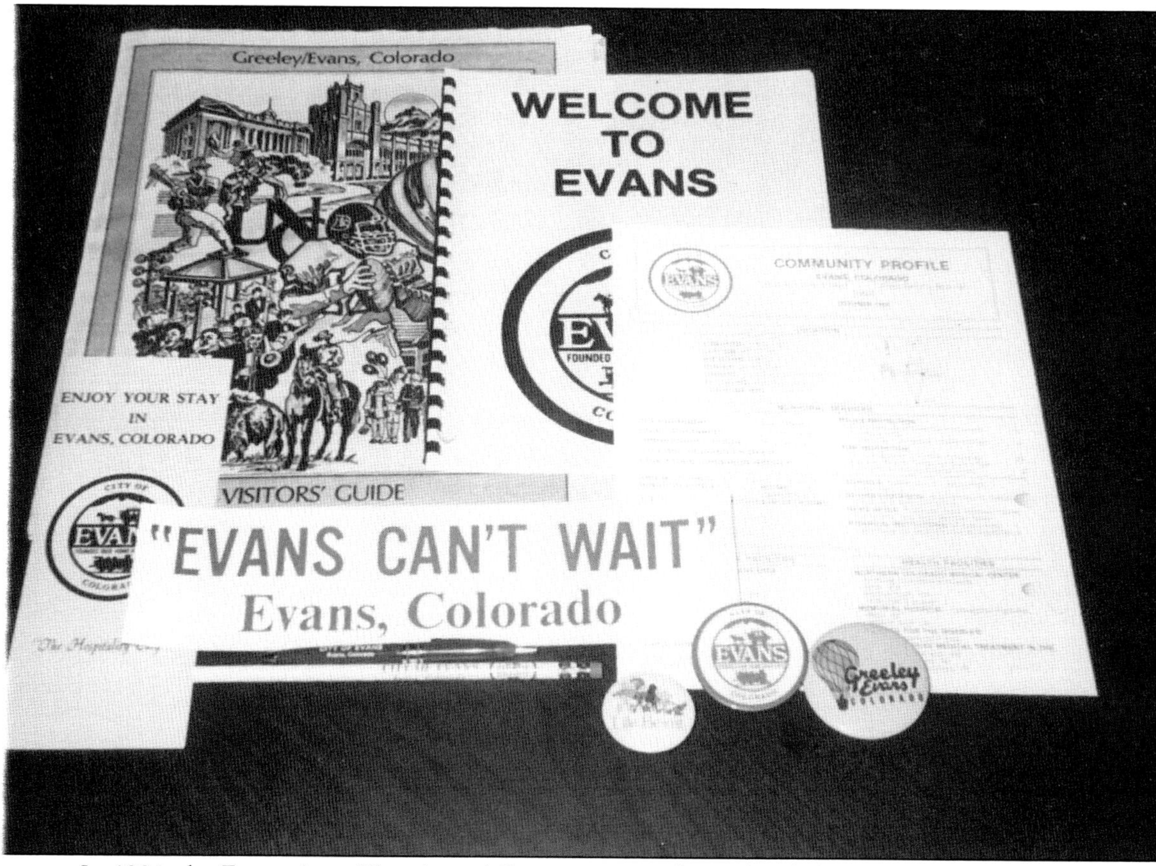


In 1984, the Evans Area Chamber of Commerce was formed and the city's new slogan, "The Hospitality City," was adopted. Brochures, stickers, and pamphlets advertising the hospitality industry were made and distributed. Another informal slogan, "Evans Can't Wait," emphasized that Evans was eager for the changes to come.

In 1984, Evans became one of 13 cities in Colorado to join Sister Cities International. The organization was founded at a White House conference on citizen diplomacy in 1956. President Eisenhower hoped the organization would help promote peace through citizen-to-citizen relationships abroad. The right certificate contains the seal of Sister Cities International and certifies that Evans is a full member of the organization. The letter pictured below, dated January 3, 1986, from Bill Gregory, a clerk to the council from Ashby-de-la-Zouch in Leicestershire, England, wrote to Evans city manager Glen Crowson to notify him that Ashby-de-la-Zouch voted to accept Evans as its sister city. Sister cities are encouraged to communicate with one another and implement programs that draw the citizens of each location together. Some of these programs included pairing up schoolchildren from each town with pen pals as well exchanging newspapers, photographs, and other information about each city.

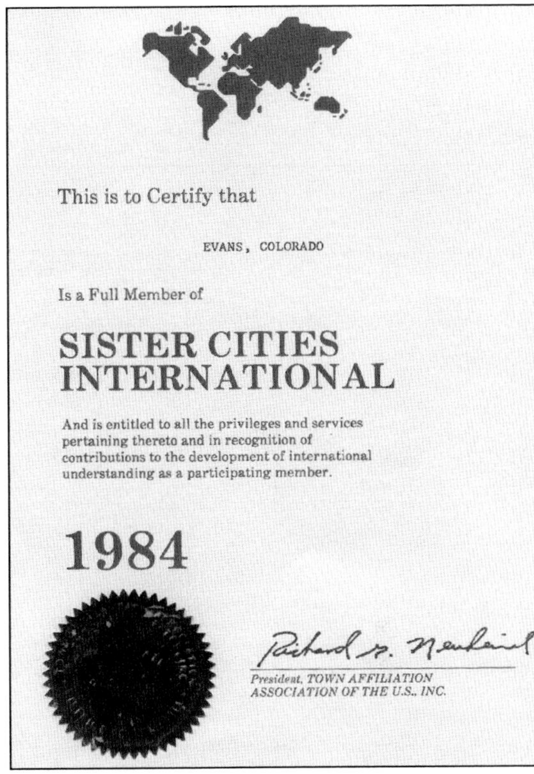
This is to Certify that

EVANS, COLORADO

Is a Full Member of

SISTER CITIES INTERNATIONAL

And is entitled to all the privileges and services pertaining thereto and in recognition of contributions to the development of international understanding as a participating member.

1984

Richard G. Neuheisel

President, TOWN AFFILIATION ASSOCIATION OF THE U.S., INC.

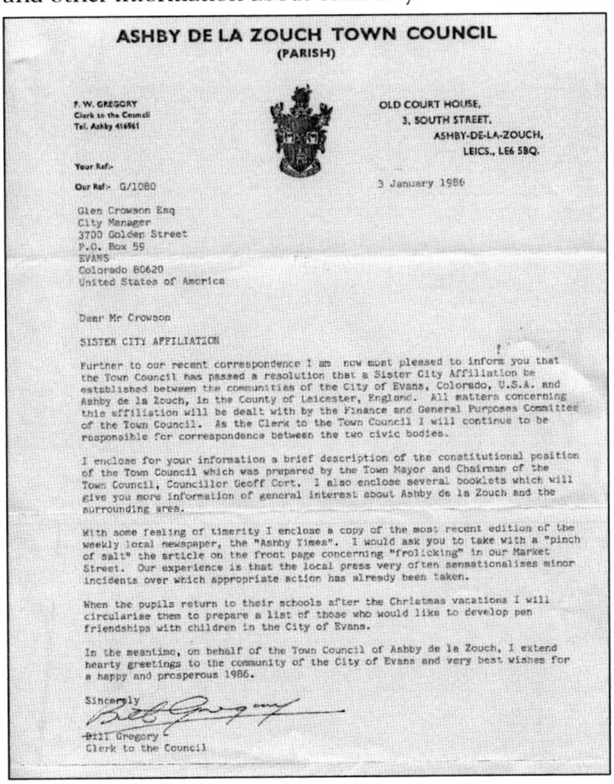
ASHBY DE LA ZOUCH TOWN COUNCIL
(PARISH)

F. W. GREGORY
Clerk to the Council
Tel. Ashby 416961

OLD COURT HOUSE,
3, SOUTH STREET,
ASHBY-DE-LA-ZOUCH,
LEICS., LE6 5BQ.

Your Ref:-

Our Ref:- G/1080

3 January 1986

Glen Crowson Esq
City Manager
3700 Golden Street
P.O. Box 59
EVANS
Colorado 80620
United States of America

Dear Mr Crowson

SISTER CITY AFFILIATION

Further to our recent correspondence I am now most pleased to inform you that the Town Council has passed a resolution that a Sister City Affiliation be established between the communities of the City of Evans, Colorado, U.S.A. and Ashby de la Zouch, in the County of Leicester, England. All matters concerning this affiliation will be dealt with by the Finance and General Purposes Committee of the Town Council. As the Clerk to the Town Council I will continue to be responsible for correspondence between the two civic bodies.

I enclose for your information a brief description of the constitutional position of the Town Council which was prepared by the Town Mayor and Chairman of the Town Council, Councillor Geoff Cort. I also enclose several booklets which will give you more information of general interest about Ashby de la Zouch and the surrounding area.

With some feeling of timerity I enclose a copy of the most recent edition of the weekly local newspaper, the "Ashby Times". I would ask you to take with a "pinch of salt" the article on the front page concerning "frolicking" in our Market Street. Our experience is that the local press very often sensationalises minor incidents over which appropriate action has already been taken.

When the pupils return to their schools after the Christmas vacations I will circularise them to prepare a list of those who would like to develop pen friendships with children in the City of Evans.

In the meantime, on behalf of the Town Council of Ashby de la Zouch, I extend hearty greetings to the community of the City of Evans and very best wishes for a happy and prosperous 1986.

Sincerely

Bill Gregory

Bill Gregory
Clerk to the Council

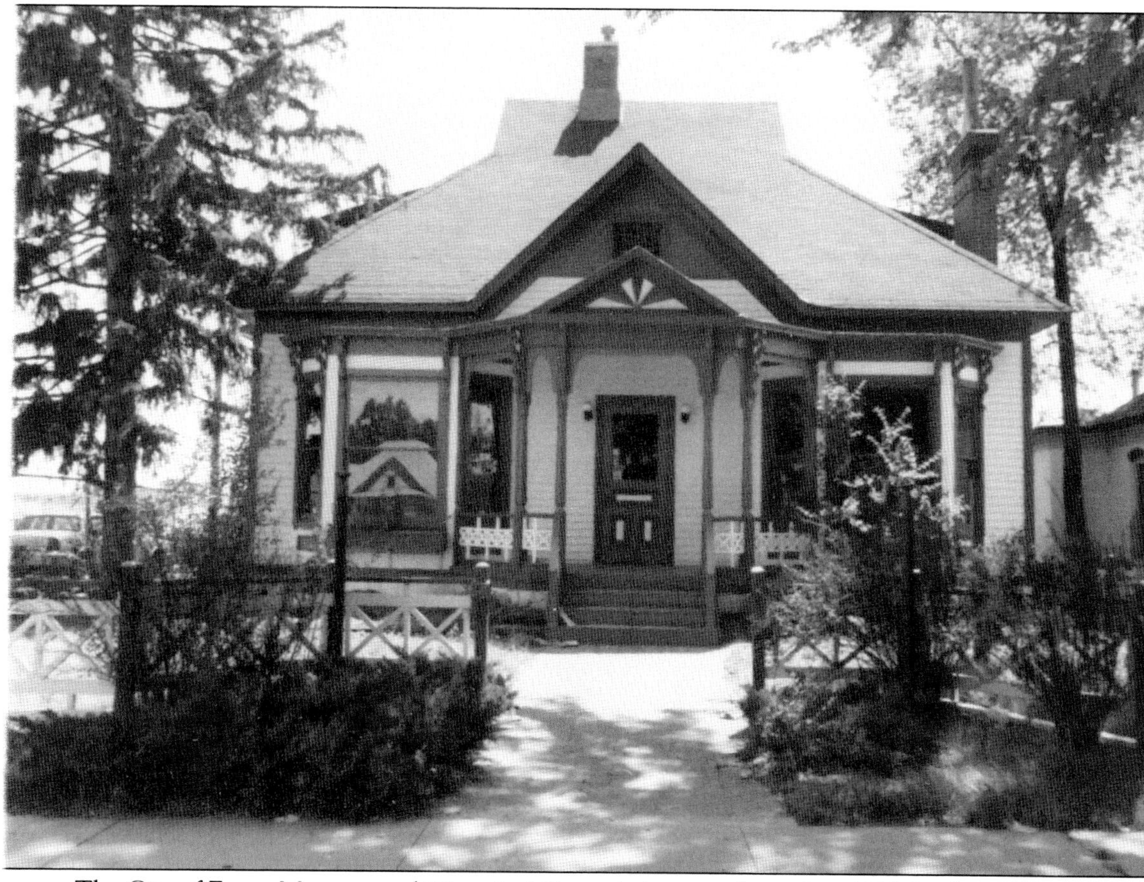

The City of Evans Museum and Historical Commission was formed in 1985 for the purpose of collecting, preserving, and displaying the town's history. Artifacts collected by the commission were on display in a front entrance area of the city hall building, but it soon became apparent that the collection would need to be moved to its own building. Just a few months after the formation of the Historical Commission, the senior coordinator and director of the Evans Museum contacted Peggy Ford at the City of Greeley Museums to help find a building to house the museum. At that time, the entire 800 block of Fifth Street in Greeley was being cleared to make way for the new Greeley Tribune building. Ford put Evans in contact with the Greeley Urban Renewal Authority, which donated a beautiful 1887 Queen Anne Victorian home to the city on the condition that the city cover the moving costs.

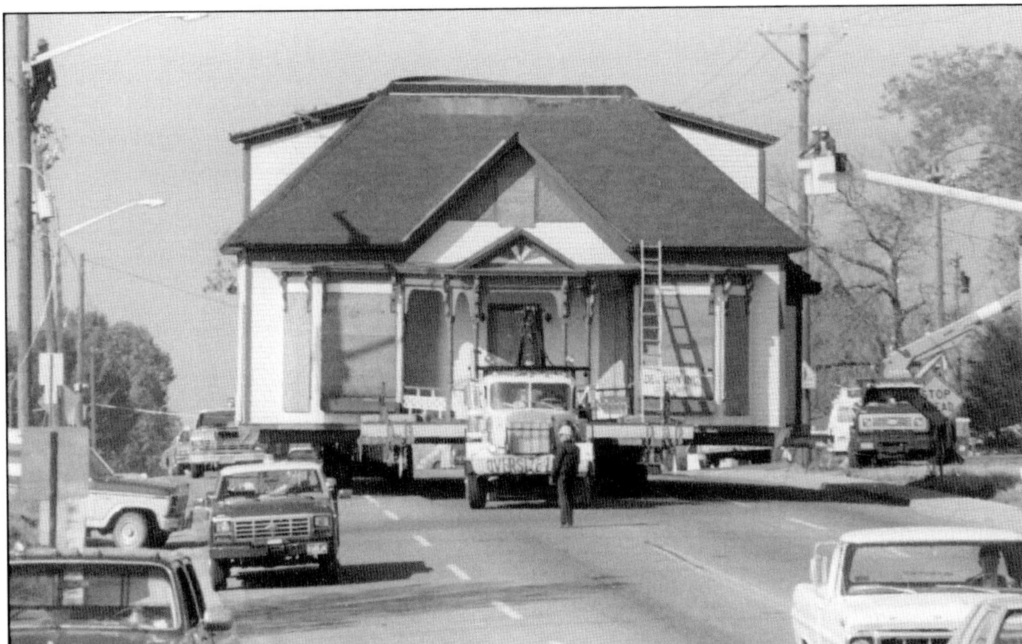

August 21, 1985, was moving day for the future Evans Historical Museum. Moving crews arrived early and started to work. Here, the home has been picked up off its foundation and is ready to make its way to a vacant lot on the corner of Eleventh Avenue and Highway 34. The building remained at that lot until the concrete foundation could be prepared at the museum grounds.

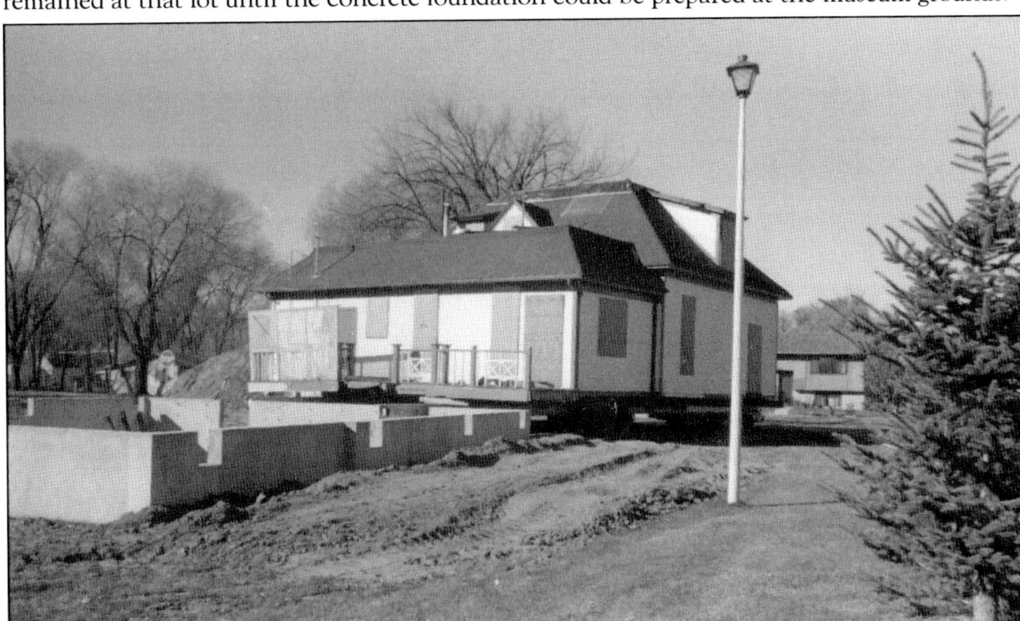

The museum building was again moved to its permanent location in the parking lot of city hall at the corner of Thirty-seventh and Golden Streets. Spectators lined the streets to watch the massive building make its way down Eleventh Avenue and around tight corners until it arrived in Evans. After all, it is not every day that a building—especially one of this size—is moved through one's neighborhood.

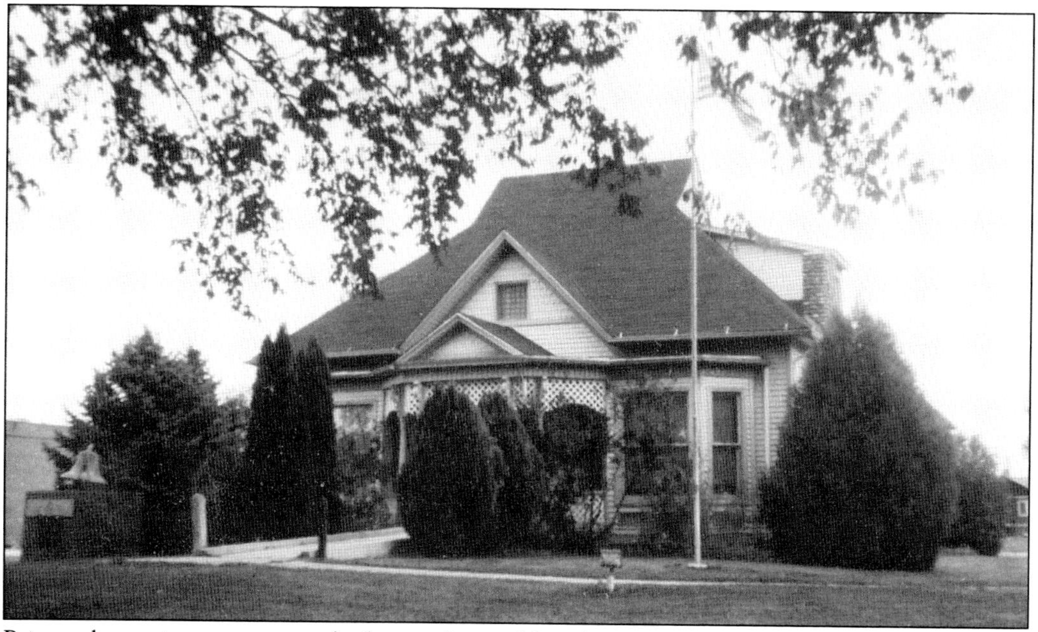

Prior to becoming a museum, the home changed hands many times over the years. The longest resident of the home, Helen Bohlender, purchased the house in 1941 and lived in it for the next 32 years. She later attended the grand opening of the museum on June 6, 1987. After Bohlender sold the house, it served as three different restaurants over the years: the Country Frenchman, the Oak Street Station, and Baltimore's.

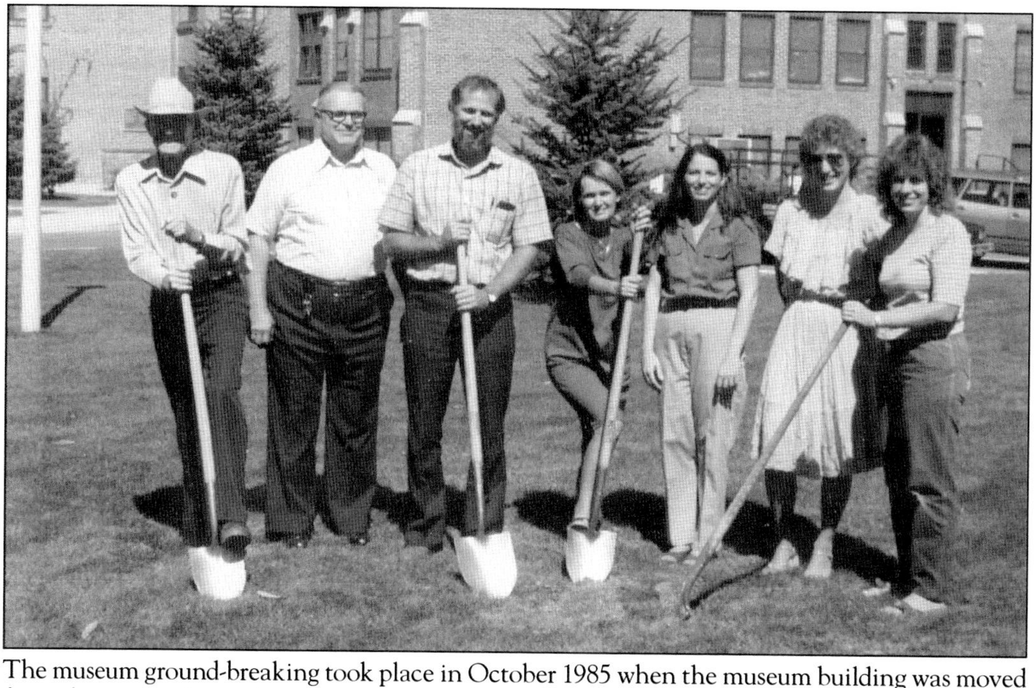

The museum ground-breaking took place in October 1985 when the museum building was moved from the vacant lot and placed on its new foundation. Visible here are several members of the Evans Museum and Historical Commission. From left to right are Doyle Bolenbaugh, Gus Ernst, Tom McMahan, unidentified, Luanne Hummels, and two unidentified people.

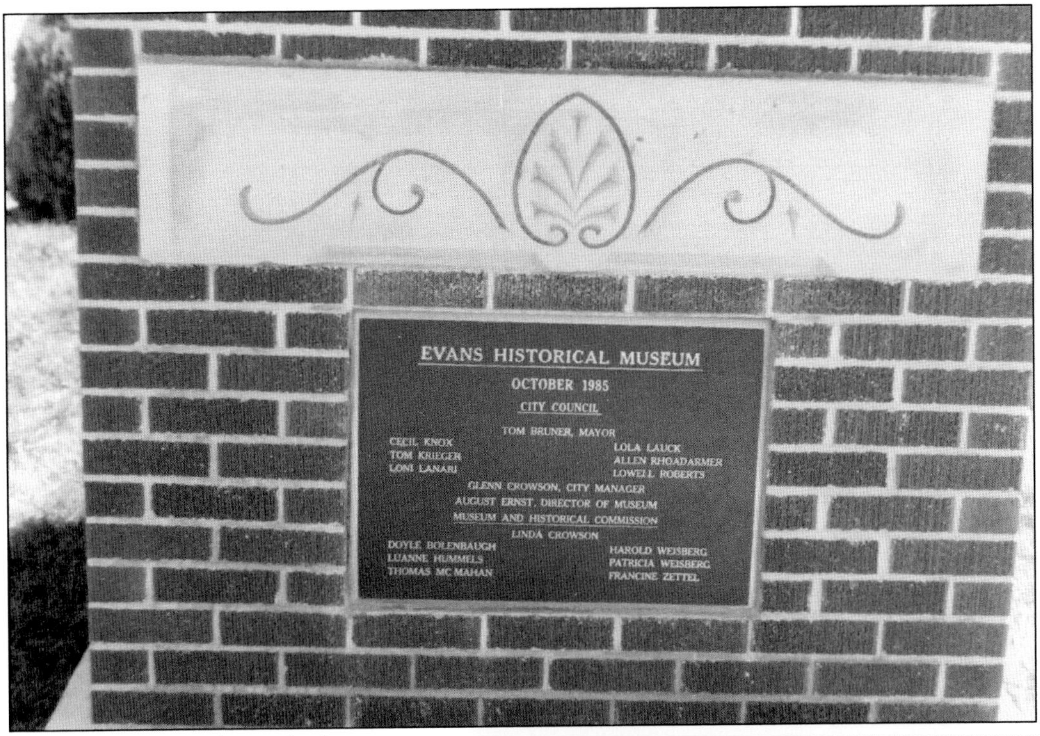


This plaque located outside the Evans Historical Museum includes two sandstone bricks that originally came from above the windows at Young's Hall. The fire department removed them before the building was torn down. The school bell from the original school also sits atop this memorial, which was dedicated in October 1985.

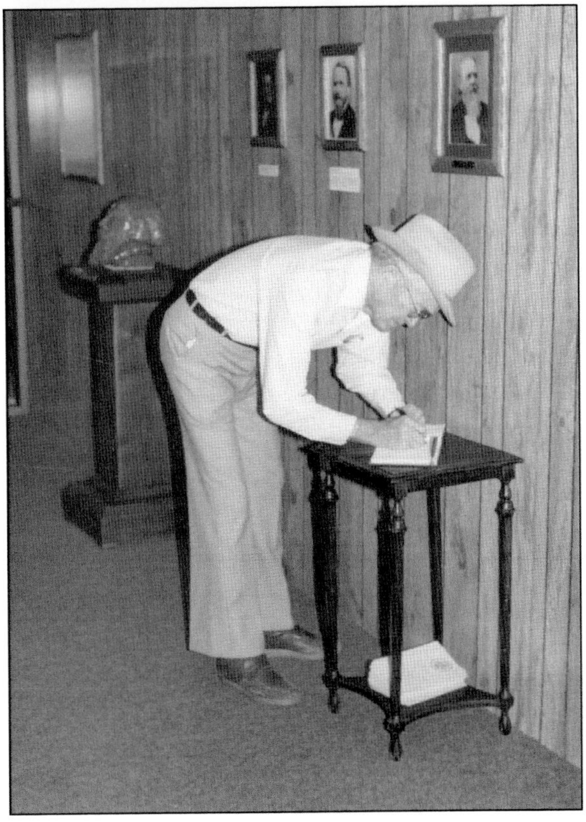

Doyle Bolenbaugh, a longtime Evans resident, was instrumental in starting the Evans Historical Museum and in collecting the town's history. In February 1993, he was honored with the RSVP, or Retired Senior Volunteer Program award, for his over 4,000 hours of volunteer work with the museum between 1988 and 1993. He continued to volunteer with the museum until he passed away in 2001.

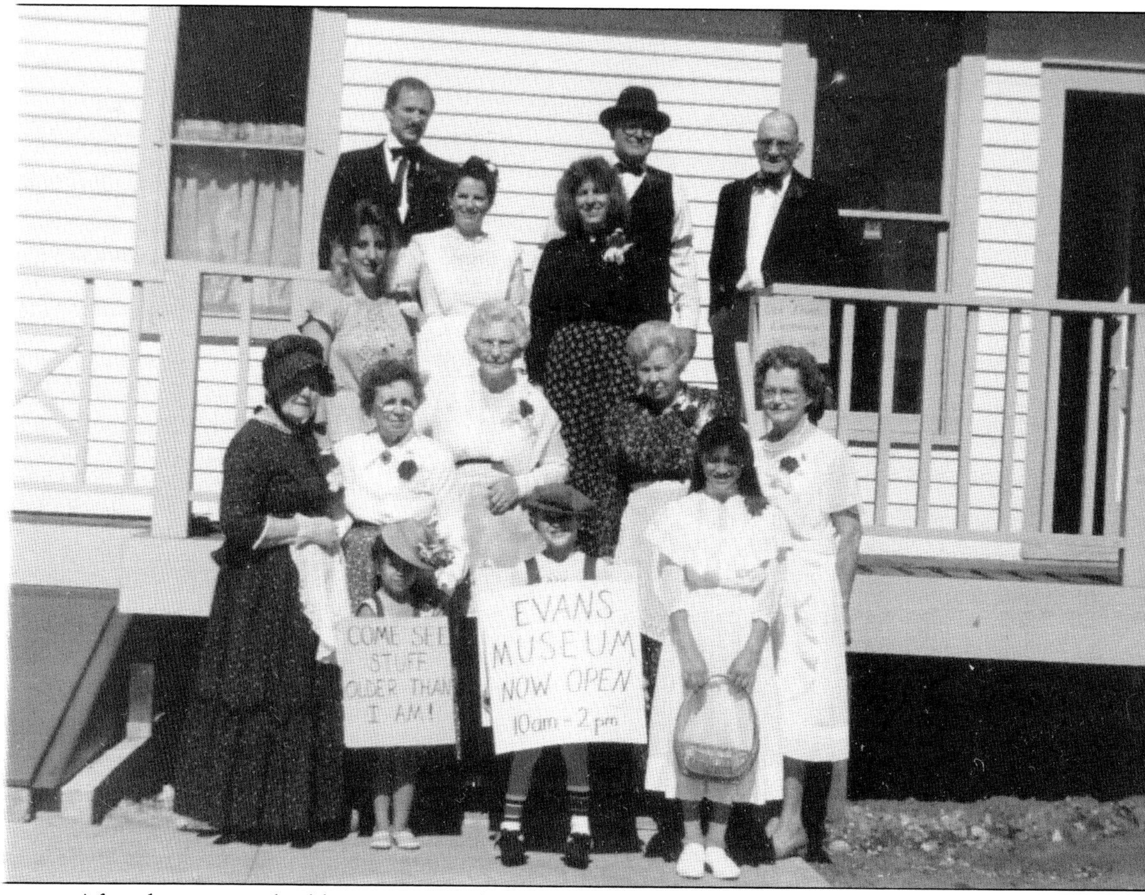


After the museum building was moved from Greeley and set on a cement foundation and repairs were made to the inside, the long-anticipated Evans Historical Museum was finally open to the public in the spring of 1986. This photograph was taken the day of the museum's grand opening. Several members of the Evans Museum and Historical Commission are posing here with some child volunteers. Vergie Crisp, who was also a member of the Bicentennial Commission in 1976, is standing on the lower left side of the steps wearing a matching dress and bonnet. Senior coordinator and museum director Gus Ernst is standing at the top of the steps wearing a hat and glasses. Doyle Bolenbaugh is standing to the right of Gus Ernst.

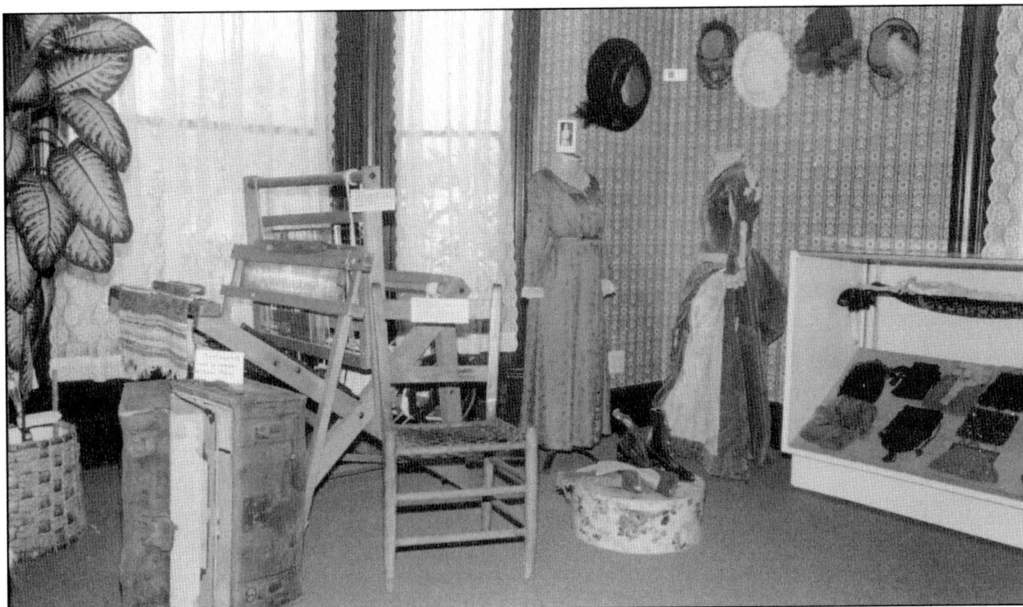

The Evans Historical Museum contained a wide variety of interesting objects. In the above photograph, the large, 100-year-old weaving loom is visible and was used by a woman in Weld County to make rugs and other textiles for the home. Pioneers who came to Colorado in a covered wagon made the chair in front of the loom. An original member of the Union Colony used the trunk that is sitting on the floor just to the left of the loom. The photograph below shows a square grand piano, sometimes called a box grand. These kinds of pianos were very common in the 18th and 19th centuries, but they are hard to come by these days. The framed artwork of a woman that is hanging above the piano is a souvenir calendar from Jack O'Grady's Saloon.

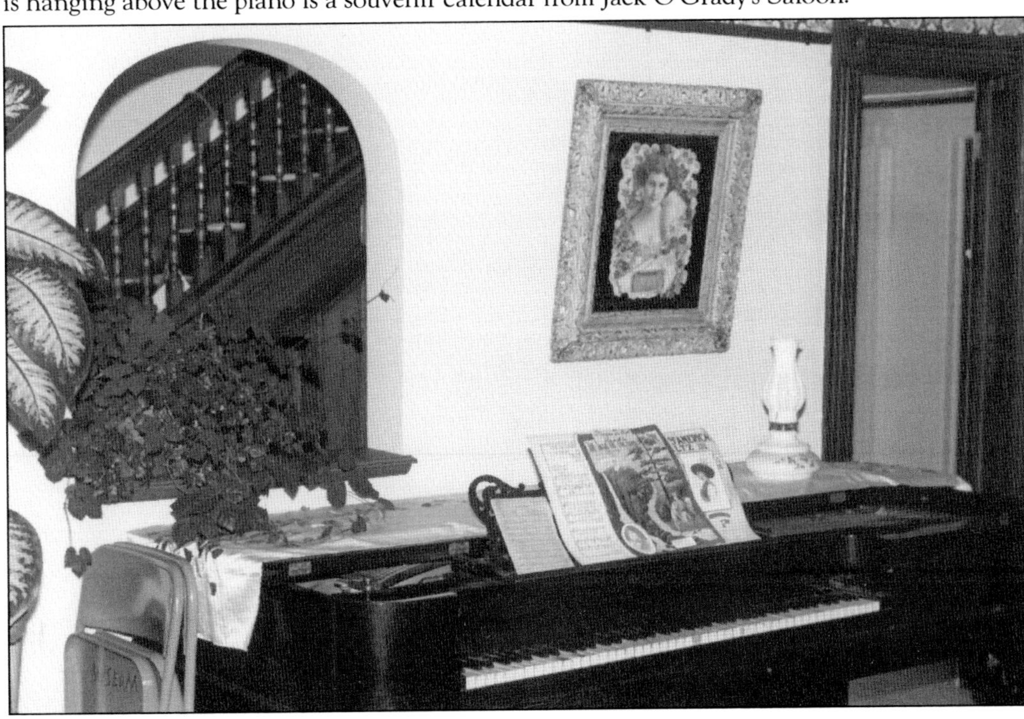

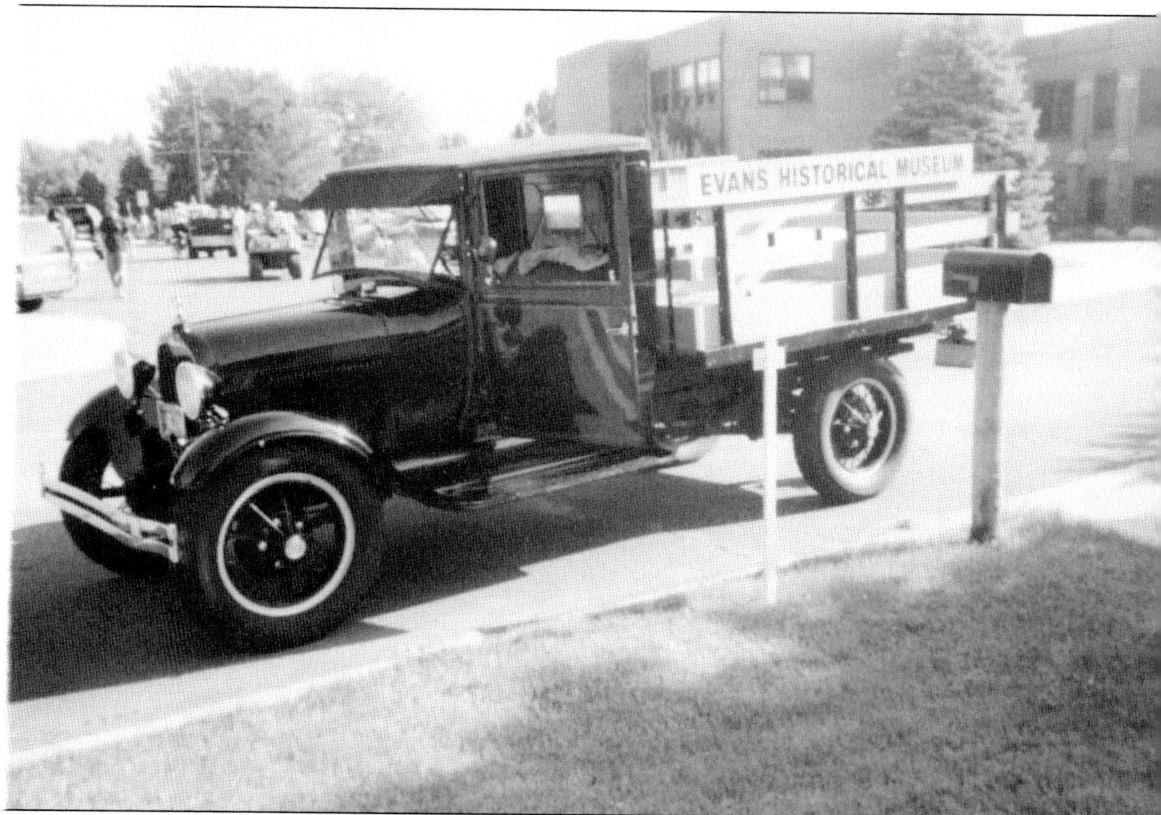


This photograph shows a historic pickup truck ridden by members of the Evans Museum and Historical Commission through town for the annual EvansFest parade in 1996. EvansFest was started in 1984 to celebrate the businesses in Evans, but over the years, it has grown to include a variety of events including a pancake breakfast, live music, a parade, and games. EvansFest fosters a sense of community and provides entertainment for all ages. The festival takes place the first Saturday following Labor Day every year.

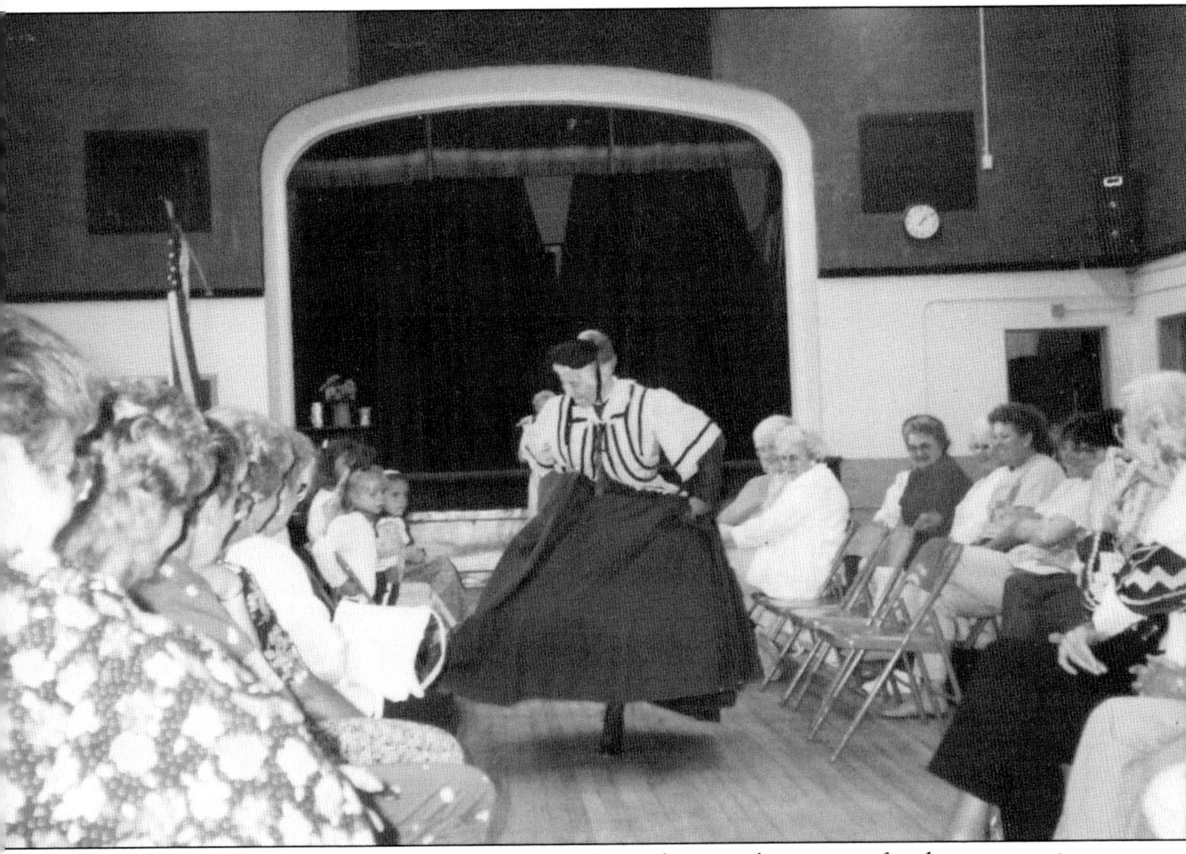

The Evans Historical Museum put on several different historical programs for the community and fundraisers over the years. On May 2, 1992, the Evans Museum and Historical Commission presented a historical fashion show in the Chappelow School gymnasium to raise money for the museum. Volunteers from the Colorado Historical Society came to Evans from Denver for the show. They wore authentic women's fashions from different time periods between the 1860s and 1960s. Over 360 volunteers were responsible for cleaning, restoring, and preserving the historic dresses that were modeled that day. Many of the garments that were showcased by the volunteers were actually worn by Colorado women. The woman in this photograph is demonstrating to the audience the fullness of her 19th-century skirt, which would have been a typical garment for a woman in that time period.

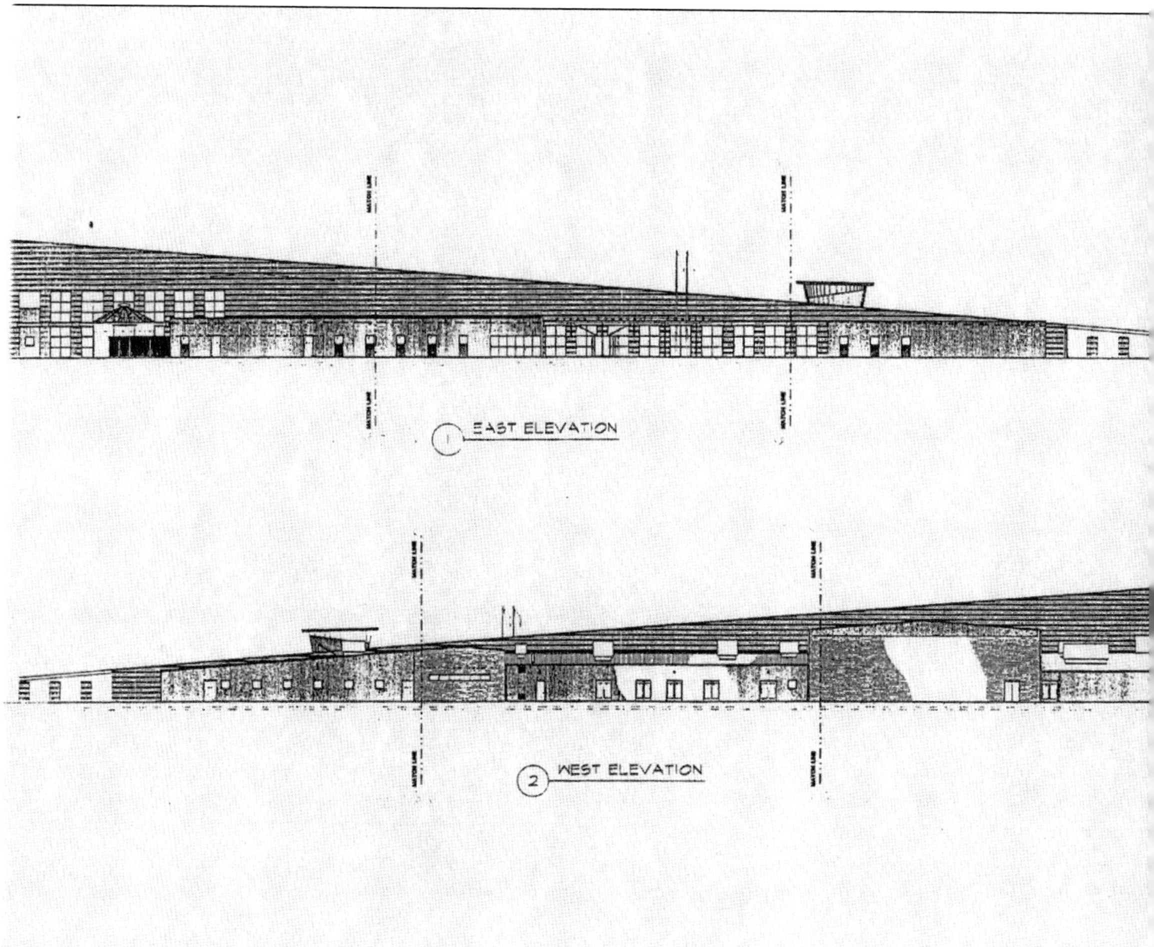


By the 1990s, the city was beginning to look for options in building a new municipal center. The old Chappelow School building that was being used for city hall was aging and had developed some structural and electrical problems over the years. In 1996, the Evans City Council hired a research group to poll 200 registered voters to determine if it would be worthwhile to hold an election to build a new city complex. The research showed that nearly 70 percent of those polled thought the current city building was in bad shape, and over half supported the construction of a new building. An election took place in the spring of 1996, and voters approved a $5.5-million referendum to build a 46,000-square-foot facility to be used as a combined public center and city offices.

The ground-breaking ceremony for the Evans Community Complex took place on March 8, 1997. The city complex at Thirty-seventh Street and Eleventh Avenue marked the first time that the city had ever built its own facility for government offices. The previous two buildings that were used as the city hall had been used for other purposes before they housed the city government.

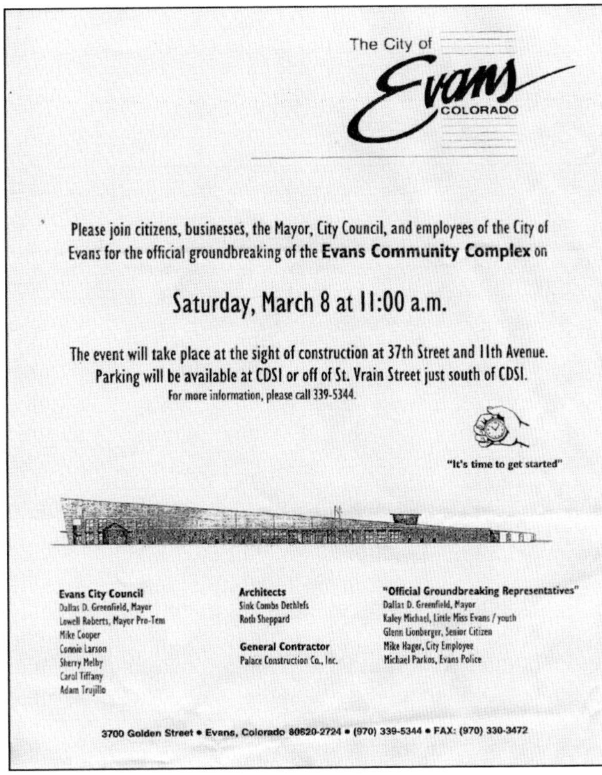

The City of
Evans
COLORADO

Please join citizens, businesses, the Mayor, City Council, and employees of the City of Evans for the official groundbreaking of the **Evans Community Complex** on

**Saturday, March 8 at 11:00 a.m.**

The event will take place at the sight of construction at 37th Street and 11th Avenue.
Parking will be available at CDSI or off of St. Vrain Street just south of CDSI.
For more information, please call 339-5344.

"It's time to get started"

**Evans City Council**
Dallas D. Greenfield, Mayor
Lowell Roberts, Mayor Pro-Tem
Mike Cooper
Connie Larson
Sherry Melby
Carol Tiffany
Adam Trujillo

**Architects**
Sink Combs Dethlefs
Roth Sheppard

**General Contractor**
Palace Construction Co., Inc.

**"Official Groundbreaking Representatives"**
Dallas D. Greenfield, Mayor
Kaley Michael, Little Miss Evans / youth
Glenn Lionberger, Senior Citizen
Mike Hager, City Employee
Michael Parkos, Evans Police

3700 Golden Street • Evans, Colorado 80620-2724 • (970) 339-5344 • FAX: (970) 330-3472

In addition to city offices and the police station, the Evans Community Complex has ball courts, weight rooms, multipurpose meeting rooms, a commercial kitchen, and a computer center run by the High Plains Library District. The recreation department offers various fitness classes for all ages, including yoga and dance. (Photograph by Sarah Arnusch.)

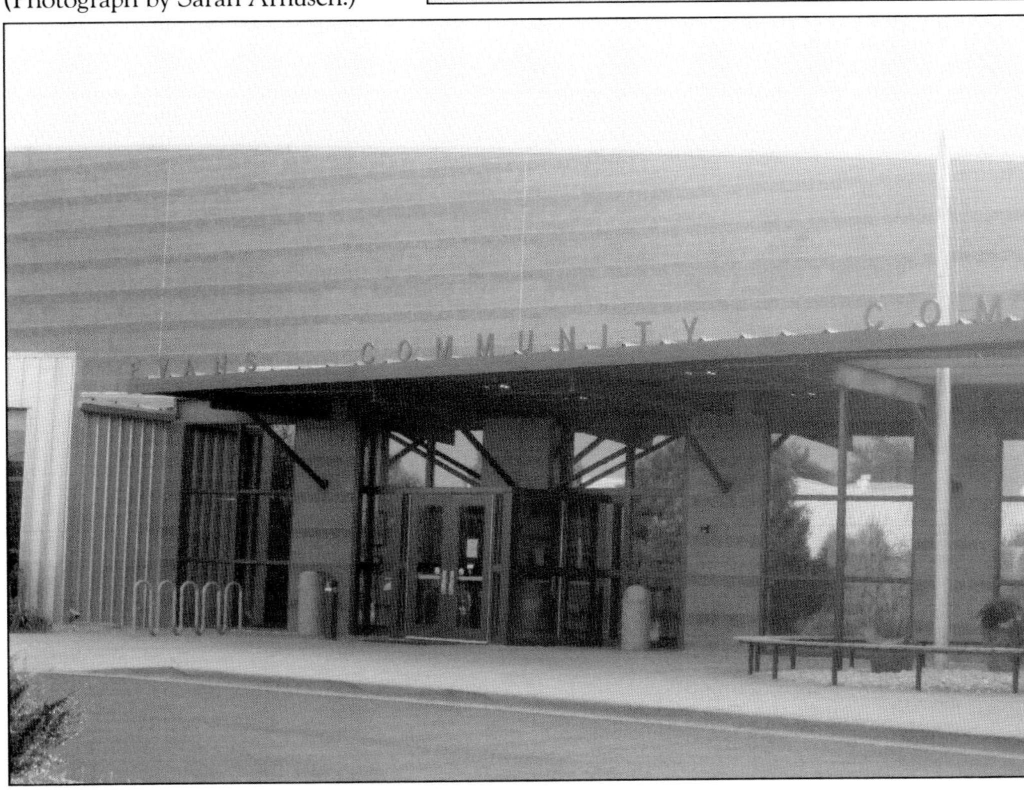

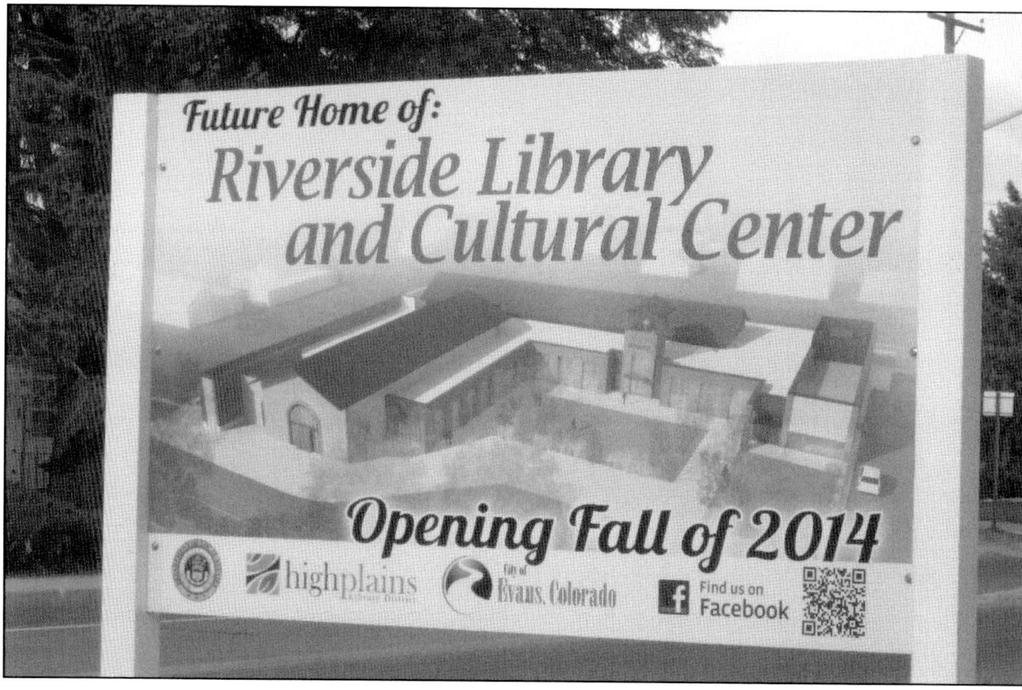


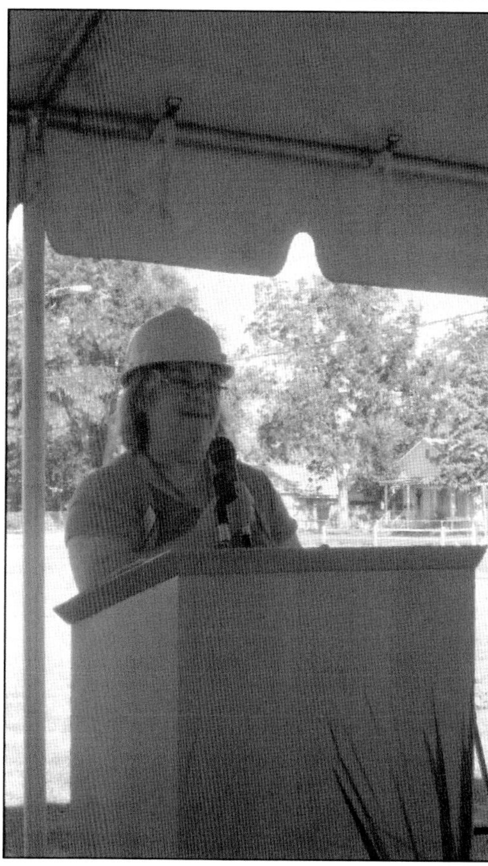

In late 2014, the High Plains Library District will open the Riverside Library and Cultural Center at Thirty-seventh and Golden Streets, the previous location of the Chappelow School and town hall. The center is a combined venture between the city and the High Plains Library District. The building will feature offices for rent to organizations, a police substation that will serve the eastern side of the city, a café, and a museum collection highlighting important people and events in Evans history. The Riverside Library and Cultural Center will be the first, but hopefully not the last, library in the city of Evans. (Photograph by Sarah Arnusch.)

The ground-breaking for the Riverside Library and Cultural Center took place on August 3, 2013, on the north lawn of the school—the future site of the library building. A crowd of community members gathered to hear the speakers and celebrate this new chapter for Evans. Librarians signed community members up for library cards and had drawings for prizes. Janine Reid, the director of the High Plains Library District, is visible here addressing the attendees at the ceremony. (Photograph by Sarah Arnusch.)

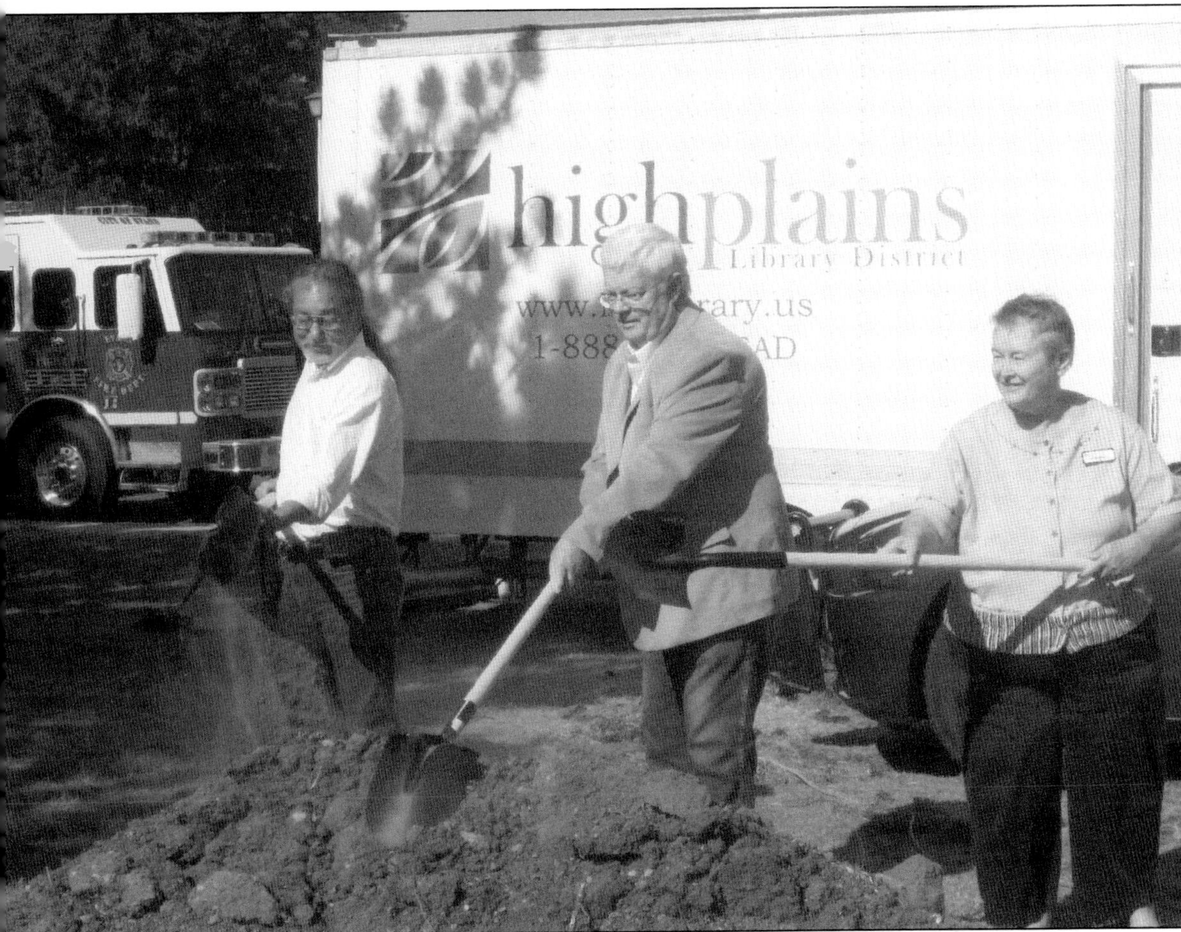


To kick off the official construction of the library, ceremonial shovels of dirt were turned by all of the High Plains Library District board members, the mayor, and Evans City Council. Pictured from left to right are Stan Sameshima (HPLD trustee), Lyle Achziger (mayor of Evans), and Lucile Arnusch (HPLD board chairwoman). Shortly after the ground-breaking ceremony, demolition work began on the old Chappelow School building. (Photograph by Sarah Arnusch.)

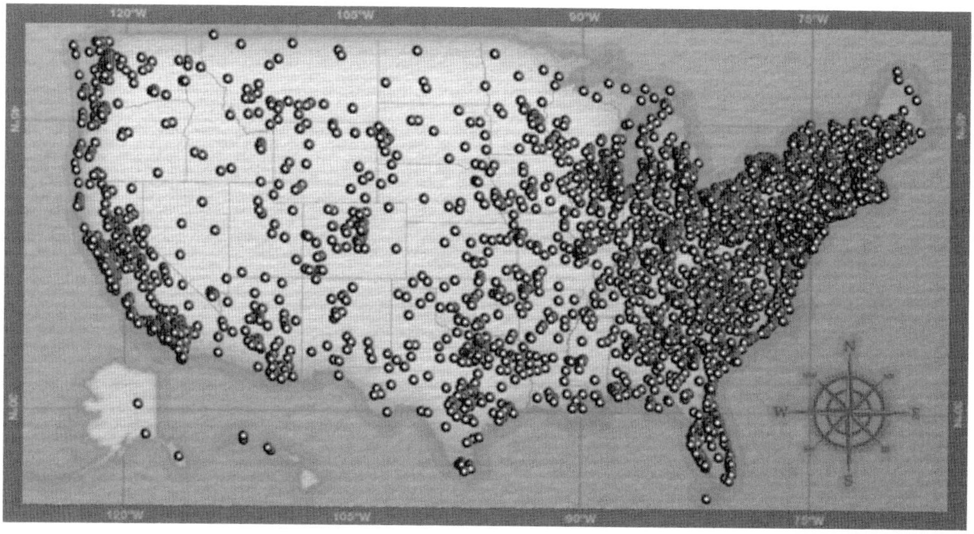